365 Snacks, Hors d'Oeuvres, and Appetizers

Other books in this series:

365 WAYS TO COOK CHICKEN
365 WAYS TO COOK PASTA
365 QUICK & EASY MICROWAVE RECIPES
365 GREAT BARBECUE & GRILLING RECIPES
365 EASY LOW-CALORIE RECIPES
365 EASY ONE-DISH MEALS
365 EASY ITALIAN RECIPES
365 GREAT CHOCOLATE DESSERTS
365 WAYS TO COOK HAMBURGER AND OTHER GROUND MEATS

365 Snacks, Hors d'Oeuvres, and Appetizers

Lonnie Gandara and Peggy Fallon

A JOHN BOSWELL ASSOCIATES BOOK

HarperCollins*Publishers*

Dear Reader:

We welcome your recommendations for future 365 Ways books. Send your suggestions and a recipe, if you'd like, to Cookbook Editor, HarperCollins Publishers, 10 East 53rd Street, New York, NY 10022. If we choose your title suggestion or your recipe we will acknowledge you in the book and send you a free copy.

Thank you for your support.

Sincerely yours,
The Editor

For information address HarperCollins Publishers, Inc., 10 East 53rd Street, New York, NY 10022.

HarperCollins books may be purchased for educational, business, or sales promotional use. For information, please write: Special Markets Department, HarperCollins Publishers, Inc., 10 East 53rd Street, New York, NY 10022.

Series Editor: Susan Wyler
Design: Nigel Rollings
Index: Maro Riofrancos

LIBRARY OF CONGRESS CATALOG CARD NUMBER 92-52585
ISBN 0-06-016536-7

94 95 96 HC 10 9 8 7 6 5 4

Contents

365 Snacks, Hors d'Oeuvres, and Appetizers

Just for Starters

In the days when we catered cocktail parties, the most requested appetizer was always "something different." Things haven't changed much since then, as we still continue to search for out-of-the-ordinary flavor combinations capable of exciting the palate in only one or two bites. We're not alone in this quest, evidently, for the hors d'oeuvre classes we've taught over the past ten years are usually filled—especially at holiday time—as others pursue "something different."

When pressed to explain what they mean by this term, we find our students merely want to avoid the pitiful displays of food that have become synonymous with the run-of-the-mill cocktail buffets we've all had to endure. Ironically, what is usually referred to as "happy hour" is more often than not a gastronomically grim occasion, featuring greasy little wads of pastry, mystery meatballs in an iridescent sauce, and a few wilted raw vegetables. This is not a tough act to follow. What all of us really crave is not something different so much as something delicious, prepared properly and presented beautifully. And that's what you'll find in *365 Snacks, Hors d'Oeuvres, and Appetizers.*

What's an appetizer? What's a nibble? What's an hors d'oeuvre? What's a starter? Do they differ from good old American snacks? With the changes in definitions that have evolved over the years, we could debate these questions forever and still reach no conclusion other than that all are foods enjoyed either in addition to or in lieu of a main meal. You'll find the terms *appetizer* and *hors d'oeuvres* used interchangeably here.

Many good cooks gained their culinary reputations by first becoming adept at appetizers. An appetizer party is a fun and practical way to entertain for both beginning and advanced cooks.

- No special equipment or utensils are required—not even tables and chairs.
- It's an informal way to provide a perfectly balanced meal to friends—even if it's only one bite at a time.
- Appetizers are easy to eat, as they are generally no more than a mouthful.
- You can serve a large number of guests for as little money as you choose to spend.
- Magnificent morsels, artfully presented, encourage guests to be adventurous eaters. With a bit of advance planning, you can

provide a little something to please everyone.

In *365 Snacks, Hors d'Oeuvres, and Appetizers* we've searched the world for the best in bites, from Garlicky Hummus to Bitty Eggs Benedict. There are plenty of instant appetizers, too, for spontaneous entertaining when there is only enough time for a quick trip to the pantry. When you want to pull out all the stops, check out our selection of Designer Originals. We've also included an array of classics as well as a few things we eat only behind closed doors: appetizers based on packaged or convenience foods that somehow end up tasting great. Our New Wave Recipes bring entertaining into the '90s with easy microwave hors d'oeuvres like Ben's Popeye Tart. Put a skip in your step with zesty salsas from our Strictly Southwestern collection. Each chapter provides variety and an inspiration to make menu planning a challenge rather than a chore.

Now that you have 365 very special recipes to try, here are a few more pointers to make your parties perfect:

- Try to achieve balance when planning appetizer menus: vary color, texture, and temperature. Guests are intrigued when they cannot predict what will emerge from your kitchen next.
- The day before your party, set out all of the serving plates and bowls you'll be using and take care of any necessary washing and polishing. Label dishes as to what they'll contain: this will eliminate last-minute panic, and it is also helpful when someone helps you assemble platters of food in the kitchen.
- For spearing, plain wooden toothpicks are generally preferable to the type with cellophane frills, and are always preferable to multicolored picks. The food should be the focal point, not the toothpicks.
- Before a dinner party, serve only one or two light appetizers—perhaps one hot and one cold—allowing two to three pieces of each per person. When appetizers are the only food being served, it is important to provide a variety. There should be at least four different types of appetizers served at a party for twenty guests; add more dishes as the party gets larger. Allow eight to ten "bites"

per person during a two- to three-hour cocktail party. Make your life easier by supplementing individual bite-size hors d'oeuvres with pâtés, mousses, nuts, olives, and cheeses.
- With mixed or soft drinks, food can be as spicy and flavorful as you dare. Better wines and champagne demand more delicate foods. And always provide an interesting selection of nonalcoholic drinks for your guests.
- Don't risk running out of ice for beverages. To be on the safe side, allow at least one pound of ice per person.

Where is it written that you have to make everything from scratch? Certainly not in *this* book. Haunt ethnic markets, supermarkets, delicatessens, and health food stores for high-quality prepared foods to serve alongside your personal creations. Purchase exotic items, such as sushi or egg rolls, ready-made from Asian restaurants.

Another nice touch is to label buffet foods with the recipe title, using the small paper place cards available in stationery stores. Guests like to know what they're eating, especially if they suffer from food allergies or follow other restricted diets. Our final bits of advice:

- Always provide plenty of cocktail napkins for a party. Allow a minimum of three per person to cover drinks and hors d'oeuvres.
- Use common sense when garnishing. Just as you wouldn't garnish a chocolate cake with a tomato rose, make sure the garnish is appropriate to the appetizer being served. Even if you are capable of making a stunning zigzag lemon cup, it has nothing to do with a Roquefort Mousse; save it for the Simply Salmon Mousse.
- When serving several hot hors d'oeuvres, choose things that bake at similar temperature. Having to heat up and cool down the oven between appetizers is a waste of time.
- When passing trays of appetizers, just serve one type at a time. Conversations are lost when guests are forced to survey an assortment of appetizers before selecting.
- Don't let guests wander around with toothpicks or crumpled cocktail napkins in hand. Provide plenty of obvious receptacles and

keep those areas as neat as possible.

- Fried hors d'oeuvres can be cooked an hour or two before guests arrive. Recrisp them in a 400°F oven until heated through.
- Small sandwiches and canapés can be made in advance, covered with a damp towel, and refrigerated up to six hours before serving.
- Candles are always lovely at an evening cocktail buffet. Short votive candles are best; if using taller ones, be sure they are out of reach to avoid accidents.
- Instead of a floral centerpiece, consider using a large lettuce-lined basket overflowing with crisp raw vegetables for nibbling. Fill in the blank spots on your buffet table with bowls or baskets of fresh fruit, especially when strawberries are in season. Fresh nontoxic green leaves from your garden, such as grape, lemon, or rose, also make good fillers.
- As soon as the doorbell rings to signal the arrival of that first guest, relax—you've done your most important work in advance and now it's your turn to have a good time!

Chapter 1

Distinctive Dips and Spreads

Once upon a time, the term dip was synonymous with dried packaged soup mix, but that's no longer the case. Today, anything goes. One taste of our Golden Caviar Dip and your crackers will take on a whole new purpose in life. Even a quick glance through this chapter should provide an appropriate dip for every taste and occasion from the simple to the sublime. Dips and spreads are generally quick and easy to prepare, especially when there's a food processor in the house. And most benefit from being made several hours in advance.

When you're bringing snacks to a friend's home for casual gatherings, this chapter's offerings are not only easy to transport, but also lend a homemade touch to the crackers, chips, or breads you can purchase as accompaniments. If time is at a premium, simply buy bite-size vegetables, already washed and cut, from a salad bar.

A moment's thought to presentation can turn a so-so spread into a fascinating conversation piece. We think plastic bowls are for storage only, so give your creation the respect it deserves by personalizing its debut. Hollowed-out vegetables such as red or green cabbages, multicolored bell peppers, oversized squash, or globe eggplants make noteworthy containers. The simplest method of all is also capable of turning a few heads; merely line a pretty bowl with decorative lettuce leaves or turnip or mustard greens before spooning in the spread. Now let's take a dip!

---

1 CREAMY DILL DIP

Prep: 5 minutes Cook: none Makes: about 1 cup

½ cup sour cream
½ cup mayonnaise
2 tablespoons chopped parsley
2 tablespoons chopped scallions
2 tablespoons minced fresh dill or 1 tablespoon dried
½ teaspoon lemon juice or vinegar
½ teaspoon salt
⅛ teaspoon pepper

In a small bowl, combine sour cream, mayonnaise, parsley, scallions, dill, lemon juice, salt, and pepper. Stir until well mixed. If made in advance, cover and refrigerate up to 3 days.

2 SPICY TOASTED ALMOND DIP

Prep: 15 minutes Cook: 7 to 10 minutes Chill: 2 hours
Makes: 1 cup

This is adapted from the classic Spanish Romesco sauce, which contains many ingredients. We find this scaled-down version from our friend Michelle Schmidt as good as any. Be sure to try it as a dipping sauce for large shrimp.

½ cup sliced almonds
2 garlic cloves, chopped
1 small tomato, peeled, seeded, and chopped
1 tablespoon red wine vinegar
½ teaspoon salt
¼ teaspoon cayenne
½ cup extra-virgin olive oil

1. Preheat oven to 325°F. Spread almonds in a single layer on a jelly-roll pan and bake 7 to 10 minutes, until lightly browned. Let cool.

2. In a food processor, combine toasted almonds, garlic, tomato, vinegar, salt, and cayenne. Puree until a coarse paste forms. With machine on, slowly add oil in a thin stream. Process until well blended. Transfer to a bowl, cover, and refrigerate at least 2 hours or as long as 2 days. Serve at room temperature.

3 ITALIAN BEAN DIP

Prep: 10 minutes Cook: none Makes: 2¼ cups

Bean dips are low in fat, high in fiber, and tops in flavor. Best of all, made with canned beans, they are quick and easy.

2 (15-ounce) cans cannellini beans (white kidney beans)
4 oil-packed sun-dried tomato halves, drained and chopped
2 tablespoons chopped fresh basil or parsley
2 tablespoons extra-virgin olive oil
2 tablespoons fresh lemon juice
2 large garlic cloves, crushed through a press
¼ teaspoon salt
⅛ teaspoon pepper
Garlic Crostini (page 151) or bread sticks

1. Place cannellini beans in a large colander and rinse thoroughly under cold running water. Drain well.

2. In a medium bowl or food processor, combine cannellini beans, sun-dried tomatoes, basil, olive oil, lemon juice, garlic, salt, and pepper. Mix until dip is well blended and beans are slightly mashed but maintain some texture. If made in advance, cover and refrigerate. Serve with garlic crostini or bread sticks.

4 GOLDEN CAVIAR DIP

Prep: 15 minutes Cook: none Makes: 1⅓ cups

Golden caviar provides a touch of elegance without the expense. It can be frozen with no loss of texture or taste until you are ready to make the dip.

1 (4-ounce) jar golden caviar
½ cup vegetable oil
½ cup sour cream
2 tablespoons chopped chives or scallions
2 tablespoons vodka
2 teaspoons ketchup
2 teaspoons lemon juice

1. In a medium bowl, whisk caviar until eggs begin to separate and mixture becomes frothy, about 2 minutes. Gradually add oil in a slow, steady stream, whisking constantly, until fully incorporated. Fold in sour cream.

2. Stir in chives, vodka, ketchup, and lemon juice until well blended. If made in advance, cover and refrigerate up to 2 days. Serve slightly chilled or at room temperature.

5 HERBED CURRY DIP

Prep: 10 minutes Cook: none Makes: 1½ cups

You'll enjoy this popular dip with its mild curry flavor. Great to serve with either vegetables or apple slices.

1 cup mayonnaise
½ cup sour cream
1 tablespoon chopped parsley
1 tablespoon grated onion
1 tablespoon lemon juice
1 teaspoon fines herbes or herbes de Provence
½ teaspoon curry powder

In a small bowl, combine all ingredients until well mixed. For best flavor, cover and refrigerate overnight before serving.

6 CURRIED CRAB DIP

Prep: 5 minutes Cook: none Makes: 2 cups

This quickly made crab dip is especially good with fresh vegetables. Be sure to use a good-quality curry powder; the difference is discernible.

1 (8-ounce) package cream cheese, softened
½ cup sour cream
1½ teaspoons curry powder
1 teaspoon lemon juice
1 garlic clove, crushed
1 (6-ounce) can crab meat, drained

In a small bowl, combine cream cheese, sour cream, curry powder, lemon juice, and garlic. Mix until well blended. Fold in crab. If made in advance, cover and refrigerate up to 2 days.

7 GARLICKY HUMMUS

Prep: 10 minutes Cook: none Makes: 2¼ cups

Hummus is a classic Middle Eastern dipping sauce, which contains tahini, a paste made from ground sesame seed. Jars of tahini are available in Middle Eastern markets, health food stores, and in the imported food section of many supermarkets. If it is not available, substitute creamy peanut butter.

- **2 (15-ounce) cans chick-peas (garbanzo beans), drained**
- **¼ cup tahini (Middle Eastern sesame seed paste)**
- **2 tablespoons extra-virgin olive oil**
- **1½ tablespoons fresh lemon juice**
- **2 large garlic cloves, crushed**
- **½ teaspoon salt**
- **Chopped parsley and paprika**
- **Pita bread**

1. In a food processor, combine chick-peas, tahini, olive oil, lemon juice, garlic, and salt. Puree until smooth. If made in advance, transfer to a bowl, cover, and refrigerate.

2. Before serving, top with chopped parsley and a dusting of paprika. Serve with pita bread.

8 PARMESAN PINE CONE

Prep: 10 minutes Cook: 7 to 10 minutes Chill: 1 hour Makes: 1¾ cups

This savory spread looks beautiful on a Christmas buffet, since it resembles a pine cone. Artificial pine sprigs make a fitting garnish.

- **1 cup sliced almonds (about 4 ounces)**
- **12 ounces cream cheese, softened**
- **½ cup grated Parmesan cheese**
- **¼ cup mayonnaise**
- **1½ teaspoons chopped fresh oregano, or ½ teaspoon dried**
- **1 small garlic clove, crushed**
- **Crackers**

1. Preheat oven to 325°F. Spread almonds in a single layer on a baking sheet. Toast in oven, shaking pan once or twice, until almonds are lightly browned, 7 to 10 minutes. Let cool.

2. In a medium bowl or in a food processor, combine cream cheese, Parmesan cheese, mayonnaise, oregano, and garlic. Blend until well mixed. Refrigerate until firm but still pliable, about 1 hour.

3. Place cheese mixture on a serving board or platter and form into shape of a pine cone. Stud top with toasted slivered almonds to complete illusion. Serve with crackers.

9 GINGER LIME DIP

Prep: 5 minutes Cook: none Makes: 1¼ cups

You'll love this piquant dipping sauce with fresh fruits, such as strawberries, chunks of cantaloupe or honeydew, slices of pear, apple, or peach.

⅔ cup mayonnaise
⅓ cup sour cream
2 tablespoons honey
2 tablespoons fresh lime juice
1 tablespoon minced crystallized ginger
1½ teaspoons grated lime zest

In a small bowl, combine mayonnaise, sour cream, honey, lime juice, ginger, and lime zest. Stir until well blended. If made in advance, cover and refrigerate up to 3 days.

10 WARM PIZZA DIP

Prep: 5 minutes Cook: 20 minutes Serves: 8 to 10

1 (8-ounce) container whipped cream cheese
1 cup pizza sauce, purchased or homemade
½ cup chopped onion
8 ounces mozzarella cheese, shredded
1 (2½-ounce) package sliced pepperoni, coarsely chopped
1 (2¼-ounce) can sliced ripe olives, drained
1 teaspoon Italian seasoning
Crackers or bread rounds

1. Preheat oven to 350°F. Spread cream cheese over bottom of a greased 9-inch round baking dish and top with layers of pizza sauce, onion, cheese, pepperoni, and olives in the order given. Sprinkle Italian seasoning evenly over top.

2. Bake until heated through, about 20 minutes. Serve warm with crackers or bread rounds.

11 ROSY SHRIMP DIP

Prep: 10 minutes Cook: none Makes: 3 cups

This tasty treat is equally good with crackers, bread rounds, or raw vegetables.

1 (8-ounce) package cream cheese, softened
1 cup mayonnaise
3 tablespoons chili sauce or ketchup
2 tablespoons lemon juice
1 small onion, grated
1 pound tiny shelled cooked shrimp

In a medium bowl, combine cream cheese, mayonnaise, chili sauce, lemon juice, and onion. Blend until well mixed. Fold in shrimp. If made in advance, cover and refrigerate up to 2 days.

12 TUNA VERDE DIP

Prep: 5 minutes Cook: none Makes: 2 cups

A new twist on tuna; add more sour cream and mayonnaise if you like a thinner dip. Just don't call this Green Tuna Dip—it loses something in the translation.

1 large avocado
1 (6½-ounce) can tuna, drained and flaked
2 tablespoons mayonnaise
2 teaspoons sour cream
1 teaspoon fresh lemon juice
1 teaspoon minced scallion
½ teaspoon salt
¼ teaspoon pepper

1. Halve avocado and discard pit. Scoop avocado into a bowl of cold water to prevent discoloration. Drain well.

2. In a medium bowl, mash avocado with tuna until well blended. Stir in mayonnaise, sour cream, lemon juice, scallion, salt, and pepper. If made in advance, cover and refrigerate up to 2 days.

13 PEGGY'S FAVORITE TAPENADE

Prep: 15 minutes Cook: none Makes: 1 cup

This recipe is short on tuna but long on flavor. Don't even *think* of omitting the anchovies; their flavor is integral to this spread, and will actually go undetected by most people.

1 (6½-ounce) jar oil-cured olives (about 1½ cups), pitted
2 garlic cloves
1 tablespoon drained capers
2 teaspoons chopped fresh thyme leaves or ½ teaspoon dried
2 flat anchovy fillets, drained
3 tablespoons extra-virgin olive oil, plus extra for topping
2 tablespoons fresh lemon juice
⅛ teaspoon freshly ground black pepper

1. Place olives in a sieve or colander and rinse thoroughly under cold running water to reduce saltiness.

2. In a food processor, mince garlic. Add about ¾ cup of the olives and process until finely chopped.

3. Add capers, thyme, and anchovies; pulse on and off 4 times. Add remaining olives, olive oil, lemon juice, and pepper and pulse until well blended. Tapenade will keep almost indefinitely in the refrigerator when topped with a thin film of olive oil before covering with plastic wrap or a lid.

14 HERBED CREAM CHEESE

Prep: 10 minutes Cook: none Makes: 2 cups

The flavor of this simple yet versatile spread mimics its expensive imported counterparts found in many cheese shops.

- **2 (8-ounce) packages cream cheese, softened**
- **1 scallion, minced**
- **1 large garlic clove, crushed through a press**
- **½ teaspoon tarragon wine vinegar or lemon juice**
- **½ teaspoon dried dill**
- **½ teaspoon dried basil**
- **½ teaspoon dried marjoram**
- **½ teaspoon dried thyme**
- **½ teaspoon Beau Monde seasoning**
- **¼ teaspoon dried tarragon**
- **Dash of salt**
- **Dash of cayenne**

In a medium bowl, combine cream cheese, scallion, garlic, vinegar, dill, basil, marjoram, thyme, Beau Monde, tarragon, salt, and cayenne until well mixed. If made in advance, cover and refrigerate up to 3 days.

15 PIQUANT ANCHOVY SPREAD

Prep: 15 minutes Cook: none Makes: 2 cups

- **2 (8-ounce) packages cream cheese, softened**
- **⅓ cup pimiento-stuffed green olives, coarsely chopped**
- **¼ cup dry sherry or white wine**
- **1 (2-ounce) can flat anchovy fillets, drained and chopped**
- **Dash of cayenne**
- **Whole-wheat or other crackers**

In a medium bowl, combine cream cheese, olives, sherry, anchovies, and cayenne. Blend until well mixed. Serve with crackers.

16 CREAMY SPINACH DIP

Prep: 10 minutes Cook: none Makes: about 3 cups

- **1 (10-ounce) package frozen chopped spinach, thawed and well drained**
- **1 cup mayonnaise**
- **1 cup sour cream**
- **½ cup chopped scallions**
- **¼ cup chopped parsley**
- **1 tablespoon fresh lemon juice**
- **1 tablespoon chopped fresh dill or 1½ teaspoons dried**
- **1 teaspoon salt**
- **½ teaspoon freshly ground pepper**

In a medium bowl, combine spinach, mayonnaise, sour cream, scallions, parsley, lemon juice, dill, salt, and pepper. Mix until well blended. Refrigerate 2 hours or as long as 2 days.

17 SUREFIRE DIP FOR SHRIMP

Prep: 5 minutes Cook: none Makes: 2 cups

This dip is guaranteed to be a favorite for shrimp or raw vegetables. It even makes a great topping for baked potatoes.

¾ cup mayonnaise
¾ cup sour cream
1 hard-boiled egg, grated
2 tablespoons white wine vinegar
2 tablespoons grated onion
1 tablespoon anchovy paste
2 teaspoons Worcestershire sauce
½ teaspoon dry mustard
1 garlic clove, crushed

1. Combine mayonnaise, sour cream, egg, vinegar, onion, anchovy paste, Worcestershire, mustard, and garlic until well mixed.

2. Serve immediately, or cover and refrigerate up to 2 days.

18 LONNIE'S RUSSIAN EGGPLANT CAVIAR

Prep: 15 minutes Cook: 2 hours Makes: 6 cups

When caviar is not in the budget, this savory eggplant spread encourages instant *glasnost*.

3 large onions, chopped
3 garlic cloves, minced
3 tablespoons vegetable oil
2 green bell peppers, cut into 1-inch squares
6 carrots, cut into 1-inch cubes
2 large eggplants (about 3 pounds total), cut into 1-inch cubes
2 cups ketchup
2 teaspoons salt
1 teaspoon freshly ground pepper
1 teaspoon sugar
½ teaspoon cayenne
½ cup chopped parsley
¼ cup chopped fresh dill

1. In a large heavy saucepan, cook onions and garlic in oil over medium heat until softened but not browned, 3 to 5 minutes. Add bell peppers and carrots and cook, stirring frequently, until crisp-tender, about 5 minutes. (If mixture begins to stick to pan, add water, about 1 tablespoon at a time.)

2. Stir in eggplant, cover, reduce heat to low, and cook, stirring frequently and adding water if necessary, until vegetables are very soft, about 1½ hours.

3. Uncover and continue cooking until liquid has evaporated, about 10 minutes. Stir in ketchup and season with salt, pepper, sugar, and cayenne. Stir in parsley and dill and cook until mixture is well blended, about 10 minutes longer. Let cool. Cover and refrigerate 2 hours or as long as 3 days. Serve with black bread or crackers.

19 LONNIE'S FAVORITE TAPENADE

Prep: 5 minutes Cook: none Makes: 2½ cups

Everyone has a favorite tapenade, and this is Lonnie's.

- **1½ cups oil-cured black olives (about ½ pound), pitted**
- **¼ cup extra-virgin olive oil**
- **1 (6½-ounce) can oil-packed tuna, drained**
- **1 (3¼-ounce) jar capers, drained**
- **2 tablespoons fresh lemon juice**
- **2 tablespoons brandy**
- **1½ teaspoons powdered mustard**
- **3 to 4 flat anchovy fillets**
- **1 garlic clove, minced**
- **½ teaspoon freshly ground pepper**
- **Pinch of ground cloves**
- **Pinch of ground ginger**
- **Pinch of grated nutmeg**

1. In a food processor, combine olives with olive oil. Chop coarsely.

2. Add tuna, capers, lemon juice, brandy, mustard, anchovies, garlic, pepper, cloves, ginger, and nutmeg. Process until mixture becomes a smooth paste. If made in advance, store well covered in the refrigerator up to 5 days.

20 CHUTNEY CHEESE SPREAD

Prep: 5 minutes Cook: none Chill: 30 minutes Serves: 8

Noted San Francisco hostess and wine lover Shirley Sarvis created this wonderful spread for crackers.

- **1 (8-ounce) package cream cheese, softened**
- **2 cups shredded sharp Cheddar cheese (about 8 ounces)**
- **2 tablespoons dry sherry**
- **1 teaspoon curry powder**
- **¼ teaspoon salt**
- **Dash of hot pepper sauce or cayenne**
- **½ cup mango chutney, finely chopped**
- **¼ cup chopped scallion**

1. In a medium bowl or in a food processor, combine cream cheese, Cheddar cheese, sherry, curry powder, salt, and hot sauce. Blend until smooth and well mixed. Spread on a serving plate and shape into a round cheesecake about ¼ inch thick. Cover and refrigerate until firm, about 2 hours.

2. At serving time, spread chutney over top and sprinkle with scallions.

21 HOT CHIPPED BEEF SPREAD

Prep: 10 minutes Cook: 30 minutes Serves: 8 to 10

Serve with toast points, bread cubes, or crackers for dipping.

- **5 or 6 ounces dried chipped beef, finely chopped**
- **2 packages (8 ounces each) cream cheese**
- **1 tablespoon minced onion**
- **1½ teaspoons Worcestershire sauce**
- **1½ cups sour cream**
- **½ teaspoon garlic salt**
- **¼ teaspoon pepper**

1. Preheat oven to 350°F. In a medium bowl, combine beef, cream cheese, onion, Worcestershire sauce, sour cream, garlic salt, and pepper. Blend well.

2. Spoon chipped beef mixture into a shallow 4-cup ovenproof dish. Bake 30 minutes.

LIVERWURST IGLOO

Prep: 15 minutes Cook: none Chill: overnight Makes: 2½ cups

- **1 (1-pound) package liver sausage**
- **1 (8-ounce) package cream cheese, softened**
- **⅓ cup minced dill pickles plus 2 tablespoons dill pickle juice**
- **¼ cup minced onion**
- **⅛ teaspoon hot pepper sauce**
- **1 small garlic clove, minced**
- **¼ cup mayonnaise**
- **1 tablespoon chopped parsley**

1. In a food processor, combine liver sausage, half the cream cheese, the dill pickles and pickle juice, onion, hot sauce, and garlic. Process until well blended. Line a 2- to 3-cup bowl with plastic wrap, pack mixture inside, cover, and refrigerate overnight.

2. In a small bowl, mix reserved cream cheese and mayonnaise until well blended.

3. Invert chilled liver mixture onto a serving plate; peel off and discard plastic wrap. With a small metal spatula, spread cream cheese mixture over molded liver to cover. Sprinkle parsley over top. Serve chilled.

23 SMOKED OYSTER DIP

Prep: 5 minutes Cook: none Makes: 1½ cups

A tin of smoked oysters in the cupboard can be your first step toward a fabulous party. What sounds like an extravagance is actually a quick assembly of convenience foods.

- **1 (8-ounce) package cream cheese, softened**
- **2 tablespoons mayonnaise**
- **1 teaspoon lemon juice**
- **¼ teaspoon garlic salt**
- **Dash of hot pepper sauce**
- **½ cup chopped ripe olives**
- **1 (9-ounce) can smoked oysters, drained and chopped**

In a small bowl, combine cream cheese, mayonnaise, lemon juice, garlic salt, and hot sauce. Mix until well blended. Fold in olives and smoked oysters. If made in advance, cover and refrigerate up to 3 days.

24 FIERY-SWEET CHEESE

Prep: 2 minutes Cook: none Makes: 1½ cups

The tingling sweet-hot flavor of pepper jelly is a perfect foil to mild cream cheese. You might also enjoy this jelly on top of a wedge of rich Brie.

- **1 (8-ounce) package cream cheese, softened**
- **½ cup green or red hot pepper jelly**
- **Unsalted crackers**

Place cheese on a serving plate and top with jelly. Serve with crackers.

25 ELEGANT ARTICHOKE SPREAD

Prep: 10 minutes Cook: none Chill: 1 hour Makes: 1½ cups

No one will ever guess how easy this is to make! All the ingredients can be kept on hand for an instant party treat.

- **1 cup sour cream**
- **1 (8-ounce) package cream cheese, softened**
- **1 (8¾-ounce) can artichoke bottoms, drained and finely diced**
- **1 (2-ounce) jar lumpfish caviar**

1. In a small bowl, combine sour cream and cream cheese. Mix until well blended. Stir in diced artichoke.

2. Drain caviar into a fine sieve and rinse under cold running water to remove black dye; drain well. Fold caviar into artichoke mixture. Cover and refrigerate 1 hour or as long as 8 hours.

26 TARAMASALATA

Prep: 5 minutes Cook: none Chill: 1 hour Makes: 1 cup

This Greek classic has been pleasing caviar lovers forever. Tarama, salted carp roe, is sold in jars in specialty food stores.

2 slices firm-textured white bread, crusts removed
¼ cup tarama (carp roe)
¼ cup fresh lemon juice
¼ to ½ cup olive oil
2 tablespoons chopped onion

1. Soak bread briefly in a small bowl of cold water and squeeze dry.

2. In a food processor, combine bread, tarama, lemon juice, 2 tablespoons olive oil, and onion. Process until well mixed. With machine on, add more olive oil until mixture is consistency of mayonnaise. Transfer to a serving bowl, cover, and refrigerate 1 hour or as long as 2 days. Serve with pita bread.

27 SMOKY SALMON BALL

Prep: 5 minutes Chill: 1 hour Cook: none Serves: 10

1 (16-ounce) can red salmon
1 (8-ounce) package cream cheese, softened
1 tablespoon fresh lemon juice
2 teaspoons minced onion
1 teaspoon prepared white horseradish
½ teaspoon liquid smoke
¼ teaspoon salt
⅓ cup chopped pecans
3 tablespoons chopped parsley

1. Drain salmon, remove bones, and flake with a fork. In a medium bowl or in a food processor, combine cream cheese, lemon juice, onion, horseradish, liquid smoke, and salt. Blend until well mixed. Mix in salmon and then form into a ball. Wrap in plastic wrap and refrigerate until firm, about 1 hour or as long as 2 days.

2. In a small bowl, combine chopped pecans and parsley. Toss until well mixed. Before serving, roll salmon ball in mixture to coat.

28 CHUTNEY CHEESE BALLS

Prep: 5 minutes Cook: none Makes: 1¼ cups

These sweet and spicy flavors meld together for a delicious appetizer. Serve with a spreading knife and crackers or apple slices.

1 (8-ounce) package cream cheese, softened
2 tablespoons minced preserved stem ginger
2 tablespoons chopped mango chutney
1 tablespoon curry powder
2 teaspoons shredded coconut
1 teaspoon ground ginger
½ cup chopped pecans

1. In a medium bowl or in a food processor, combine cream cheese, preserved ginger, chutney, curry, coconut, and ground ginger. Blend until well mixed.

2. Form into 1 or 2 balls and roll in pecans. If made in advance, cover and refrigerate up to 3 days.

29 SMOKED SALMON SPREAD WITH SCOTCH AND CHIVES

Prep: 10 minutes Cook: none Makes: 2 cups

For spreads such as this, where the fish will be chopped or pureed, ask for smoked salmon trimmings, which are often less expensive than picture-perfect slices of salmon. Serve with pumpernickel bread, mini-bagels, or cucumber slices.

1 (8-ounce) package cream cheese, softened
½ pound smoked salmon
2 tablespoons Scotch whisky
2 teaspoons lemon juice
½ teaspoon prepared white horseradish
Dash of cayenne
2 tablespoons chopped fresh chives or scallions

1. In a food processor, combine cream cheese, smoked salmon, Scotch, lemon juice, horseradish, and cayenne. Process until well mixed. Add chives and pulse to mix them in.

2. Store, well covered, in refrigerator up to 3 days. Serve at cool room temperature.

30 SOY SESAME CREAM CHEESE

Prep: 2 minutes   Cook: none   Marinate: 10 minutes   Makes: 1 cup

Soy sauce stains the exterior of the cheese a rich mahogany color, giving the illusion of more exotic fare.

¼ cup soy sauce
1 (8-ounce) package cream cheese
2 tablespoons toasted sesame seeds
Unsalted crackers

1. Pour soy sauce into a shallow dish and marinate cheese, turning frequently, until all sides have been colored, about 10 minutes.

2. Remove cheese from marinade, drain, and place on serving plate. Top with sesame seeds and serve with unsalted crackers.

31 SPEEDY SHRIMP SPREAD

Prep: 5 minutes   Cook: none   Makes: 2 cups

Here's an instant appetizer that seems too easy to be true. We admit to being skeptical the first time we encountered it at a party, but we changed our minds when we saw how quickly it was devoured. See for yourself.

1 (8-ounce) package cream cheese
½ cup cocktail sauce
1 (4½-ounce) can shrimp, drained
Crackers

Place cheese on a serving plate and cover with sauce. Top with shrimp. Serve with crackers.

32 PICK-O-THE-PANTRY

Prep: 2 minutes   Cook: none   Makes: 1 cup

Pickapeppa Sauce is a spicy tomato-based condiment from Jamaica. Look for its distinctive dark green bottle in the imported foods section of your supermarket.

1 (8-ounce) package cream cheese
¼ cup Pickapeppa Sauce
Crackers

Place cheese on a serving plate and top with sauce. Serve with crackers.

33 YOGURT CHEESE ITALIANO

Prep: 15 minutes Cook: none Makes: about 16

At under 20 calories per tablespoon, we can afford to use yogurt cheese lavishly in many recipes. As lean as it is, this visually appealing appetizer adds nothing but flavor to make a memorable and guilt-free treat.

1¼ cups Yogurt Cheese (recipe follows)
3 tablespoons finely chopped roasted red bell pepper
1 tablespoon chopped fresh basil or oregano, or 1 teaspoon dried
1 garlic clove, crushed
½ teaspoon salt
¼ teaspoon pepper
⅓ cup minced parsley
16 small inner leaves of radicchio, or Bibb or romaine lettuce, or Belgian endive

1. In a medium bowl or in a food processor, combine yogurt cheese, roasted red pepper, basil, garlic, salt, and pepper. Blend well. Form mixture into balls about ¾ inch in diameter and roll in parsley to cover.

2. Gently press 1 yogurt cheese ball onto the base of each radicchio or lettuce leaf. If made in advance, cover and refrigerate up to 1 hour.

34 YOGURT CHEESE

Prep: 5 minutes Chill: 24 hours Cook: none
Makes: about 1¼ cups

Modern calorie counters know that just as yogurt makes an acceptable substitute for sour cream, yogurt cheese can be successfully used in place of cream cheese for most dips and spreads. The taste of yogurt cheese is less tart than plain yogurt, and it has a creamy, spreadable consistency. Check your supermarket or health food store for a good-quality yogurt that does not contain gelatin, as gelatin prevents the liquid (whey) from draining off.

4 cups (2 pounds) plain lowfat or nonfat yogurt without gelatin, agar, or pectin

1. Line a large sieve with a double thickness of damp cheesecloth. Place sieve over a deep bowl to catch whey. (To allow for adequate drainage, be sure sieve does not touch bottom of bowl.)

2. Empty yogurt into sieve and let drain, covered, in refrigerator until thickened yet still soft, 24 to 48 hours. If made in advance, cover and refrigerate up to 1 week. Serve plain as a substitute for cream cheese, or flavor to taste with herbs, garlic, and or spices.

35 GARDEN FRESH YOGURT CHEESE

Prep: 5 minutes Cook: none Serves: 6

Although we prefer this crunchy spread on slices of dark pumpernickel, it is equally good with an assortment of raw vegetables.

- **1¼ cups Yogurt Cheese (page 19)**
- **1 pound radishes, coarsely chopped**
- **6 scallions, chopped**
- **¾ teaspoon freshly ground pepper**
- **½ teaspoon salt**

In a medium bowl, combine yogurt cheese, radishes, scallions, pepper, and salt. Stir until well blended. If made in advance, cover and refrigerate up to 2 days.

36 SPICY ANCHOVY MAYONNAISE

Prep: 10 minutes Cook: none Chill: 1 hour Makes: 1¼ cups

This is as good with crisp raw vegetables as it is with shrimp or fish kebabs.

- **1 cup mayonnaise**
- **1 hard-boiled egg, chopped**
- **1 tablespoon chopped parsley**
- **1 tablespoon chopped anchovies**
- **1 tablespoon drained capers**
- **1 teaspoon Dijon mustard**
- **Dash of cayenne**

In a small bowl, combine all ingredients. Stir until well mixed. Cover and refrigerate 1 hour or as long as 2 days.

37 ZESTY HORSERADISH SAUCE

Prep: 5 minutes Cook: none Chill: 1 hour Makes: 1⅓ cups

This is particularly good with roast beef as well as fish kebabs. You'll love it with smoked salmon and mini bagels, too.

- **1 cup sour cream**
- **⅓ cup prepared horseradish**
- **1 tablespoon fresh lemon juice**
- **Dash of white pepper**

In a small bowl, combine all ingredients. Stir until well mixed. Cover and refrigerate 1 hour or as long as 3 days.

38 CURRIED HONEY DIP

Prep: 10 minutes Cook: 5 minutes Makes: 1 cup

We will admit to having been rather skeptical about how this would taste, but one delicious spoonful turned us into true believers. You'll love this with an assortment of crisp vegetables.

1 cup honey
1 tablespoon curry powder
2 tablespoons mayonnaise

1. In a small saucepan, combine honey and curry, stirring to blend well. Cook over low heat, stirring occasionally. Transfer to a small bowl and let cool 5 minutes.

2. Whisk mayonnaise into honey mixture until well blended. Serve immediately, or cover and refrigerate as long as 3 days.

39 CURRIED LEMON MAYONNAISE

Prep: 5 minutes Cook: none Chill: 2 hours Makes: about 1 cup

Serve as a dip with a basket of crudités.

½ cup mayonnaise
½ cup sour cream
3 tablespoons fresh lemon juice
1½ teaspoons curry powder, or more to taste
Dash of salt
Dash of cayenne

1. In a small bowl, combine mayonnaise and sour cream. Mix until well blended. Stir in lemon juice, curry powder, salt, and cayenne. Taste for seasoning, adding more curry powder if necessary.

2. Cover and refrigerate 2 hours or as long as 3 days.

40 HERBED OLIVE OIL

Prep: 5 minutes Cook: none Makes: 3/4 cup

This herbaceous oil is great drizzled over steamed or raw vegetables or served on the side as a dipping sauce. Store it in the refrigerator for keeping, but be sure to let it return to room temperature before using.

3 tablespoons chopped parsley
1 tablespoon chopped fresh rosemary or 1 teaspoon dried
1½ tablespoons chopped fresh marjoram or 1½ teaspoons dried
1½ tablespoons chopped fresh sage or 1¾ teaspoons dried
1½ tablespoons chopped fresh savory or 1¾ teaspoons dried
1 garlic clove, crushed through a press
1 teaspoon salt
½ teaspoon fresh ground peppercorns
½ cup extra-virgin olive oil

In a food processor or blender, combine parsley, rosemary, marjoram, sage, savory, garlic, salt, and pepper. Process until herbs are finely minced. Add olive oil and blend well. Let stand 10 minutes before serving or transfer to a covered jar and store in refrigerator up to 1 week.

41 OLIVE AÏOLI

Prep: 10 minutes Cook: none Makes: 1 cup

This lusty garlic mayonnaise is from our friend Marlena Spieler, who cooks and writes about the hot and spicy cuisines of the world. She serves this as a dipping sauce for tiny steamed new potatoes and other vegetables, as a sandwich spread, or even drizzled over roast leg of lamb. We find it irresistible.

4 large garlic cloves
1 tablespoon coarsely chopped fresh rosemary, or 1 teaspoon dried
⅓ cup mayonnaise
¼ cup olive paste* or tapenade
2 teaspoons fresh lemon juice
⅛ teaspoon freshly ground pepper
¼ cup extra-virgin olive oil

1. In a food processor, finely chop garlic and rosemary. Add mayonnaise, olive paste, lemon juice, and pepper. Process until well mixed.

2. With machine on, gradually add oil in a thin stream until blended. Use immediately, or cover and refrigerate for as long as 1 week.

* *Available in small jars in Italian or international markets, or in the imported condiment section of many supermarkets.*

Chapter 2

Not Too Hot to Handle

There is something very comforting about warm appetizers. These melt-in-the-mouth morsels show your guests you care enough to spend a few extra moments in the kitchen. And if, in the process, your house is perfumed from their baking, all the better.

Pastry is flakiest, cheese creamiest, and meats their tastiest while still hot from the oven. Since recipes like Cheesy Artichoke Squares adapt equally well to being served either warm or at room temperature, you'll have to be the one who decides which way is divine and which way is merely delicious.

The warm and satisfying hors d'oeuvres in this chapter, such as Bacon-Wrapped Water Chestnuts, Clam, Corn, and Chile Fritters, and Buffalo Chicken Wings play double duty by squelching hunger pangs while simultaneously stimulating the appetite. In fact, you might be tempted to make a meal out of several of these delectable dishes. Go right ahead. Small samplings of several light appetizers is a great way to dine.

So many recipes in this chapter can be prepared hours or even days in advance that your guests will marvel at how one seemingly quick trip to the kitchen produced such elaborate-looking appetizers.

42 CHEESY CHILE SQUARES

Prep: 15 minutes Cook: 45 to 50 minutes Makes: 36

This is our version of a popular recipe that first appeared in Marlene Sorosky's *Cookery for Entertaining*. Once you've tasted it, you'll understand why it became a classic in our catering days.

4 tablespoons butter
5 eggs
¼ cup flour
½ teaspoon baking powder
⅛ teaspoon salt
Dash of cayenne
2 cups shredded Monterey Jack or Cheddar cheese (about 8 ounces)
1 cup small-curd cottage cheese
1 (4-ounce) can diced green chiles

1. Preheat oven to 400°F. Melt butter in a 9-inch square baking pan in oven.

2. In a large bowl, whisk eggs until well blended. Stir in flour, baking powder, salt, and cayenne. Tip baking pan to coat bottom and sides; add melted butter to egg mixture. Add Monterey Jack cheese, cottage cheese, and chiles and blend well.

3. Pour mixture into buttered pan and bake 15 minutes. Reduce oven temperature to 350° and bake 30 to 35 minutes longer, until top is lightly browned and a knife inserted into center shows no evidence of uncooked egg. Let cool on a rack at least 10 minutes. Cut into 1½-inch squares. (If made in advance, cover and refrigerate up to 2 days. Freeze for longer storage.) Serve warm or at room temperature.

43 BROCCOLI BITES

Prep: 15 minutes Cook: 15 minutes Freeze: 3 hours Makes: 50

2 (10-ounce) packages frozen chopped broccoli
2 cups herb stuffing mix
1 cup grated Parmesan cheese (4 ounces)
6 eggs, beaten
1½ sticks (6 ounces) butter or margarine, softened
½ teaspoon salt
¼ teaspoon pepper

1. Cook broccoli according to package directions; drain well. In a medium bowl, combine cooked broccoli, stuffing mix, cheese, eggs, butter, salt, and pepper.

2. Roll mixture into small balls, about 1 inch in diameter. Freeze, well covered, for at least 3 hours.

3. Preheat oven to 350°F. Place frozen balls on lightly greased cookie sheet. Bake until brown, about 15 minutes.

44 ARTICHOKE BALLS

Prep: 10 minutes Cook: 10 minutes Makes: 24

Easy and quick, but elegant enough for company, these tasty hors d'oeuvres can be made ahead and refrigerated for up to six hours before being baked in Step 3. Allow an extra five minutes' cooking time if they have been chilled.

- **1 (8¾-ounce) can artichoke hearts, drained and finely chopped**
- **1 cup seasoned bread crumbs**
- **2 eggs**
- **2 tablespoons olive oil**
- **2 tablespoons grated Parmesan cheese**
- **1 tablespoon fresh lemon juice**
- **2 garlic cloves, minced**
- **¼ cup grated Parmesan cheese**

1. Preheat oven to 350°F. In a medium bowl, combine chopped artichoke, bread crumbs, eggs, olive oil, 2 tablespoons Parmesan cheese, lemon juice, and garlic.

2. Form mixture into 24 small balls 1 inch in diameter and roll in remaining Parmesan cheese. Set on a lightly greased baking sheet.

3. Bake artichoke balls until eggs are set throughout and balls are heated through, about 10 minutes.

45 CHEESY ARTICHOKE SQUARES

Prep: 10 minutes Cook: 30 minutes Makes: 36

- **2 (6-ounce) jars marinated artichoke hearts**
- **½ medium onion, minced**
- **1 garlic clove, minced**
- **4 eggs**
- **¼ cup fine dry bread crumbs**
- **¼ teaspoon salt**
- **⅛ teaspoon dried oregano**
- **⅛ teaspoon freshly ground black pepper**
- **⅛ teaspoon hot pepper sauce**
- **2 cups shredded Cheddar cheese (about 8 ounces)**
- **2 tablespoons chopped parsley**

1. Preheat oven to 325°F. Drain artichoke hearts, reserving marinade from one jar. Finely chop drained artichokes. In a large frying pan, cook onion and garlic in reserved marinade over medium heat until soft, about 5 minutes. Remove from heat and set aside to cool slightly.

2. In a medium bowl, beat eggs until blended. Stir in chopped artichokes, bread crumbs, salt, oregano, pepper, and hot sauce until well mixed. Stir in cheese, parsley, and onion and garlic with marinade. Pour into a greased 7x11-inch baking pan.

3. Bake until center feels firm to the touch, about 30 minutes. Remove from oven and let cool 15 minutes before cutting into 1-inch squares. Serve warm or at room temperature.

46 ARTICHOKE CLAM PUFFS

Prep: 15 minutes Cook: 20 to 22 minutes Makes: about 36

For easy serving, spear each artichoke diagonally with a toothpick before topping with clam mixture.

2 (9-ounce) packages frozen artichoke heart halves
1 (8-ounce) package cream cheese, softened
2 tablespoons fresh lemon juice
¼ teaspoon hot pepper sauce
1 (6½-ounce) can minced clams, drained
Paprika

1. Preheat oven to 400°F. Cook artichoke hearts according to package directions, about 10 minutes. Drain well. Arrange cut-sides up on a greased baking sheet.

2. In a small bowl, combine cream cheese, lemon juice, and hot sauce. Stir in clams.

3. Spoon clam mixture onto cut sides of artichokes and sprinkle with paprika. Bake until clam mixture is lightly browned and bubbly, 10 to 12 minutes.

47 CLAM, CORN, AND CHILE FRITTERS

Prep: 10 minutes Cook: 4 minutes Makes: 18

1 (8-ounce) can minced clams, drained
3 eggs
1 cup corn kernels
½ cup soda cracker crumbs
½ teaspoon salt
½ teaspoon pepper
1 fresh jalapeño pepper, seeded and minced, or ½ teaspoon crushed hot red pepper
2 to 4 cups corn or peanut oil

1. Drain clams, reserving liquid. In a medium bowl, beat eggs until well mixed. Stir in clams, corn, cracker crumbs, salt, pepper, and jalapeño pepper. If mixture is very dry, moisten with reserved clam juice to make a thick batter.

2. In a wok or large heavy saucepan, heat 2 inches of oil to 375°F on a deep-frying thermometer. Using 2 tablespoons, scoop up a heaping mound of batter with one spoon and slide off bowl of spoon with the other. Drop into hot oil. Fry, a few at a time, turning once, until golden brown, about 4 minutes total. Remove fritters with a slotted spoon, drain on paper towels, and serve at once.

48 MAKE-AHEAD CHEESE PILLOWS

Prep: 10 minutes Cook: 10 to 15 minutes Freeze: 2 hours Makes: 48

Here is the perfect use for a loaf of day-old bread. These rich and creamy appetizers can be made well in advance and baked frozen.

- **1 unsliced sandwich loaf of white bread**
- **2 cups shredded sharp Cheddar cheese (about 8 ounces)**
- **1 cup heavy cream**
- **1 stick (4 ounces) butter, softened**
- **Dash of cayenne**

1. Freeze bread loaf until firm, about 1 hour. Trim off crust. Cut bread into 1½-inch cubes.

2. In a double boiler set over simmering water, combine cheese, cream, butter, and cayenne. Heat, stirring occasionally, until cheese and butter are melted and mixture is well blended, about 5 minutes.

3. Spear each bread cube with the tines of a fork and swirl in warm cheese mixture until thoroughly coated. Transfer to a baking sheet lined with wax paper and repeat until all bread cubes have been coated. Place tray of cheese cubes in freezer for about 1 hour. Cheese cubes can now be stored in plastic bags in the freezer for up to 2 months.

4. To serve, preheat oven to 450°F. Arrange frozen cheese cubes on a baking sheet and bake until heated through and barely browned at edges, 5 to 10 minutes. Serve hot.

49 OLIVE-FILLED CHEDDAR NUGGETS

Prep: 15 minutes Cook: 15 minutes Makes: 48

Unbaked nuggets can be frozen, thawed in the refrigerator for a few hours, and baked just before serving.

- **2 cups shredded sharp Cheddar cheese (8 ounces)**
- **4 tablespoons butter, softened**
- **1 cup flour**
- **1½ teaspoons paprika**
- **Dash of cayenne**
- **1 (8½-ounce) jar pimiento-stuffed olives**
- **1 egg**
- **1 tablespoon cream or milk**
- **¼ cup sesame or poppy seeds**

1. Preheat oven to 350°F. In a food processor, combine cheese and butter. Process until well blended. Add flour, paprika, and cayenne and process until smooth.

2. Drain olives and pat dry. Wrap about 1 teaspoon of dough around each olive, pinching to seal any cracks. Form into balls and arrange on a parchment or foil-lined baking sheet.

3. In a small bowl, beat egg and cream until well blended; brush over tops of pastries. Sprinkle with sesame seeds and bake until just golden, about 15 minutes. Serve hot, warm, or at room temperature.

50 CLAM AND PROSCIUTTO PUFFS

Prep: 20 minutes Cook: 18 minutes Makes: 24

You'll want to serve these on small plates with cocktail forks. To save work, ask your fish market to shuck the clams for you, reserving the shells.

1 dozen hard-shelled clams, such as littleneck or razor clams
4 tablespoons butter
½ cup chopped scallions
2 cups chopped fresh mushrooms (about ½ pound)
3 tablespoons flour
¼ pound prosciutto or Black Forest ham, chopped (about 1 cup)
½ teaspoon Dijon mustard
¼ teaspoon salt
½ teaspoon freshly ground pepper
4 egg whites

1. Preheat oven to 400°F. Scrub and shuck clams, reserving shells. Separate shells, lightly butter both halves, and set aside. Coarsely chop clams.

2. In a large skillet, melt remaining butter over medium heat. Add scallions and mushrooms and cook until softened but not browned, about 3 minutes. Stir in chopped clams, flour, prosciutto, mustard, salt, and pepper. Cook, stirring, until thickened, about 5 minutes. Spoon into buttered clam shells.

3. Beat egg whites until stiff but not dry. Spoon over clams and bake until lightly browned, about 10 minutes. Serve warm.

51 HERBED PIZZA BISCUITS

Prep: 10 minutes Cook: 10 minutes Makes: 24

1 cup biscuit baking mix, such as Bisquick
1 (8-ounce) can tomato sauce
1 tablespoon Italian seasoning
24 thin slices of pepperoni, 1 inch in diameter (about 1¾ ounces)

1. Preheat oven to 350°F. In a small bowl, combine biscuit mix, tomato sauce, and Italian seasoning; blend well. Pinch off about 2 teaspoons of dough, roll into a ball, and place on a lightly greased baking sheet. Repeat until all dough has been used.

2. Top each ball of dough with a slice of pepperoni; press to flatten slightly. Bake until pepperoni is bubbly hot and biscuit is golden around the edges, about 10 minutes.

52 SAVORY MUSHROOM CUPS

Prep: 25 minutes Cook: 27 to 32 minutes Makes: 24

When we were catering, this hot hors d'oeuvre was one of our most popular appetizers. The versatile filling keeps several days in the refrigerator, and it is equally good baked in puff pastry, filo, or cream cheese pastry.

4 tablespoons butter
3 shallots, minced
½ pound mushrooms, finely chopped
2 tablespoons flour
½ cup heavy cream
3 tablespoons chopped fresh or freeze-dried chives
2 tablespoons chopped parsley
½ teaspoon salt
½ teaspoon lemon juice
⅛ teaspoon cayenne
Toast Cups (recipe follows)
2 tablespoons grated Parmesan cheese or chopped parsley

1. In a large frying pan, melt butter over medium heat. Add shallots and cook until softened but not browned, about 2 minutes. Add mushrooms and cook, stirring occasionally, until nearly all the liquid has cooked away, 10 to 15 minutes.

2. Sprinkle flour over mushroom mixture, and cook, stirring, 2 minutes. Increase heat to high and stir in cream, mixing well. Cook until mixture comes to a boil, about 3 minutes. Remove from heat and stir in chives, parsley, salt, lemon juice, and cayenne. If made in advance, store well covered in refrigerator up to 3 days.

3. Preheat oven to 350°F. Mound about 1 tablespoon of mushroom mixture in each toast cup and top with ¼ teaspoon grated Parmesan cheese or parsley. Bake until tops are golden and mushroom mixture is bubbling hot, about 10 minutes.

53 TOAST CUPS

Prep: 10 minutes Cook: 10 minutes Makes: 24

It's a good idea to keep a batch of these in the freezer. They make great containers for many of the hot or cold fillings found in this book.

2 tablespoons butter, softened
1 (1-pound) loaf of thin sliced firm-textured white bread

1. Preheat oven to 400°F. Butter insides of 2 gem-size (1½-inch) muffin tins (24 cups).

2. Using a plain or fluted 2½- to 3-inch biscuit cutter, cut a round from each slice of bread and gently press into muffin cups to line bottom and sides. Bake until edges are golden brown, about 10 minutes. Let cool on a rack. Store airtight up to 3 days, or freeze.

54 SPICY OLIVE BITES

Prep: 25 minutes Cook: 26 to 32 minutes Makes: 32

- **¾ cup thinly sliced scallions**
- **2 garlic cloves, minced**
- **1 tablespoon olive oil**
- **4 eggs**
- **1 (4-ounce) can diced green chiles**
- **1 (2¼-ounce) can sliced ripe olives, drained**
- **¼ cup fresh bread crumbs**
- **2 tablespoons chopped fresh cilantro or parsley**
- **¼ teaspoon salt**
- **¼ teaspoon ground cumin**
- **⅛ teaspoon cayenne**
- **1½ cups shredded Cheddar or Monterey Jack cheese (about 6 ounces)**

1. Preheat oven to 325°F. In a medium frying pan, cook scallions and garlic in olive oil over medium heat until softened but not browned, 1 to 2 minutes. Remove from heat and let cool.

2. In a medium bowl, beat eggs until well blended. Add chiles, olives, bread crumbs, cilantro, salt, cumin, and cayenne. Mix well. Stir in cheese and cooked scallions and garlic. Pour mixture into a greased 8-inch square baking pan.

3. Bake until a knife inserted into center shows no evidence of runny egg, 25 to 30 minutes. Let cool on a rack at least 10 minutes. (If made in advance, cover and refrigerate up to 2 days.) Cut into 1x2-inch pieces. Serve warm or at room temperature.

55 SMOKED SALMON AND PARMESAN CREAM CUPS

Prep: 10 minutes Cook: 5 minutes Makes: 32

This is our adaptation of a recipe found in *The Frog Commissary Cookbook.* It's hard to improve upon perfection.

- **8 ounces natural cream cheese, softened***
- **¾ cup grated Parmesan cheese (about 3 ounces)**
- **¼ teaspoon hot pepper sauce**
- **Dash of lemon juice**
- **3 ounces thinly sliced smoked salmon**
- **32 Toast Cups (page 29)**
- **32 tiny sprigs of fresh dill or parsley**

1. Preheat oven to 400°F. In a small bowl or food processor, combine cream cheese, Parmesan cheese, hot sauce, and lemon juice. Blend well.

2. Cut smoked salmon into 32 pieces and place a piece inside each toast cup. Spoon or pipe about 2 teaspoons of cheese mixture over salmon and top each with a sprig of dill. Bake until cheese is just softened, about 5 minutes. Serve warm.

* *Available in delicatessens and specialty food shops.*

56 BLUE CHEESE STUFFED MUSHROOMS

Prep: 20 minutes Cook: 15 minutes Makes: 24

In keeping with Miss Piggy's dictum that one should never eat more than one can lift—as well as our theory that appetizers should be no more than a mouthful—we prefer to use small or medium-size mushrooms for stuffing.

24 medium mushrooms (about 1 pound)
3 tablespoons butter or olive oil
1 shallot, minced
2 tablespoons cooked and crumbled bacon (about 2 slices)
4 ounces blue cheese, crumbled (about 1 cup)
1 (3-ounce) package cream cheese, softened
1 teaspoon brandy or lemon juice
½ teaspoon dried thyme leaves

1. Preheat oven to 375°F. Remove stems from mushrooms and finely chop. In a medium skillet, melt 1 tablespoon butter over medium heat. Add shallot and mushroom stems and cook until mushroom liquid is exuded and then evaporates, about 3 minutes. Scrape mixture into a medium bowl. Add bacon, blue cheese, cream cheese, brandy, and thyme and blend well.

2. In same skillet, melt remaining 2 tablespoons butter over medium heat. Immediately remove from heat and toss mushroom caps in melted butter until well coated. Arrange caps stem-end up on a baking sheet and mound about 2 teaspoons blue cheese filling in each. (If made in advance, cover with plastic wrap and refrigerate up to 8 hours).

3. Bake until cheese is bubbly hot and mushrooms are tender but still hold their shape, about 10 minutes.

SWISS SHRIMP FANTASIES

Prep: 10 minutes Cook: 8 to 10 minutes Makes: 42

The topping can be made a day in advance if covered well and stored in the refrigerator. Spread over the rye bread shortly before baking to prevent sogginess.

½ pound tiny shelled cooked shrimp
1 cup mayonnaise
4 ounces Swiss cheese, shredded (about 1 cup)
⅓ cup chopped scallions
1 tablespoon fresh lemon juice
1½ teaspoons chopped fresh dill or ½ teaspoon dried
Dash of cayenne
42 slices of petit cocktail rye

1. In a medium bowl, combine shrimp, mayonnaise, cheese, scallions, lemon juice, dill, and cayenne. If made in advance, cover and refrigerate.

2. Preheat oven to 450°F. Top each bread slice with about 1 tablespoon of shrimp mixture and arrange in a single layer on a greased baking sheet. Bake until topping is golden brown and bubbly, 8 to 10 minutes. Serve at once.

58 UPTOWN POTATO SKINS

Prep: 30 minutes Cook: 51 to 52 minutes Makes: 24

These potato skins have gotten all dressed up for the party. Fortunately, most of the preparation can be done well in advance.

12 tiny red (new) potatoes, about 1½ inches in diameter
2 to 4 cups peanut or corn oil
½ cup sour cream or crème fraîche
Optional toppings: Salsa and chopped fresh cilantro, crisp crumbled bacon and minced scallions, caviar and minced chives, chopped ripe olives and finely shredded Cheddar cheese

1. Preheat oven to 400°F. Pierce each potato with a fork and bake until tender, about 40 minutes. Let cool.

2. Halve potatoes. Cut a thin slice from the rounded bottom of each potato half so it will stand upright. Using a melon baller or a small spoon, scoop out center from each potato half, leaving a shell about ¼ inch thick; reserve potato for another use.

3. In a wok or large heavy saucepan, heat oil to 360° on a deep-fry thermometer. Cook potato shells, in batches without crowding, until just golden, 1 to 2 minutes. Drain on paper towels. (If made in advance, cover and refrigerate as long as 24 hours.)

4. Preheat oven to 400°. Using a small spoon or a pastry bag fitted with a star tip, fill each potato cavity with 2 teaspoons sour cream. Arrange on a baking sheet and cook until heated through, about 10 minutes. Top with desired toppings and serve warm.

59 SWEET POTATO BITES

Prep: 20 minutes Cook: 25 minutes Makes: about 30

Sweet potato slices make a delicious edible base for this colorful appetizer. Be sure to allow at least 3 per person.

1 pound sweet potatoes, about 2 inches in diameter
2 tablespoons vegetable oil
⅓ cup sour cream
Optional toppings: Caviar, chopped fresh chives or scallions, crystallized ginger, crumbled bacon, chopped fresh dill or thyme

1. Preheat oven to 400°F. Scrub sweet potatoes and trim ends. Cut into ¼-inch rounds. Oil a jelly-roll pan and arrange sweet potato slices in a single layer; brush tops with remaining oil. Bake 15 minutes, or until slices are golden brown on the bottom. Turn slices over and cook 10 minutes longer, or until both sides are nicely browned.

2. Transfer potato slices to a serving plate and spoon or pipe about ½ teaspoon sour cream onto each. Top with 1 or more optional toppings. Serve hot, warm, or at room temperature.

---

60 PASTA AND PEPPER FRITTATA

Prep: 15 minutes Cook: 35 to 45 minutes Serves: 6 to 8

Pasta gives this unusual frittata extra substance and an interesting texture. If you are lucky enough to have leftovers, refrigerate and serve the next day with salad for a light meal.

- **6 ounces angel hair or other thin pasta**
- **1 tablespoon olive oil**
- **1 small red bell pepper, chopped**
- **2 garlic cloves, minced**
- **1 cup shredded fontina cheese (about 4 ounces)**
- **2 tablespoons chopped parsley**
- **1 tablespoon chopped fresh oregano or 1 teaspoon dried**
- **5 eggs**
- **¼ cup heavy cream**
- **1 teaspoon salt**
- **¼ teaspoon freshly ground pepper**

1. Preheat oven to 325°F. In a large pot of boiling salted water, cook pasta over high heat until tender but still firm to the bite, about 2 minutes. Drain, rinse well under cold water, and drain again.

2. In a medium skillet, heat olive oil over medium heat. Add pepper and garlic and cook until softened but not browned, about 3 minutes. Scrape into a large bowl.

3. Add pasta, cheese, parsley, and oregano to bowl. Toss well. Turn pasta mixture into a greased 9-inch quiche or pie plate. In same bowl, beat eggs, cream, salt, and pepper until well blended. Pour egg mixture over pasta.

4. Bake 30 to 40 minutes, or until a knife inserted into center shows no evidence of uncooked egg. Let cool 15 minutes or as long as 2 hours before cutting into wedges. Serve warm or at room temperature.

61 DEEP-FRIED TORTELLONI WITH PUTTANESCA SAUCE

Prep: 10 minutes Cook: 10 minutes Serves: 8 to 10

2 (9-ounce) packages fresh or frozen tortelloni
2 to 4 cups peanut or corn oil
Puttanesca Sauce (recipe follows)

1. Cook tortelloni according to package directions. Rinse under cold water, drain, and pat dry.

2. Fill a wok or heavy saucepan with 2 inches of oil and heat over medium-high heat until oil reaches 350°F on a deep-frying thermometer. Deep-fry tortelloni in batches without crowding, turning once, until crisp and lightly golden, 2 to 3 minutes. Remove with a skimmer or slotted spoon and drain well on paper towels. Serve individually with toothpicks, or thread one or two tortelloni on skewers for dipping in sauce.

PUTTANESCA SAUCE

Makes about 2 cups

1 (15-ounce) can tomato sauce
½ cup kalamata olives, pitted and chopped
1 (2-ounce) tin flat anchovy fillets, drained and chopped
2 tablespoons drained capers
1 tablespoon extra-virgin olive oil (or oil from anchovies)
2 garlic cloves, minced
⅛ teaspoon crushed hot red pepper
¼ cup chopped parsley

In a small saucepan, combine tomato sauce with olives, anchovies, capers, oil, garlic, and hot pepper. Simmer over medium-low heat until flavors have blended, about 10 minutes. Stir in parsley and serve warm with Tortelloni (above) or Polenta Sticks (recipe follows).

62 POLENTA STICKS

Prep: 15 minutes Cook: 25 to 30 minutes Chill: 1 hour Makes: 32

Serve these "Italian fries" with Blue Cheese Dip (page 37) or Puttanesca Sauce (above), for dipping.

2 cups chicken broth or water
½ teaspoon salt
½ cup instant polenta or yellow cornmeal
2 tablespoons olive oil

1. Use a 20-inch piece of plastic wrap to line the inside of an 8-inch square baking pan, letting excess plastic drape over edges.

2. In a medium saucepan, combine chicken broth and salt over high heat. When mixture boils, gradually whisk in polenta in a slow, steady stream. Reduce heat to medium and cook, stirring, 5 minutes, or until polenta is thickened to consistency of hot cereal. Pour into prepared pan, pressing mixture to an even thickness. Cover with excess plastic wrap and let cool. Refrigerate until firm, about 1 hour, or as long as 2 days.

3. Preheat oven to 450°F. Unmold polenta onto a clean work surface and discard wrap. Cut polenta crosswise in half, then cut vertically into sticks ½ inch wide. Arrange polenta sticks on a greased foil- or parchment-lined baking sheet. Brush sticks generously with olive oil and bake 20 to 25 minutes, until golden and crusty. Serve warm.

---

63 GARLIC POTATO CUPS WITH FRESH SAGE

Prep: 25 minutes Cook: 20 to 30 minutes Makes: about 32

These tiny twice-baked potatoes fill the need to have something substantial with drinks. If you have never cooked garlic in this manner, you'll be surprised at its sweet, nutty flavor.

- **1 pound small red new potatoes (creamers), 1 to 1½ inches in diameter**
- **4 large garlic cloves (with skins left on)**
- **1 (3-ounce) package cream cheese, softened**
- **2 tablespoons buttermilk or sour cream**
- **1½ tablespoons minced fresh sage leaves, or 1 teaspoon dried**
- **¼ teaspoon salt**
- **⅛ teaspoon freshly ground pepper**
- **Paprika**

1. In a medium saucepan, combine potatoes and garlic with cold salted water to cover. Bring to a boil and cook until potatoes and garlic are tender, 10 to 15 minutes; drain into a colander.

2. Preheat oven to 425°F. When cool enough to handle, cut potatoes in half. Using a melon baller or small spoon, scoop out and reserve centers, leaving a ¼-inch-thick shell.

3. Peel garlic cloves. In a medium bowl, mash reserved potato centers, garlic, cream cheese, buttermilk, sage, salt, and pepper until well blended. Using a spoon or pastry bag fitted with a large plain tip, mound potato mixture back into potato shells and sprinkle with paprika. Arrange filled potatoes, mashed-side up, on a baking sheet. (If made in advance, let stand at room temperature up to 2 hours, or cover and refrigerate up to 8 hours.)

4. Bake potatoes until filling is heated through and lightly browned on top, 10 to 15 minutes. Serve warm.

64 "WURST" ONION CUPS

Prep: 20 minutes Cook: 15 minutes Makes: 24

Dough cups can be shaped ahead and kept covered in the refrigerator for an hour before filling and baking.

1 (4¾-ounce) can liverwurst spread
½ cup plus 1 tablespoon sour cream
½ teaspoon lemon juice
½ cup crumbled canned French-fried onions
1 (8-ounce) can refrigerated crescent dinner rolls

1. Preheat oven to 375°F. Combine liverwurst spread, 1 tablespoon sour cream, lemon juice, and crumbled onions. Unroll dough and cut into 4 rectangles. Cut each rectangle into 6 equal pieces, then roll each piece into a ball. Place 1 ball of dough in each of 24 gem-size (1½-inch) ungreased muffin cups.

2. Press dough to evenly cover bottom and sides of muffin cups. Fill each with 1 generous teaspoon liverwurst mixture, keeping level with edge of dough. Top each with 1 teaspoon sour cream and bake until crust is golden brown, about 15 minutes.

65 CHEDDAR CLOUDS

Prep: 10 minutes Cook: 20 minutes Serves: 10 to 12

6 eggs, lightly beaten
¾ cup flour
1 teaspoon baking powder
½ teaspoon salt
¼ cup chopped scallions
2 tablespoons chopped fresh or freeze-dried chives
2 cups shredded Cheddar cheese (about 8 ounces)
2 to 4 tablespoons peanut or corn oil
½ cup sour cream
Black olive paste* or salsa

1. In a medium bowl, whisk together eggs, flour, baking powder, and salt until well blended. Stir in scallions, chives, and Cheddar cheese.

2. In a medium skillet, heat 1½ tablespoons oil over medium heat. Drop tablespoons of batter into hot oil without crowding and cook, turning once or twice, until both sides are golden brown, about 3 minutes total. Remove with a spatula and continue cooking tablespoons of remaining egg mixture, adding more oil as necessary. (If made in advance, refrigerate up to 2 days and reheat for 5 minutes in a 400°F oven.)

3. To serve, top each Cheddar Cloud with ½ teaspoon sour cream and a dab of black olive paste or salsa. Serve hot or at room temperature.

**Available in small jars in Italian or international markets, or in the imported condiment section of many supermarkets.*

66 BUFFALO CHICKEN WINGS

Prep: 20 minutes Cook: 10 minutes Makes: 48

This American classic originated at the Anchor Bar in Buffalo, New York, where it is still a favorite with locals and tourists alike. Tradition dictates that these spicy morsels be served with crisp celery sticks and creamy blue cheese dressing to cool the fire.

24 whole chicken wings (about 4 pounds)
Salt and pepper
2 to 4 cups corn or peanut oil
4 tablespoons butter
2 to 5 tablespoons Frank's Louisiana Red Hot Sauce or other hot pepper sauce
1 tablespoon distilled white vinegar
Celery sticks
Blue Cheese Dip (recipe follows)

1. Rinse chicken with cold water and pat dry. Cut off and discard pointed tip of each wing and halve wings at the main joint. Season chicken with salt and pepper to taste. In a wok or large heavy saucepan, heat 2 inches of oil to 375°F on a deep-frying thermometer. Cook the wings, in batches without crowding, until crisp and golden, about 10 minutes. Drain well on paper towels.

2. In a small saucepan, melt butter over medium-low heat. Stir in hot sauce and vinegar. Mound wings on a serving plate and pour hot butter sauce over them. Serve at once, with celery sticks and blue cheese dip.

67 BLUE CHEESE DIP

Prep: 5 minutes Cook: none Makes: 1¾ cups

1 cup crumbled blue cheese (4 ounces)
½ cup sour cream
½ cup mayonnaise
1 scallion, chopped
1 tablespoon distilled white vinegar
1 garlic clove, crushed through a press

In a small bowl, combine blue cheese, sour cream, mayonnaise, scallion, vinegar, and garlic. Stir until well mixed. If made in advance, cover and refrigerate up to 3 days.

68 CAJUN CHICKEN WINGS

Prep: 20 minutes Marinate: overnight Cook: 20 minutes
Makes: 48

24 whole chicken wings (about 4 pounds)
1 tablespoon cayenne
2 tablespoons paprika
2 tablespoons garlic powder
1 tablespoon dried oregano
1 tablespoon dried thyme leaves
1 tablespoon onion powder
1 tablespoon salt
½ teaspoon freshly ground white pepper
½ teaspoon freshly ground black pepper
¼ cup olive or other vegetable oil

1. Rinse chicken with cold water and pat dry. Cut off and discard pointed tip of each wing and halve wings at the main joint.

2. In a food processor or blender, combine cayenne, paprika, garlic powder, oregano, thyme, onion powder, salt, white pepper, and black pepper. Process until well blended. With machine on, slowly pour in oil and process until a thick paste forms. In a large bowl, combine chicken wings and spice paste. Toss until wings are well coated. Cover and refrigerate overnight.

3. Preheat broiler. Arrange wings on broiler pan about 4 inches from heat. Broil, turning once, until nicely browned outside and cooked through, about 20 minutes total. Serve warm or at room temperature.

69 CHICKEN KEBABS WITH MUSTARD CRUST

Prep: 15 minutes Cook: 5 to 7 minutes Makes: 24 skewers

Tangy Dijon mustard complements the flavor of juicy chicken nuggets in this easily assembled appetizer.

1 tablespoon vegetable oil
5 skinless, boneless chicken breast halves (about 1½ pounds)
½ cup Dijon mustard
1 tablespoon minced shallot
2 cups fresh bread crumbs
¼ cup chopped parsley

1. Preheat oven to 450°F. Line a baking sheet with foil or parchment paper, brush with oil, and set aside. Soak 24 bamboo skewers in water for at least 30 minutes to prevent burning.

2. Rinse chicken breasts with cold water and pat dry. Cut each piece of chicken into ¾-inch chunks.

3. In a medium bowl, combine mustard and shallot. In another medium bowl, combine bread crumbs and parsley. Toss chicken pieces in mustard mixture to coat, then dredge in parslied bread crumbs. Thread 2 or 3 chunks onto end of each skewer and place on prepared baking sheet. Bake until chicken is cooked through but still juicy, 5 to 7 minutes. Serve warm.

70 SCALLION BEEF ROLLS

Prep: 20 minutes   Marinate: 15 minutes   Cook: 2 minutes
Makes: 12

These make a wonderful addition to any party. The flavors of fermented black beans and fresh ginger are addicting, so be sure to make plenty.

- **½ pound flank steak or top round**
- **1 egg white**
- **½ teaspoon salt**
- **1 teaspoon cornstarch**
- **1 teaspoon Chinese fermented black beans,* rinsed, drained, and minced**
- **6 garlic cloves, minced**
- **1 tablespoon minced fresh ginger**
- **½ teaspoon sugar**
- **1 tablespoon soy sauce**
- **1 tablespoon dry red wine or vermouth**
- **12 scallions**
- **2 tablespoons Asian sesame oil**

1. Cut steak into 2-inch squares. Cut each square horizontally in half so meat is about ¼ inch thick. Pound each square until flattened to ⅛ inch. In a medium bowl, combine egg white, salt, and cornstarch. Beat until well mixed. Add steak and toss to coat. Marinate 15 minutes.

2. In a small bowl, combine black beans, garlic, ginger, sugar, soy sauce, and red wine. Mix well.

3. Cut off white scallion bulbs and set aside for another use. Cut remaining light and dark green parts into 2-inch lengths. In a small heatproof bowl, pour boiling water over dark green part of scallions to soften. Drain, rinse with cold water, and drain again.

4. Spread 1 teaspoon of black bean mixture on each piece of steak, then place light green part of scallion on top. Roll up and tie with dark green part of scallion. Brush with sesame oil. Broil, turning once, until lightly browned, about 1 minute on each side. Serve hot.

* *Chinese fermented black beans are available in Asian markets and the imported food sections of many supermarkets.*

71 JERK CHICKEN WINGS

Prep: 25 minutes Marinate: overnight Cook: 20 minutes
Makes: 48

Don't worry, be happy! The name of this recipe is no reflection on the cook; jerk is a fiery Jamaican marinade for chicken, pork, or beef.

24 whole chicken wings (about 4 pounds)
8 scallions, cut into 1-inch pieces
4 fresh jalapeño peppers, seeded and coarsely chopped
2 tablespoons distilled white vinegar
1 tablespoon ground allspice
4 garlic cloves, chopped
2 teaspoons dried thyme
1 teaspoon salt
½ teaspoon freshly ground pepper
¼ teaspoon cayenne
¼ cup vegetable oil
Lime wedges

1. Rinse chicken with cold water and pat dry. Cut off and discard pointed tip of each wing and halve wings at the main joint.

2. In a food processor, combine scallions, jalapeño peppers, vinegar, allspice, garlic, thyme, salt, pepper, and cayenne. Process until well blended. With machine on, slowly pour in oil and puree until a thick paste forms.

3. In a large bowl, combine chicken wings and jerk paste. Toss until wings are well coated. Cover and refrigerate overnight.

4. Preheat broiler. Arrange wings on broiler pan about 6 inches from heat and broil, turning once, until nicely browned outside and cooked through, about 20 minutes total. Serve warm or at room temperature with lime wedges and lots of napkins.

72 CANDIED BACON KNOTS

Prep: 30 minutes Cook: 15 to 20 minutes Makes: 42 to 48

With the exception of an occasional vegetarian, we have yet to meet a person who can eat only one of these. Be sure to make plenty!

Vegetable cooking spray
1½ cups packed light brown sugar
1½ pounds thinly sliced bacon

1. Preheat oven to 350°F. Line a broiler pan with aluminum foil to facilitate cleanup. Position broiler rack on top and coat with vegetable cooking spray.

2. Place brown sugar in a shallow dish. Tie each bacon slice into a loose knot. Press one side of bacon into brown sugar to coat well. Arrange in a single layer, sugared-side up, on prepared broiler rack.

3. Bake until bacon is crisp and sugar is bubbly, 15 to 20 minutes. Transfer, sugar-side up, to paper towels to drain and cool. Candied bacon knots can be held up to 3 hours at cool room temperature. Serve in a napkin-lined basket.

73 CHIPPER BURGER BITES

Prep: 20 minutes Cook: 10 minutes Makes: 36

As an alternative to toothpicks, thin pretzel sticks make ideal picks for serving these savory meatballs.

- **2 eggs, beaten**
- **2 tablespoons cornstarch**
- **1 tablespoon soy sauce**
- **1 medium onion, finely chopped**
- **¼ teaspoon pepper**
- **3 cups (about 4 ounces) corn tortilla chips, crumbled**
- **1 pound ground sirloin (90% lean)**

1. In a medium bowl, combine eggs, cornstarch, soy sauce, onion, and pepper. Blend well. Stir in crumbled corn chips and let stand 20 minutes to soften. Add beef and blend well.

2. Preheat broiler. Shape beef mixture into 1-inch balls and arrange 1 inch apart on a foil-lined baking sheet. Broil about 6 inches from heat 10 minutes, or until browned outside but still pink and juicy inside.

74 PEANUTTY MEATBALLS

Prep: 10 minutes Cook: 5 to 7 minutes Makes: 24

- **½ pound ground round (80% lean)**
- **½ cup peanut butter, smooth or crunchy, to taste**
- **¼ cup minced onion**
- **½ cup plus 2 tablespoons chili sauce or ketchup**
- **½ teaspoon salt**
- **⅛ teaspoon pepper**
- **1 egg, beaten**
- **Dash of cayenne**
- **About ¼ cup peanut or corn oil**

1. In a medium bowl, combine ground beef, peanut butter, onion, 2 tablespoons chili sauce, salt, pepper, egg, and cayenne. Blend until well mixed. Shape mixture into 24 meatballs, about ¾ inch in diameter.

2. In a large frying pan, heat 2 tablespoons oil over medium-high heat. Add meatballs in batches without crowding and cook, turning, until browned all over, 5 to 7 minutes; add more oil as needed to prevent sticking. Serve hot with wooden toothpicks, with remaining ½ cup chili sauce for dipping on the side.

75 PEPPERED BACON KNOTS

Prep: 30 minutes Cook: 15 to 20 minutes Makes: 42 to 48

Spicy black pepper works beautifully against the sweetness of honey and the saltiness of the bacon.

Vegetable cooking spray
1 cup honey or maple syrup
1½ pounds thinly sliced bacon
Coarsely ground black peppercorns

1. Preheat oven to 350°F. Line a broiler pan with aluminum foil to facilitate cleanup. Position broiler rack on top and coat with vegetable cooking spray.

2. Tie each bacon slice into a loose knot and place in a single layer on prepared broiler rack. Brush with honey and top with a generous grinding of black pepper.

3. Bake until bacon is crisp and honey is bubbly, 15 to 20 minutes. Transfer, honey-side up, to paper towels to drain and cool. Peppered bacon knots can be held up to 3 hours at cool room temperature. Serve in a napkin-lined basket.

76 BACON-WRAPPED WATER CHESTNUTS

Prep: 15 minutes Cook: 15 to 20 minutes
Marinate: 15 minutes Makes: 18 to 24

The number of water chestnuts in a can varies from brand to brand, which is the reason for the range in the yield of this recipe.

¼ cup soy sauce
1 tablespoon brown sugar
1 (8-ounce) can whole water chestnuts, drained
9 to 12 thin slices of bacon

1. In a small bowl, mix soy sauce and brown sugar until sugar dissolves and mixture is well blended. Stir in water chestnuts and marinate, stirring occasionally, 15 minutes.

2. Preheat oven to 400°F. Line a baking sheet with aluminum foil to facilitate cleanup. Cut bacon slices crosswise in half. Drain water chestnuts and wrap each in a bacon slice; secure with a toothpick. Arrange on prepared baking sheet and bake until bacon is nicely browned, 15 to 20 minutes. Drain and serve warm.

77 LAMB BROCHETTES WITH PANCETTA AND MINT PESTO SAUCE

Prep: 30 minutes   Marinate: 4 hours   Cook: 7 to 10 minutes
Makes: 65

- **1 leg of lamb, 4½ to 5 pounds, boned and trimmed of all excess fat**
- **2 tablespoons fresh lemon juice**
- **2 to 3 large garlic cloves, crushed through a press**
- **1 teaspoon salt**
- **½ teaspoon freshly ground pepper**
- **¼ cup extra-virgin olive oil**
- **2 tablespoons chopped fresh mint or 1 teaspoon dried**
- **½ pound thinly sliced pancetta or bacon***
- **Mint Pesto Sauce (recipe follows)**

1. Cut lamb into ¾-inch cubes. In a medium bowl, combine lemon juice, garlic, salt, and pepper. Whisk until blended. Whisk in oil and mint. Add lamb and toss until well coated. Cover and marinate in refrigerator, tossing occasionally, at least 4 hours or as long as 2 days.

2. If using bamboo skewers, soak in water at least 30 minutes to prevent burning. Preheat oven to 500°F. Stack pancetta slices and cut into thirds. Thread 2 pieces of lamb and 1 piece of pancetta on each skewer and arrange on a baking sheet. Cook until lamb is nicely browned outside yet still pink and juicy inside, 7 to 10 minutes. Serve with mint pesto sauce for dipping.

* *If using bacon, blanch in a large saucepan of simmering water for 5 minutes. Drain and pat dry before using.*

78 MINT PESTO SAUCE

Prep: 10 minutes   Cook: none   Makes: 1½ cups

- **2 cups loosely packed fresh mint leaves**
- **½ cup loosely packed chopped parsley**
- **½ cup grated Parmesan cheese**
- **¼ cup extra-virgin olive oil**
- **¼ cup pine nuts (pignoli) or walnuts**
- **1 tablespoon fresh lemon juice**
- **2 garlic cloves, chopped**
- **¼ teaspoon salt**
- **⅛ teaspoon pepper**
- **¼ cup yogurt, sour cream, or mayonnaise**

In a food processor or blender, combine mint, parsley, Parmesan cheese, olive oil, pine nuts, lemon juice, garlic, salt, and pepper. Process until a coarse paste forms. Add yogurt and mix until blended. If made in advance, cover and refrigerate up to 3 days.

79 CORN PUPPIES

Prep: 25 minutes Cook: 3 to 5 minutes Makes: 16

Here is a home version of all-American state fair corn dogs, a heartland special. To make them, you'll need 16 wooden popsicle sticks, which are available at craft stores and in some supermarkets.

1 cup yellow cornmeal
1 cup flour
1 tablespoon sugar
1 tablespoon baking powder
1 teaspoon salt
1 teaspoon chili powder
Dash of cayenne
1 cup milk
2 eggs
¼ cup vegetable oil plus 2 to 4 cups oil, for frying
8 frankfurters (1 pound)
Mustard, as accompaniment

1. In a medium bowl, combine cornmeal, flour, sugar, baking powder, salt, chili powder, and cayenne. Stir or whisk gently until well mixed. In a separate bowl, combine milk, eggs, and ¼ cup oil. Beat until well blended. Stir liquid mixture into dry ingredients until smooth.

2. In a wok or large heavy saucepan, heat 2 inches oil over medium-high heat until it reaches 360°F on a deep-frying thermometer.

3. Cut frankfurters crosswise in half and pat dry. Skewer cut end of each frankfurter with a wooden popsicle stick. Using stick as a handle, dip into batter to coat evenly. Fry frankfurters, a few at a time, in hot oil until batter is cooked through and golden brown outside, 3 to 5 minutes. Drain on paper towels, and serve warm, with mustard for dipping.

80 PORK SATÉ

Prep: 20 minutes Marinate: 2 hours Cook: 8 to 10 minutes Makes: 16

1 pound boneless pork loin
2 tablespoons smooth peanut butter
2 tablespoons soy sauce
⅓ cup minced onion
1 garlic clove, minced
1 tablespoon fresh lime or lemon juice
2 teaspoons brown sugar
Dash of hot pepper sauce
1 tablespoon vegetable oil

1. Trim all excess fat from pork and cut meat into ½-inch cubes. In a medium bowl, combine peanut butter, soy sauce, onion, garlic, lime juice, brown sugar, hot sauce, and oil. Mix until well blended. Add pork and toss to coat. Marinate 2 hours at room temperature or overnight in refrigerator.

2. If using bamboo skewers, soak in water at least 30 minutes to prevent burning. Thread 3 pieces of pork onto each skewer.

3. Broil satés 4 inches from heat, turning occasionally, until nicely browned outside and still juicy but with no trace of pink inside, 8 to 10 minutes.

81 POLENTA AND PEPPERONI SQUARES

Prep: 10 minutes Cook: 15 to 17 minutes Chill: 2 hours
Makes: 128

2 cups chicken broth
2 cups milk
1 tablespoon butter
½ teaspoon salt
1 cup instant polenta or yellow cornmeal
1 cup shredded sharp provolone or fontina cheese (about 3 ounces)
1 (3-ounce) package pepperoni, chopped
¼ cup grated Parmesan cheese
¼ cup chopped parsley
¼ teaspoon freshly ground pepper

1. Line two 8-inch square baking pans with sheets of plastic wrap about 16 inches long, so there is plenty of overhang.

2. In a medium saucepan, combine chicken broth, milk, butter, and salt. Bring to a boil over medium-high heat. Gradually add polenta in a slow, steady stream and cook, stirring frequently, until mixture is creamy and well blended, 5 to 7 minutes. Remove from heat and stir in provolone, pepperoni, Parmesan, parsley, and pepper. Divide mixture between 2 prepared pans and cover with ends of plastic wrap. Let cool and refrigerate until firm, at least 2 hours or as long as 48 hours.

3. Preheat oven to 400°F. Pull back plastic wrap and unmold polenta squares onto a clean work surface. Remove remaining plastic wrap and cut polenta into 1-inch squares. Bake on a parchment- or foil-lined baking sheet until golden brown at the edges, about 10 minutes.

82 BACON-WRAPPED WAFERS

Prep: 15 minutes Cook: 10 to 12 minutes Makes: 24

This appetizer became all the rage when it was reported that the Duchess of Windsor served it at one of her famous parties.

12 strips of thinly sliced bacon (about 6 ounces)
24 buttery crackers, such as Waverly wafers

1. Preheat oven to 350°F. Cut bacon strips in half crosswise and wrap a piece around center of each cracker, pressing bacon edges together to seal.

2. Place wrapped wafers, seam-side down, on a broiler rack to allow fat to drip down. Bake until bacon is crisp, 10 to 12 minutes. Drain on paper towels and serve warm.

83 GLAZED COCKTAIL RIBS

Prep: 10 minutes Cook: 1 to 1¼ hours Serves: 10 to 12

For appetizer-size portions, ask your butcher to saw the ribs in half crosswise. These oven-barbecued tidbits are messy to eat, but are always a hit. Be sure to provide lots of napkins as well as a receptacle for bones.

1 cup chili sauce or ketchup
3 tablespoons honey
2 tablespoons soy sauce
2 garlic cloves, minced
1 rack of pork spareribs (3 to 4 pounds), cut crosswise

1. Preheat oven to 350°F. In a small bowl, combine chili sauce, honey, soy sauce, and garlic. Stir until well blended.

2. Arrange ribs in a single layer in a foil-lined baking pan. Pour chili sauce mixture over meat. Cook, uncovered, until meat is browned and tender and no longer pink at bone, 1 to 1¼ hours. To serve, cut into individual ribs. Serve warm or at room temperature.

84 DOUBLE PORK MEATBALLS

Prep: 10 minutes Cook: 1 hour Makes: 48

1 pound cooked ham, finely chopped or ground (about 1½ cups)
1½ pounds fresh pork sausage
2 cups fresh bread crumbs
1 cup milk
1 cup packed brown sugar
1 teaspoon dry mustard
½ cup cider vinegar

1. Preheat oven to 350°F. In a large bowl, combine ham, sausage, bread crumbs, and milk. Blend until well mixed. Form into balls about 1 inch in diameter and place in a large baking pan.

2. In a small nonreactive saucepan, combine brown sugar, mustard, vinegar, and ½ cup water. Cook over medium heat, stirring, until sugar is dissolved, about 3 minutes. Pour sauce over meatballs and bake uncovered, basting frequently, until cooked through, about 1 hour.

Chapter 3

Cool and Easy

Here are some of the recipes that make your life simple. Served cold or at room temperature, these are appetizers that will wait for you and your guests, that are not at all temperamental, and that can be made well in advance. Pickled vegetables, stuffed eggs, and easy salami cornucopias are the types of dishes you'll find in this chapter. Not a few would be perfect for a picnic.

When planning your party menu, intersperse these patient foods with fancier creations and hot hors d'oeuvres, which must be timed right. Some cool appetizers, such as Eggplant Antipasto, Smoked Clam Log, and Sweet and Tangy Tomatoes, might do best on a buffet table. Others, such as Chicken Drum Pops and Salmon Cucumber Cups, deserve to be passed.

Keep the recipes in this chapter in mind also when you are asked to bring a dish to a friend's party or a group gathering. It is always thoughtful to choose a cold appetizer and leave the oven free to the host.

---

85 SMOKED CLAM LOG

Prep: 10 minutes Cook: none Chill: 3 hours Makes: 24 slices

- **1 (8-ounce) package cream cheese, softened**
- **1½ tablespoons mayonnaise**
- **1 teaspoon Worcestershire sauce**
- **⅛ teaspoon freshly ground white pepper**
- **Dash of hot pepper sauce**
- **1 (4-ounce) can smoked clams, drained and chopped**
- **Chopped parsley**

1. In a medium bowl or in a food processor, combine cream cheese, mayonnaise, Worcestershire sauce, pepper, and hot sauce. Blend well. Spread mixture on a sheet of wax paper to form a 6 x 10-inch rectangle about ¼ inch thick. Cover and refrigerate 1 hour.

2. Spread clams over cream cheese mixture and roll up from a long side, jelly-roll fashion, into a thick log. Twist ends of paper to seal roll. Refrigerate at least 2 hours. Before serving sprinkle parsley over roll and cut into ½-inch slices.

86 CHILES WITH CHEESE

Prep: 10 minutes Cook: none Makes: 32

Low-fat string cheese makes this recipe low in calories as well. If string cheese is unavailable in your area, substitute mozzarella, cut into thin, matchstick-size pieces.

8 ounces Armenian string cheese
8 Anaheim chiles

1. Pull string cheese into very fine threads. (If done in advance, cover and refrigerate up to 3 days. Let return to room temperature before serving.)

2. Remove chile stems; cut in half lengthwise and discard seeds. Cut each piece in half crosswise. Arrange chiles, cut-side up, around outside of a platter and mound string cheese in center. To eat, fill a chile section with cheese and pop in your mouth.

87 CHICKEN DRUM POPS

Prep: 15 minutes Marinate: 24 hours Cook: 1 hour Makes: 48

Terrific tiny tidbits. These wings can be refrigerated for up to three days ahead of time.

1¼ cups soy sauce
⅔ cup dry sherry
1 cup hoisin sauce*
⅔ cup Chinese plum sauce*
1 cup minced white and tender green scallions (about 12)
5 large garlic cloves, minced
⅔ cup cider vinegar
⅓ cup honey
5 pounds chicken drumettes or wings separated into sections with tips discarded
½ cup sesame seeds

1. In a medium nonreactive saucepan, bring soy sauce, sherry, hoisin, plum sauce, scallions, garlic, vinegar, and honey to a boil over medium heat. Reduce heat to low and simmer 5 minutes. Remove from heat and let cool to room temperature.

2. In a large bowl, combine chicken with sauce mixture. Cover and refrigerate overnight.

3. Preheat oven to 350°F. Line a baking pan with foil to facilitate cleanup. Roll marinated wings in sesame seeds and bake in a single layer until just cooked through, about 1 hour. Serve at room temperature.

* *Available in Chinese groceries, specialty food stores, and the Asian foods section of many supermarkets.*

88 EGGPLANT ANTIPASTO

Prep: 15 minutes Cook: 12 to 20 minutes Makes: 2½ cups

Stir-frying in a wok requires much less oil than a frying pan. You can buy red peppers already roasted and covered with oil in the specialty section of the supermarket.

1½ pounds narrow Asian eggplants (about 6)
About ½ cup plus 1 tablespoon olive oil
2 teaspoons coarse (kosher) salt
⅓ cup chopped roasted red bell pepper or pimiento
¼ cup chopped parsley
1 tablespoon chopped fresh marjoram or oregano, or 1 teaspoon dried
2 teaspoons balsamic vinegar
¼ teaspoon crushed hot red pepper
Garlic Crostini (page 151) or rounds of French bread

1. Cut eggplant crosswise on the diagonal into slices about ⅛ inch thick. In a wok or large frying pan, heat 1½ tablespoons oil over medium-high heat. Add about one-fourth of eggplant seasoned with ½ teaspoon salt and cook, tossing often, until eggplant is nicely browned and fork-tender, 3 to 5 minutes. Transfer to a medium bowl and repeat with remaining eggplant, salt, and oil in 3 more batches.

2. Add roasted red bell pepper, parsley, marjoram, 1 tablespoon olive oil, balsamic vinegar, and hot pepper to eggplant. Stir until well mixed. (If made in advance, cover and refrigerate as long as 2 days.) Serve eggplant antipasto spread at room temperature, mounded in the center of a platter and surrounded with garlic crostini.

89 CREAM CHEESE–STUFFED CUCUMBERS

Prep: 10 minutes Cook: none Chill: 24 hours Makes: 36

3 medium English (hothouse) cucumbers, scrubbed
1 (8-ounce) package cream cheese, softened
½ cup pimiento-stuffed olives, chopped
¼ cup chopped chives

1. Remove ends from cucumbers and cut in half lengthwise. Using a melon baller or grapefruit spoon, remove seeds from both halves. In a small bowl, combine cream cheese, olives, and chives. Blend until well mixed.

2. Stuff each cucumber half with cheese mixture and reassemble halves, pressing together gently. Wrap in plastic wrap and refrigerate overnight. Cut into ¼-inch slices to serve.

90 CURRIED CHUTNEY BALLS

Prep: 15 minutes Cook: 7 to 12 minutes Makes: 24

- **1 (4-ounce) bag shredded coconut (1⅓ cups)**
- **1 (8-ounce) package cream cheese, softened**
- **1 tablespoon mango chutney, finely chopped**
- **1 teaspoon curry powder**

1. Preheat oven to 350°F. Spread coconut on a jelly-roll pan and bake, stirring frequently, until lightly toasted, 7 to 12 minutes. Let cool.

2. In a small bowl or food processor, combine cream cheese, chutney, and curry powder. Blend well. Pinch off about 1 heaping teaspoon cheese mixture at a time and form into 24 balls. (If made in advance, cover and refrigerate up to 3 days.) Just before serving, roll in toasted coconut.

91 ENDIVE WITH BRANDIED GORGONZOLA CREAM

Prep: 15 minutes Cook: 10 minutes Makes: about 24

- **¼ cup sliced almonds**
- **1 cup crumbled Gorgonzola or other blue cheese (about 4 ounces), softened**
- **1 (3-ounce) package cream cheese, softened**
- **2 teaspoons brandy**
- **3 to 4 medium heads Belgian endive**

1. Preheat oven to 325°F. Spread out almonds in a small baking dish and toast until lightly browned, 7 to 10 minutes. Let cool. Chop coarsely.

2. In a small bowl or food processor, combine Gorgonzola, cream cheese, and brandy. Blend well.

3. Cut root end from endives to separate leaves. Place 1 heaping teaspoon cheese mixture on base of each leaf. Top with almonds. Arrange endive leaves on a serving platter in concentric circles, with tips facing out.

92 STUFFED KUMQUATS AND LITCHI NUTS

Prep: 20 minutes Cook: none Makes: 50

Here is a new twist on the classic fruit and cream cheese combo.

- **1 (8-ounce) package cream cheese, softened**
- **⅛ teaspoon salt**
- **1 tablespoon dry sherry**
- **3 tablespoons chopped nuts (walnuts, pecans, almonds, or macadamias)**
- **1 (20-ounce) can litchi nuts, drained**
- **1 (15½-ounce) jar whole preserved kumquats (or about 25 fresh kumquats)**

1. Place cream cheese in a small bowl. Add salt, sherry, and nuts. Blend well.

2. Stuff each litchi nut with about 1 teaspoon cream cheese filling.

3. With a sharp knife, cut kumquats in half and remove seeds. Fill one half of each kumquat with 1 teaspoon of filling and sandwich halves together with unfilled halves.

4. Arrange stuffed kumquats and litchis on a serving platter. Serve at room temperature or slightly chilled.

93 ASPARAGUS DEVILED EGGS

Prep: 10 minutes Cook: none Makes: 12

Arrange these colorful stuffed eggs on a bed of curly lettuce or a nest of alfalfa sprouts just before serving. They are good for calorie counters, especially if you use a reduced-calorie mayonnaise.

- **6 hard-boiled medium eggs**
- **2½ tablespoons mayonnaise**
- **2 teaspoons grated lemon zest**
- **¼ teaspoon salt**
- **⅛ teaspoon curry powder**
- **⅛ teaspoon dry mustard**
- **12 cooked asparagus tips**
- **1 canned pimiento**

1. Halve the eggs lengthwise. Remove and mash the yolks. Add mayonnaise, lemon zest, salt, curry powder, and mustard. Mix until creamy.

2. Fill egg whites with flavored yolk mixture, leveling each to flat edge of egg. Place one asparagus tip across the center of each half.

3. Cut pimiento in thin strips and place 2 strips across each asparagus tip.

94 ENDIVE WITH CURRIED CRAB

Prep: 15 minutes Cook: none Makes: about 24

The attractive leaves of Belgian endive make a natural container for many types of spreads. This is one of our favorites.

- **1 cup crab meat, picked over (about 6 ounces)**
- **¼ cup mayonnaise**
- **2 tablespoons chopped water chestnuts**
- **2 teaspoons curry powder**
- **⅛ teaspoon freshly ground pepper**
- **3 to 4 medium heads Belgian endive**

1. In a small bowl, combine crab, mayonnaise, water chestnuts, curry powder, and pepper. Stir until well mixed.

2. Cut root end from endives to separate leaves. Place 1 heaping teaspoon crab mixture on base of each leaf. Arrange endive leaves on a serving platter in concentric circles, with tips facing out.

95 POTATO TART WITH FRESH CHILES AND CUMIN

Prep: 15 minutes Cook: 1 hour Cool: 30 minutes Serves: 8

You'll want to serve this appetizer on small plates with forks. A dab of sour cream on top of each slice would not be out of place.

- **1 large garlic clove, minced**
- **¼ cup olive oil**
- **1 teaspoon ground cumin**
- **1 teaspoon salt**
- **½ teaspoon freshly ground pepper**
- **1 mild fresh chile, such as Anaheim, or ½ green bell pepper, minced**
- **1 jalapeño pepper or other fresh green chile, seeded and minced**
- **2½ pounds baking potatoes, peeled and thinly sliced**
- **½ cup dry white wine or chicken broth**

1. Preheat oven to 425°F. In a small saucepan, cook garlic in olive oil over low heat until just fragrant, 1 to 2 minutes. Remove from heat and stir in cumin, salt, and pepper. In a small bowl, combine mild chiles and jalapeño and toss until well mixed.

2. Arrange a thin layer of potato slices in a greased 9-inch quiche or pie plate. Brush potatoes with seasoned oil and top with 1 to 2 teaspoons chiles. Repeat layers, ending with a layer of potato slices. Drizzle wine over potatoes and brush with remaining oil.

3. Bake until crispy brown on top and tender in center when pierced with tip of a knife, about 1 hour. Transfer to a rack and immediately top with a piece of parchment or wax paper, a plate, and heavy cans to weigh down tart. Let stand until cool and pressed flat, about 30 minutes. Cut into pie-shaped wedges and serve at room temperature.

96 STUFFED GRAPE LEAVES

Prep: 40 minutes Cook: 55 minutes Chill: 4 hours
Makes: about 50

Cooked ground lamb can be added to the filling, but this vegetarian version is a real winner. The number of grape leaves varies wildly from jar to jar, but you can be sure there will be at least fifty in an eight-ounce jar.

1 (8-ounce) jar grape leaves, drained
1¼ cups olive oil
2 medium onions, chopped
2 carrots, chopped
2 garlic cloves, minced
1 tomato, peeled, seeded, and chopped
1 cup rice
1 cup boiling water
½ cup chopped parsley
⅓ cup fresh lemon juice
1 tablespoon chopped fresh dill or 1½ teaspoons dried
1½ teaspoons chopped fresh mint
2 teaspoons salt
1 medium baking potato, peeled
Fresh lemon wedges

1. Rinse grape leaves and soak in a large bowl of cold water for at least 1 hour to remove some of the brine; drain. If leaves have stems, remove them with kitchen shears or a sharp knife.

2. In a large saucepan, heat 1 cup of olive oil and cook onions, carrots, and garlic over medium heat until softened but not browned, 2 to 3 minutes. Add tomato and rice and stir until well mixed. Add boiling water, cover, and reduce heat to low. Cook until rice is just tender, about 20 minutes. Remove from heat and stir in parsley, 2 tablespoons lemon juice, dill, mint, and salt. Let cool. (If made in advance, cover and refrigerate up to 2 days.)

3. Cut potato into slices ¼ to ⅜ inch thick and arrange in a single layer on bottom of a 5-quart saucepan or flameproof casserole. (The potato thickens the sauce and prevents grape leaves from sticking to the pan.) Place several grape leaves, rib-side up, on a flat work surface. Place about 1 tablespoon rice filling at stem end of leaf, in center. Turn stem end up and over filling, then fold in sides; roll up to form a cylinder. Arrange completed grape leaves seam-side down on top of potato slices. Repeat with remaining grape leaves and rice filling.

4. Pour remaining lemon juice, olive oil, and 1 cup water over grape leaves and weight down with a large heatproof plate. Cover and cook over low heat until leaves are tender, about 30 minutes. Remove from heat and let cool, partially covered; then refrigerate until well chilled, at least 4 hours or as long as 2 days. To serve, let return to cool temperature. Arrange grape leaves on a serving plate. Discard potato slices or eat separately. Drizzle cooking juices over stuffed grape leaves and garnish with lemon wedges.

97 OLIVE AND CHEESE BALLS

Prep: 15 minutes Cook: none Makes: 24

Quick to make; quick to disappear. You can also use this as a spread on toast.

1 (8-ounce) package cream cheese, softened
1 (4½-ounce) can chopped ripe olives
½ cup chopped parsley
½ cup finely chopped walnuts
Thin pretzel sticks or toothpicks

1. In a medium bowl, combine cream cheese and olives until well blended. In a small bowl, toss parsley and walnuts until well mixed.

2. Pinch off about 1 teaspoon of cheese mixture at a time and form into balls. (If made in advance, cover and refrigerate up to 3 days.) Just before serving, roll in parsley and walnuts. Spear with pretzel sticks or toothpicks.

POTATO TORTILLA

Prep: 15 minutes Cook: 38 to 45 minutes Serves: 6 to 8

The Spanish tortilla is a thick, firmly cooked omelet, similar to the Italian frittata. Teleme is a creamy white cheese produced in California. If you are unable to find it in your area, substitute Monterey Jack.

1 medium onion, thinly sliced
2 medium baking potatoes, peeled and thinly sliced (about ¾ pound total)
¼ cup olive oil
2 garlic cloves, minced
2 teaspoons salt
⅛ teaspoon freshly ground pepper
6 eggs
1 tablespoon chopped fresh oregano or 1 teaspoon dried
3 drops of hot pepper sauce
½ cup shredded Teleme or Monterey Jack cheese
1 (2-ounce) jar diced pimientos, drained and coarsely chopped

1. Preheat oven to 300°F. In a large frying pan, cook onion and potatoes in olive oil over medium-low heat until vegetables are tender but not browned, 7 to 9 minutes. Add garlic, salt, and pepper and cook until garlic is just fragrant, 1 minute longer. Let cool for 5 minutes, then turn mixture into a greased 9- or 10-inch round baking dish.

2. In a large bowl, beat eggs until well blended. Beat in oregano, hot sauce, cheese, and pimiento. Pour over potatoes.

3. Bake until top is golden brown and eggs are set throughout, 30 to 35 minutes. Let stand at least 5 minutes. Cut tortilla into pie-shaped wedges or small squares and serve at room temperature.

99 CAVIAR POTATOES

Prep: 10 minutes Cook: 10 to 15 minutes Makes: 24

Using three different types of caviar makes a sparkling presentation.

- **12 tiny red (new) potatoes, about 1½ inches in diameter**
- **Salt and freshly ground pepper**
- **½ cup sour cream or crème fraîche**
- **1 ounce black, red, and/or golden caviar**

1. In a medium saucepan, cook potatoes in boiling salted water over medium-high heat until tender, 10 to 15 minutes. Drain and let cool.

2. Halve potatoes. Cut a thin slice from the rounded bottom of each potato half so it will stand upright. Using a melon baller, remove center from each potato half, leaving a shell about ¼ inch thick. Season cavities with salt and pepper.

3. Using a small spoon or a pastry bag fitted with a star tip, fill potato cavities with sour cream. Top each with a dab of caviar.

100 SALAMI CORNUCOPIA WITH DILLED CREAM CHEESE

Prep: 30 minutes Chill: 1 hour Cook: none Makes: 48

Genoa salami is available in most delicatessens.

- **24 thin slices of Genoa salami (about ½ pound)**
- **2 (8-ounce) packages cream cheese, softened**
- **3 tablespoons minced parsley**
- **3 tablespoons minced chives**
- **3 tablespoons minced fresh dill or 1½ tablespoons dried**
- **1 teaspoon lemon juice**
- **Dash of salt**

1. Stack salami slices and cut in half. Roll each piece into a cone shape, pressing ends to seal.

2. Arrange salami cornucopia in a single layer with sealed sides down on a platter or baking sheet and refrigerate until firm, about 1 hour.

3. In a food processor, combine cream cheese, parsley, chives, dill, lemon juice, and salt. Process until well blended. Using a large star tip, pipe mixture into cornucopia. If made in advance, cover and refrigerate up to 2 days.

101 DEVILED EGGS WITH CAVIAR

Prep: 10 minutes Cook: none Makes: 10

For a party or a fancy picnic appetizer, try stuffed eggs topped with caviar. Depending upon the occasion and your budget, choose the caviar that seems appropriate at the moment: salmon, golden, lumpfish, or imported beluga.

5 hard-boiled medium eggs
2 teaspoons lemon juice
2½ tablespoons sour cream
½ teaspoon salt
¼ teaspoon pepper
About 2½ teaspoons caviar: lumpfish, golden, salmon, or beluga

Cut eggs in half lengthwise and remove yolks. Mash egg yolks to a paste with lemon juice, sour cream, salt, and pepper. Pipe or spoon yolk mixture into egg whites; make a small depression in the center of each. Fill each hollow with about ¼ teaspoon caviar.

102 STEAK TARTARE

Prep: 15 minutes Cook: none Makes: 36

As a safety measure, olive oil is substituted here for the traditional raw egg yolk, keeping the richness with no loss in flavor. Forming the tartare mixture into bite-sized balls makes it perfect for a party. These will always be popular with your steak-loving guests.

1 pound beef sirloin or tenderloin, trimmed of all fat
½ cup minced onion
1 tablespoon extra-virgin olive oil
1½ teaspoons salt
1 teaspoon freshly ground pepper
1 small garlic clove, minced
1 cup chopped parsley
Optional garnishes:
Capers, sieved hard-boiled eggs, chopped anchovies
Cocktail rye or pumpernickel, as accompaniment

1. Using a large sharp knife or a food processor, mince beef. In a medium bowl, combine beef, onion, olive oil, salt, pepper, and garlic. Mix gently until well blended. Form mixture into 1-inch balls and roll in parsley. Serve immediately, or cover and refrigerate up to 8 hours.

2. Serve steak tartare balls, well chilled, with toothpicks. Garnish platter with capers, sieved hard-boiled eggs, and chopped anchovies and serve a basket of bread alongside.

103 WON TON PLEASURES

Prep: 20 minutes Cook: 8 to 10 minutes Makes: 36

You'll love this tropical shrimp salad encased in its own crunchy won ton cup.

2 tablespoons vegetable oil
36 won ton wrappers*
½ pound tiny shelled cooked shrimp
2 scallions, chopped
2 tablespoons finely chopped celery
2 tablespoons chopped green bell pepper
2 tablespoons mayonnaise
2 tablespoons sour cream
1 teaspoon curry powder
1 teaspoon fresh lime or lemon juice
Dash of salt
Dash of cayenne
3 tablespoons well-drained canned crushed unsweetened pineapple
2 tablespoons shredded coconut
Chopped cilantro or parsley

1. Preheat oven to 350°F. Use vegetable oil to grease 36 gem-sized (1½-inch) muffin tins. Press 1 won ton wrapper into each to form a cup. Bake, in batches if necessary, until just crisp and golden, 8 to 10 minutes. Let cool. (If made in advance, store airtight up to 3 days or freeze. If frozen, bake for 5 minutes in a 350° oven to recrisp.)

2. In a medium bowl, combine shrimp, scallions, celery, green pepper, mayonnaise, sour cream, curry powder, lime juice, salt, cayenne, and pineapple. Fold gently until well mixed. (If made in advance, cover and refrigerate up to 8 hours.) Just before serving, use a slotted spoon to mound shrimp mixture in won ton cups. Top with shredded coconut and chopped cilantro.

* *Available in Asian markets or in the refrigerated produce or frozen food section of many supermarkets.*

104 SALMON CUCUMBER CUPS

Prep: 15 minutes Cook: none Makes: 36

This appetizer is as pretty as it is delicious.

3 English (hothouse) cucumbers (about 1½ pounds)
2 cups Herbed Cream Cheese (page 11) or Boursin
⅓ pound smoked salmon, cut into thin strips ½ inch long

1. Scrub cucumbers but do not peel. Score with tines of a fork if you like. Slice cucumbers into ½-inch rounds.

2. With a melon baller, scoop out center of each round, leaving bottom intact, to make shallow cups. Using a pastry bag or a spoon, fill cucumber cavities with cheese and top each with a strip of salmon.

105 SWEET AND TANGY TOMATOES

Prep: 10 minutes Cook: none Marinate: 48 hours Makes: 4 cups

These will keep several weeks in the refrigerator. They are great for snacking.

2 pints cherry tomatoes (about 2 pounds), stemmed
2 cups cider vinegar or red wine vinegar
¼ cup sugar
2 tablespoons coarse (kosher) salt
1 tablespoon whole cloves
6 bay leaves

1. Using the tip of a sharp knife, puncture each tomato several times to allow for absorption of marinade.

2. In a medium bowl, combine vinegar, sugar, salt, cloves, bay leaves, and 1 cup of water. Stir to dissolve sugar and salt. Add tomatoes, cover, and refrigerate 48 hours or as long as 4 days before serving.

106 CHERRY TOMATOES WITH PASTA AL PESTO

Prep: 25 minutes Cook: 5 to 7 minutes Drain: 20 minutes Makes: about 24

⅓ cup orzo (rice-shaped pasta) or other pastina
Salt
⅓ cup pesto, homemade or purchased
1 pint cherry tomatoes, stemmed (about 1 pound)

1. Cook pasta in a medium pot of boiling salted water until tender but still firm, 5 to 7 minutes. Drain in a sieve or colander and cool under cold running water; drain well. In a small bowl, combine pasta with pesto. Toss until mixed.

2. Using a small serrated knife, cut a thin slice from the bottom end of each tomato so they will stand upright. Scoop out tomato seeds and pulp with a small spoon, grapefruit knife, or melon baller. Lightly salt tomato cavities and let drain upside down on paper towels 20 minutes at room temperature or as long as overnight, well covered in refrigerator.

3. Using a small spoon, fill tomato cavities with pasta al pesto. Refrigerate up to 2 hours before serving.

107 BACON-STUFFED CHERRY TOMATOES

Prep: 30 minutes   Cook: 5 to 7 minutes   Drain: 20 minutes
Makes: about 24

The flavor of this appetizer will remind you of the ever popular BLT—without the bread.

½ pound bacon (about 8 slices)
1 pint cherry tomatoes, stemmed (about 1 pound)
Salt
4 scallions, finely chopped
½ cup mayonnaise

1. In a large skillet, cook bacon over medium heat until browned, 5 to 7 minutes. Drain on paper towels and chop finely.

2. Using a small serrated knife, cut a thin slice from the bottom end of each tomato. (The stem end serves as a flat bottom so tomatoes will stand upright.) Scoop out tomato seeds and pulp with a small spoon, grapefruit knife, or melon baller. Lightly salt tomato cavities and let drain upside down on paper towels 20 minutes or at room temperature as long as overnight, well covered in refrigerator.

3. In a small bowl, combine bacon, scallions, and mayonnaise. Stir until well mixed. Using a small spoon, stuff mixture into tomato cavities, mounding slightly. Refrigerate up to 2 hours before serving.

108 ALMOND DEVILED EGGS

Prep: 10 minutes   Cook: none   Makes: 18

We like to use smaller eggs for stuffing, so they are closer to bite-size. Feel free to substitute any nut you like for the almonds. The crunch is a complement to the velvety egg filling.

9 hard-boiled medium eggs
3 tablespoons mayonnaise
3 tablespoons sour cream
1 teaspoon salt
2 teaspoons coarse grainy mustard
¼ cup chopped salted almonds

1. Cut eggs in half lengthwise and remove yolks. Mash egg yolks. Add mayonnaise, sour cream, salt, and mustard and blend well.

2. Press yolk mixture through a pastry tube with a star-shaped tip, or use 2 teaspoons to fill egg whites. Sprinkle almonds on top.

109 SHRIMP TOSTADITAS

Prep: 20 minutes Cook: none Makes: 48

Assemble these miniature tostadas shortly before serving so the tortilla chips remain crisp. They may be tiny, but the taste is terrific.

48 tiny shelled cooked shrimp (about ½ pound), patted dry
1½ tablespoons fresh lime or lemon juice
¼ teaspoon salt
⅛ teaspoon cayenne
1 (12-ounce) bag round tortilla chips
2 cups guacamole, purchased or homemade (page 87)
Fresh cilantro leaves

1. In a medium bowl, combine shrimp, lime juice, salt, and cayenne. Toss until well mixed.

2. Spoon about 2 teaspoons guacamole onto each tortilla chip. Top each with a shrimp and garnish with a small cilantro leaf.

110 PITA AND YOGURT CHEESE ROLL-UPS

Prep: 15 minutes Cook: none Chill: 1 hour Makes: about 36

Middle Eastern pita bread is low in fat and cholesterol and makes perfectly delicious sandwiches.

3 (6-inch) plain or whole wheat pita breads
1½ cups Garden Fresh Yogurt Cheese (page 20)
¾ cup alfalfa sprouts

1. Split each pita bread horizontally in half to form 6 rounds. If bread is not pliable, soften between 2 damp towels for a few minutes. Place bread rounds, rough-side up, on a clean work surface; cover each with about ⅓ cup garden fresh yogurt cheese. Top each with about 2 tablespoons alfalfa sprouts.

2. Roll pita rounds jelly-roll fashion, gently but firmly to avoid air pockets. Wrap rolls securely in plastic wrap and refrigerate 1 hour, or as long as overnight.

3. Remove plastic wrap and use a serrated knife to trim ends and cut rolls diagonally into slices about ¾ inch thick. Arrange flat on a platter and serve slightly chilled.

Chapter 4

Designer Originals

If you purchase a designer dress, you don't expect to walk into a party and face five carbon copies. So it is with the recipes in this chapter. Here we feature genuine knockouts, not knockoffs. These are the recipes to turn to when the boss is coming for cocktails and only the best will do.

These are also recipes that feature ingredients that may be more expensive or harder to find. Some, such as Wild Rice Pancakes with Smoked Salmon, Scotch Quail Eggs with Honey Mustard Sauce, or Mussels with Black Walnut Sauce, may require a trip to a specialty food shop. Others, such as Shrimp Extravaganza or Bite-Size Beef Wellingtons, will take extra time in the kitchen. But all are exceptional, and do-ahead tips for advance preparation are noted wherever possible.

For a large party, you might wish to serve one of these special hors d'oeuvres as a star accent with a larger selection of dips, cheeses, and simpler creations. Or you might choose one of the more substantial hors d'oeuvres, such as Buckwheat Blini with Caviar or Oregon Crab and Leek Pie, to serve as a starter at an elegant sit-down dinner. However you use them, these are the dishes that are designed to dazzle.

111 BITE-SIZE BEEF WELLINGTONS

Prep: 30 minutes Chill: 4 hours Cook: 20 to 28 minutes
Makes: 48

This is not the sort of thing we'd serve to a roomful of hungry sports fans working their way through a second keg of beer. But for other festive occasions, when you have a captive audience, this is the ticket. They require a bit of work, but much of it can be done in advance. The raves you receive will make it all worthwhile.

1 pound center-cut beef fillet, chilled
1 tablespoon olive oil
½ teaspoon salt
¼ teaspoon freshly ground pepper
Flour
2 (17¼-ounce) packages frozen puff pastry sheets, thawed as package directs
Mushroom Duxelles (recipe follows)
48 watercress leaves

1. Preheat a medium cast-iron skillet or other heavy-bottomed frying pan over high heat. Rub beef with olive oil and season with salt and pepper. Place beef in hot pan and cook, turning once or twice, until crusty brown outside but still quite rare inside, 4 to 5 minutes total. Remove to a plate and let cool. Cover and refrigerate until well chilled, about 4 hours or as long as 2 days.

2. On a lightly floured work surface, roll each pastry sheet to a thickness of about ⅛ inch. Using an oval biscuit cutter, preferably with a crinkled edge, make a total of 96 (2¼-inch) pastry ovals. Arrange half of them 1 inch apart on foil- or parchment-lined baking sheets and brush lightly with water. Using a small round biscuit cutter, remove a ¾- to 1-inch circle from centers of remaining pastry ovals. Gently place each hollow oval on top of moistened pastry, aligning edges to form a sandwich. Cover and refrigerate until thoroughly chilled, 30 minutes or as long as 2 days. Preheat oven to 400°F.

3. Bake chilled pastry until puffed and golden brown, 15 to 20 minutes. Transfer to a rack and let cool. If any of the center indentations have puffed up, press down with a wooden spoon handle. (If made in advance, store airtight at room temperature up to 2 days. Freeze for longer storage.)

4. Remove any visible fat from chilled beef and cut into ¼- to ½-inch chunks to fit inside pastries. Top with about ½ teaspoon mushroom duxelles. Bake until pastry is crisp and mushroom topping bubbly hot, 5 to 8 minutes. Garnish each with a watercress leaf. Serve warm.

112 MUSHROOM DUXELLES

Prep: 15 minutes Cook: 15 to 20 minutes Makes: 1½ cups

4 tablespoons butter
3 shallots, minced
½ pound mushrooms, finely chopped
2 tablespoons flour
½ cup heavy cream
3 tablespoons minced fresh or freeze-dried chives
2 tablespoons chopped parsley
½ teaspoon fresh lemon juice
½ teaspoon salt
⅛ teaspoon cayenne

1. In a large frying pan, melt butter over medium heat. Add shallots and cook until softened but not browned, about 2 minutes. Add mushrooms and cook, stirring occasionally, until nearly all liquid has cooked away, 10 to 15 minutes.

2. Sprinkle flour over mushrooms and cook, stirring, until well blended, about 2 minutes. Increase heat to high, add cream, and cook, stirring well, until mixture comes to a boil, about 3 minutes. Remove from heat and stir in chives, parsley, lemon juice, salt, and cayenne. Let cool. If made in advance, cover and refrigerate up to 3 days. Freeze for longer storage.

113 BROCCOLI AND CHEESE MINI QUICHE

Prep: 30 minutes Cook: 15 minutes Makes: 24

Vegetable cooking spray
¼ pound Easy Cream Cheese Pastry (page 189)
1 cup chopped or shredded Gruyère or other Swiss cheese (about 4 ounces)
1 (10-ounce) package frozen chopped broccoli, thawed and well drained
2 eggs
½ cup heavy cream
⅛ teaspoon salt
Dash of cayenne
Dash of grated nutmeg

1. Preheat oven to 400°F. Oil insides of 2 gem-size (1¾-inch) muffin tins (24 cups) with vegetable cooking spray. Press 1½ teaspoons cream cheese pastry evenly into each muffin cup to line bottom and sides.

2. Distribute cheese evenly among pastry shells. In a food processor or blender, combine broccoli, eggs, cream, salt, cayenne, and nutmeg until well blended. Using a ladle or a turkey baster, fill unbaked shells about ¾ full. Bake until filling is puffed and pastry is lightly browned, about 15 minutes. Serve warm or at room temperature. (Baked Mini Quiche can be refrigerated up to 3 days or frozen. Reheat in a 400° oven for 5 to 10 minutes before serving.)

114 BUCKWHEAT BLINI WITH CAVIAR

Prep: 10 minutes Rise: 1 hour Cook: about 24 minutes Makes: 24

Buckwheat has a pleasing nutty flavor, and these Russian crepes are a perfect vehicle for caviar. For a traditional but extravagant treat, drizzle a little melted sweet butter over the blini before topping with sour cream and caviar. Iced vodka is the classic accompaniment to this sumptuous hors d'oeuvre.

2 cups all-purpose flour
½ cup buckwheat flour
1 (¼-ounce) envelope active dry yeast
2 teaspoons sugar
2 egg yolks
3 cups lukewarm milk (105° to 115°)
3 egg whites
2 tablespoons butter
½ cup sour cream
2 ounces caviar

1. In a medium bowl, combine all-purpose flour and buckwheat flour. Whisk gently until well mixed. Stir in yeast and sugar. Make a well in center of flour mixture and drop in egg yolks. Gradually stir in warm milk until well blended. Cover bowl with a towel and place in a warm spot. Let batter rise until doubled in bulk, about 1 hour.

2. In a large bowl, beat egg whites until soft peaks form. Fold beaten whites into batter.

3. In a large frying pan, melt butter over medium heat. Form blini by dropping batter, 1 heaping tablespoon at a time, into hot pan. Cook, turning once, until golden brown, about 3 minutes total. Top each blini with 1 teaspoon sour cream and a dab of caviar. Serve warm or at room temperature.

115 EASY MINI QUICHE LORRAINE

Prep: 45 minutes Cook: 15 minutes Makes: 48

Once you discover how easily these are made, you'll know why they are a favorite of all caterers. For a distinctly American flavor variation, substitute crumbled cooked bacon and Cheddar for the Canadian bacon and Gruyère cheese.

Vegetable cooking spray
½ pound Easy Cream Cheese Pastry (page 189)
1 (6-ounce) package Canadian bacon, chopped
1 cup chopped or shredded Gruyère or other Swiss cheese (about 4 ounces)
4 eggs
1 cup heavy cream
⅛ teaspoon salt
Dash of cayenne
Dash of grated nutmeg

1. Preheat oven to 400°F. Oil insides of 4 gem-size (1¾-inch) muffin tins (48 cups) with vegetable cooking spray. Press 1½ teaspoons cream cheese pastry evenly into each muffin cup to line bottom and sides.

2. Distribute Canadian bacon and cheese evenly among pastry shells. In a medium bowl, mix eggs, cream, salt, cayenne, and nutmeg until well blended. Using a ladle or a turkey baster, fill unbaked shells about ¾ full.

3. Bake 15 minutes, or until filling is puffed and golden and pastry is lightly browned. Serve warm or at room temperature. (Baked mini quiche can be refrigerated up to 3 days or frozen. Reheat in a 400° oven for 5 to 10 minutes before serving.)

116 WHITE BEAN PÂTÉ WITH SUN-DRIED TOMATOES AND SAGE

Prep: 20 minutes Cook: 48 to 50 minutes Stand: 45 minutes Serves: 12 to 16

Use this vegetarian pâté as a spread for crackers, bread rounds, or Garlic Crostini (page 151).

1 medium onion, chopped
3 celery ribs, chopped
3 garlic cloves, minced
4 tablespoons butter or olive oil
2 (15-ounce) cans cannellini beans, well rinsed and drained
2 eggs
½ cup fine dry bread crumbs
½ cup heavy cream
¼ cup oil-packed sun-dried tomato halves, drained and chopped
¼ cup dry white wine or vermouth
¼ cup chopped parsley
2 tablespoons chopped fresh sage leaves or 2 teaspoons dried
¾ teaspoon salt
¼ teaspoon freshly ground pepper
2 to 3 whole sage leaves, for garnish

1. Preheat oven to 400°F. In a large frying pan, cook onion, celery, and garlic in butter over medium heat until softened but not browned, 3 to 5 minutes.

2. In a food processor, puree beans until smooth. Add eggs and process until well blended.

3. In a large mixing bowl, combine sautéed vegetables with pureed bean mixture. Add bread crumbs, cream, sun-dried tomatoes, wine, parsley, chopped sage, salt, and pepper. Blend well. Spoon mixture into a greased shallow 9-inch baking dish and top with fresh sage leaves. Top with a buttered piece of parchment or wax paper and cover with foil.

4. Bake until center is cooked through, about 45 minutes. Let cool on a rack 45 minutes, stacking cans on top of foil cover to weight the pâté. Serve warm or at room temperature.

117 CARPACCIO CIGARETTES

Prep: 30 minutes Cook: none Chill: 2 to 3 hours Makes: 24

Carpaccio is the Italian word for raw meat or fish that has been pounded paper thin. Be sure to use the freshest, best-quality beef. To make this even easier, have your butcher slice and pound the meat for you and skip to step 2.

6 ounces beef fillet, well trimmed, in one piece
⅓ cup mayonnaise
2 tablespoons capers, drained
1 tablespoon Dijon mustard
1 teaspoon fresh lemon juice
24 small sprigs of watercress or parsley
Freshly ground pepper
2 ounces Parmesan cheese, in one piece
Lemon wedges
Garlic Crostini (page 151)

1. Chill beef, well wrapped, in the freezer until nearly frozen, 2 to 3 hours. Remove from freezer and slice paper thin. Pound slices even thinner between two sheets of wax paper.

2. In a small bowl, combine mayonnaise, capers, mustard, and lemon juice.

3. Spread 1 teaspoon of mayonnaise mixture over each slice of beef and top with a sprig of watercress, trimming so that only a bit of the leafy part will peek through one end. Roll beef slices into tight cylinders to resemble cigarettes.

4. Arrange "cigarettes" on a platter and season generously with pepper. Using a vegetable peeler, shave thin slices of Parmesan cheese over meat. Garnish with lemon wedges and serve with garlic crostini.

118 COCKTAIL CRAB CAKES WITH CHILI MAYONNAISE

Prep: 20 minutes Cook: 10 to 12 minutes Makes: 36

⅓ cup lightly packed parsley leaves
1 celery rib, cut into 1-inch pieces
2 scallions, cut into 1-inch pieces
½ pound crab meat, picked over
3 tablespoons plain or Chili Mayonnaise (recipe follows)
1 egg
2 tablespoons plus ⅓ cup fresh bread crumbs
Salt to taste
⅓ cup Chili Mayonnaise

1. Preheat oven to 400°F. Generously butter a baking sheet.

2. In a food processor, combine parsley, celery, and scallions. Process until finely chopped. Add crab meat, 3 tablespoons mayonnaise, egg, 2 tablespoons bread crumbs, and salt. Pulse until well mixed.

3. Form tablespoons of crab mixture into balls and roll in ⅓ cup bread crumbs. Arrange 1½ inches apart on prepared baking sheet and press down lightly to form patties.

4. Bake until firm and cooked through, 10 to 12 minutes. To serve, flip the crab cakes with a spatula so that browned side shows. Using a spoon or a pastry bag, top each crab cake with ½ teaspoon chili mayonnaise.

CHILI MAYONNAISE

Makes: about ½ cup

2 teaspoons fresh lemon juice
2 teaspoons chili powder
1 teaspoon ground cumin
⅛ teaspoon cayenne
Dash of salt
½ cup mayonnaise

In a small bowl, combine lemon juice, chili powder, cumin, cayenne, and salt. Stir until well blended. Blend in mayonnaise. If made in advance, cover and refrigerate up to 4 days.

---

119 OREGON CRAB AND LEEK PIE

Prep: 15 minutes Cook: 55 minutes Serves: 8

A favorite of Cleve Boehi, one of Oregon's best cooks, this makes a wonderful starter that your guests will never forget.

1 (9-inch) unbaked tart or pie shell
¼ cup slivered almonds
2 tablespoons butter
2 medium leeks (white and tender green), well rinsed, chopped
1½ cups shredded Swiss cheese (about 6 ounces)
½ pound crab meat, picked over
4 eggs
1 cup light cream
¼ teaspoon salt
¼ teaspoon dry mustard
2 tablespoons lemon juice
½ teaspoon grated lemon zest

1. Preheat oven to 425°F. Prick pastry with a fork, then press a sheet of foil directly onto pie shell, covering surface. Bake 6 minutes, remove foil, and bake until just golden, about 4 minutes longer. Remove from oven. Reduce oven temperature to 325°.

2. Spread out almonds in a shallow baking pan and toast in oven 7 to 10 minutes, until lightly browned. Meanwhile, in a large skillet, melt butter over medium heat. Add leeks and cook until softened but not brown, about 5 minutes; remove from heat and let cool slightly. Sprinkle half of cheese over bottom of pastry shell. Gently mix leeks with crab meat and spoon over cheese-lined shell.

3. In a large bowl, beat eggs with cream, salt, mustard, lemon juice, and lemon zest. Pour over crab mixture and sprinkle remaining cheese on top. Scatter toasted almonds over all.

4. Bake 55 minutes, or until custard appears firm when pan is gently shaken. Serve warm or at room temperature, cut into wedges.

120 CAVIAR ROULADE

Prep: 25 minutes Cook: 45 to 47 minutes Serves: 10

Spring for the best caviar you can afford for this—it's worth it! Serve on small plates with forks for a truly elegant first course any time of year.

4 tablespoons butter
½ cup sifted flour
2 cups milk, heated
4 eggs, separated
Pinch of salt
1 (3-ounce) package cream cheese, softened
1 cup sour cream
4 ounces caviar*

1. Preheat oven to 325°F. Line a 10x15-inch jelly-roll pan with heavy-duty aluminum foil cut to allow an overlapping margin. Carefully fold overlapping edges of foil around corners of pan to keep foil from slipping. Grease foil with butter.

2. In a medium saucepan, melt butter over medium heat. Add flour and cook, whisking often, 1 to 2 minutes without allowing flour to color. Whisk in milk and bring to a boil, whisking until thickened and smooth, about 2 minutes. Reduce heat to a simmer and cook, stirring, 2 to 3 minutes longer. Remove from heat.

3. In a small bowl, beat egg yolks until well blended. Whisk about ½ cup hot sauce into yolks. Whisk egg yolk mixture into remaining sauce in pan. In a large bowl, beat egg whites with salt until stiff but not dry. Fold into warm sauce. Pour batter into greased pan and smooth top with a spatula.

4. Bake until mixture rebounds to the touch and is golden brown on top, about 40 minutes. Turn out onto a clean kitchen towel.

5. Meanwhile, in a small bowl, combine cream cheese with 3 tablespoons of sour cream. Beat until well blended. Spread lightly over roulade. Roll up jelly-roll fashion from one of short sides.

6. Using a serrated knife, carefully slice off rough ends of roll. Cut roll into slices 1 inch thick and serve warm or cold with a spoonful of remaining sour cream and a dollop of caviar.

* *If using lumpfish caviar, drain into a fine sieve and rinse under cold running water to remove dye.*

121 CAVIAR MOUSSE

Prep: 15 minutes Chill: 2 hours Serves: 12

¾ cup sour cream
¼ cup finely chopped onion
3 hard-boiled eggs, chopped
¼ cup lemon juice
3 tablespoons mayonnaise
1½ teaspoons salt
½ teaspoon Worcestershire sauce
¼ teaspoon white pepper
5 to 7 drops of hot pepper sauce
1 (¼-ounce) envelope unflavored gelatin
2 ounces black lumpfish caviar

1. In a medium bowl, combine sour cream, onion, eggs, lemon juice, mayonnaise, salt, Worcestershire sauce, white pepper, and hot sauce. Stir until well blended.

2. In a small saucepan, soften gelatin in 2 tablespoons cold water, then warm over low heat until dissolved. Fold gelatin into sour cream mixture until well blended.

3. Place caviar in a fine sieve and rinse under cold water to remove black dye. Drain well and fold into sour cream mixture. Turn into a 3-cup mold. Refrigerate for at least 2 hours or up to 3 days.

122 MUSSELS WITH BLACK WALNUT SAUCE

Prep: 20 minutes Cook: 5 minutes Chill: 1 hour Makes: 24

This is a great way to serve mussels, as there is no last-minute fussing. Black walnuts lend a distinctive flavor to this piquant sauce. One taste will make you wonder why we so seldom see nuts combined with shellfish.

24 large mussels
¼ cup chopped black walnuts
½ cup olive oil
¼ cup fresh bread crumbs
2 teaspoons red wine vinegar
1 teaspoon balsamic vinegar
Dash of hot pepper sauce
Salt and freshly ground pepper

1. Scrub mussels and remove heavy brown beards. Discard any open shells that will not close when tapped. In a large pot with a steam rack, bring about 2 inches of water to a boil over medium-high heat. Add mussels, cover, and cook until mussels open, about 5 minutes. Discard any mussels that do not open. Let cool, then remove and discard top shells.

2. In a food processor, combine black walnuts, olive oil, bread crumbs, red wine vinegar, balsamic vinegar, and hot sauce. Puree until smooth. Season with salt and pepper to taste. Spoon sauce over each mussel. Cover and refrigerate for 1 hour or as long as 4 hours. Serve slightly chilled.

123 SCOTCH QUAIL EGGS WITH HONEY MUSTARD SAUCE

Prep: 25 minutes Cook: 20 to 25 minutes Makes: 24

Quail eggs are the perfect size for appetizers. Fresh quail eggs are available at Asian markets and in the poultry section of some supermarkets.

12 fresh quail eggs *
1 pound fresh sausage
¾ cup fine dry bread crumbs
Honey Mustard Sauce (recipe follows)

1. Place quail eggs in a medium saucepan. Add enough water to cover by 2 inches and bring to a boil over high heat. Reduce heat to low and simmer 5 minutes. Immerse eggs in cold water. Tap shells to crack, then pull off.

2. Preheat oven to 400°F. In a food processor or blender, puree sausage to a smooth paste. Divide into 12 equal portions. Flatten sausage in your hand and wrap around each egg to cover. Roll in bread crumbs and arrange 1 inch apart on a jelly-roll pan.

3. Bake until sausage is browned and cooked through, 15 to 20 minutes. Let cool to room temperature. (If made in advance, cover and refrigerate as long as 24 hours.) Cut each egg in half and serve cool or at room temperature with honey mustard sauce.

* *Canned or bottled quail eggs can be substituted; look for them in gourmet shops. Be sure to rinse them with cold water and dry well before using.*

HONEY MUSTARD SAUCE

Makes: about ¾ cup

½ cup mayonnaise
2 tablespoons Dijon mustard
1 tablespoon honey

In a small bowl, combine mayonnaise, mustard, and honey. Mix until well blended. If made in advance, cover and refrigerate up to 5 days.

124 CORN-A-COPIAS

Prep: 20 minutes Stand: 2 hours Cook: 1 to 3 minutes
Makes: about 24

Cornmeal gives added texture to these miniature crepes. The flavor of corn complements a number of fillings, so let your imagination run wild. Possible fillings include cream cheese and hot pepper jelly or corn relish; slivers of roast duck and Chinese plum sauce; slivers of turkey or chicken with cranberry chutney; cream cheese, dill, and smoked salmon; Herbed Cream Cheese (page 11) and prosciutto or Black Forest ham; cream cheese blended with blue cheese, port wine, and golden raisins.

- **½ cup cold buttermilk or milk**
- **2 eggs**
- **¼ teaspoon salt**
- **½ cup flour**
- **½ cup polenta or yellow cornmeal**
- **½ teaspoon sugar**
- **2 tablespoons melted butter, plus more for cooking**

1. In a blender or food processor, combine buttermilk, eggs, salt, flour, polenta, sugar, 2 tablespoons melted butter, and ½ cup cold water. Process until well blended. Transfer batter to a bowl, cover, and let rest 2 hours at cool room temperature. (Batter can be refrigerated up to 8 hours, but let return to room temperature before proceeding with recipe.)

2. Heat a 6- to 7-inch crepe pan or nonstick frying pan over medium heat until hot. Brush pan lightly with butter. When butter is hot, remove pan from heat and pour in 2 tablespoons of batter. Tilt and rotate pan to cover bottom with batter. Return pan to heat, loosen edges with a spatula, and cook crepe until bottom is lightly browned, 1 to 2 minutes. Turn crepe over and cook until spotted brown on other side, 30 seconds to 1 minute longer. Transfer cooked crepe to a plate. Repeat with remaining batter, stacking crepes and adding more butter only if pan begins to stick. (If made in advance, stack crepes in plastic wrap and refrigerate up to 3 days or freeze.)

3. Cut stack of crepes in half. Fill each half with one of the fillings suggested above and roll up into a small cone, using some of the filling to seal edges together. Serve at room temperature.

125 BITTY EGGS BENEDICT

Prep: 40 minutes Cook: 6 to 9 minutes Makes: 30

Nowadays a full order of eggs Benedict seems like the ultimate indulgence, but who could resist just one delicious mouthful? Although some last-minute preparation is involved, many of the elements can be prepared in advance.

1 (1-pound) loaf sliced English Muffin Toasting Bread or other firm-textured white bread
4 tablespoons melted butter or olive oil
6 ounces thinly sliced boiled ham, at room temperature (about 6 slices)
10 to 12 hard-boiled small or medium-size eggs, at room temperature
¾ cup hollandaise sauce, purchased or homemade (recipe follows)
Optional garnishes: Sliced ripe black olives, paprika, or chopped parsley

1. Preheat oven to 400°F. Using a 1¾-inch biscuit cutter, cut out 30 bread rounds. Brush both sides with butter and arrange on a baking sheet. Bake, turning once, until lightly toasted, 5 to 8 minutes. Let cool. (If made in advance, store airtight at room temperature up to 2 days. Freeze for longer storage.) Increase oven temperature to 450°.

2. With same biscuit cutter, cut out 30 ham rounds. Using an egg slicer or a sharp knife, cut at least 30 egg slices, discarding ends.

3. Top each toasted bread round with 1 ham slice and then 1 egg slice no larger than the bread. (If made in advance, cover and refrigerate as long as 24 hours. Let return to room temperature before proceeding.) Spread about 1 teaspoon hollandaise sauce over each egg slice to cover completely. Top with an olive slice, if desired. Bake until sauce is just bubbly, 1 to 2 minutes. Serve warm, garnished with a dusting of paprika or a sprinkling of chopped parsley.

126 FOOD PROCESSOR HOLLANDAISE SAUCE

Prep: 5 minutes Cook: none Makes: about 1 cup

A quick hollandaise always comes in handy. Keep in mind, however, the risk of salmonella in uncooked eggs.

4 egg yolks, at room temperature
2 tablespoons fresh lemon juice
1 teaspoon Dijon mustard
½ teaspoon salt
Dash of cayenne
1 stick (4 ounces) unsalted butter, cut into bits

1. In a food processor, combine egg yolks, lemon juice, mustard, salt, and cayenne. Process until well blended.

2. In a small saucepan, melt butter over medium heat until bubbling hot. With machine on, slowly pour hot butter in a thin stream into egg mixture until a thick sauce is formed. Serve at once.

127 OYSTER SAUSAGES

Prep: 20 minutes Cook: 15 minutes Makes: 8

You will need to order sausage casings from your butcher in advance. Serve these whole as a first course or cut into 1-inch pieces and skewer on toothpicks for passing, accompanied by a savory tarragon mustard.

- **2 cups minced raw oysters (about 1 pound)**
- **1½ cups finely chopped beef suet (about ¾ pound)**
- **1½ cups fresh bread crumbs**
- **1½ teaspoons fresh lemon juice**
- **2 eggs**
- **⅛ teaspoon ground allspice**
- **⅛ teaspoon grated nutmeg**
- **¼ teaspoon salt**
- **¼ teaspoon freshly ground pepper**
- **1 or 2 sausage casings, cut into 8 pieces 8 inches long**
- **2 tablespoons butter**
- **2 tablespoons oil**

1. In a medium bowl, combine oysters, suet, bread crumbs, lemon juice, eggs, allspice, nutmeg, salt, and pepper. Blend well. Using a pastry bag fitted with a large metal tip, force mixture into sausage casings. Tie one end of casing, making sausages about 4 to 5 inches long. Squeeze stuffing to eliminate any air pockets. Twist casing and tie with string.

2. Prick sausages with a fork and poach in a large skillet of salted water 10 to 15 minutes, or until firm; drain. Refrigerate for up to a day if not serving immediately.

3. When ready to serve, melt butter and oil in a large frying pan over medium-high heat. Add sausages and cook, turning, until browned all over, about 8 minutes. Serve at once.

128 PETIT PARMESAN PALMIERS

Prep: 25 minutes Cook: 17 to 20 minutes Chill: 2 hours
Makes: 36

Palmiers are French palm leaf–shaped cookies made from sweetened puff pastry. We've borrowed the basic concept, scaling them down in size and giving them a savory pesto or mushroom filling to create a tasty and unusual appetizer.

1 (17¼-ounce) package frozen puff pastry sheets, thawed, as package directs
Creamy Pesto Filling or Creamy Mushroom Filling (recipes follow)
¼ cup grated Parmesan cheese

1. Unfold 1 pastry sheet on a clean work surface. Spread with an even layer of half the filling of choice. Sprinkle with 2 tablespoons Parmesan cheese. Tightly roll up long ends of pastry sheet on both sides, jelly-roll fashion, until they meet in center. Repeat with second pastry sheet and remaining filling. Wrap each roll tightly in plastic wrap, place on a baking sheet, and refrigerate until firm, 1 hour or as long as 2 days.

2. Remove plastic wrap from pastry rolls. Using a thin, sharp knife, cut each roll into ½-inch-thick slices. Arrange unbaked palmiers flat, 2 inches apart on foil- or parchment-lined baking sheets. Cover with plastic wrap and refrigerate until firm, about 1 hour.

3. Preheat oven to 400°F. Bake 10 minutes; then turn palmiers over and continue baking until crisp and golden brown outside and fully cooked inside, 7 to 10 minutes longer. Let cool on a wire rack. Serve warm or at room temperature. (If made in advance, cover and refrigerate up to 2 days; freeze for longer storage. To serve, reheat in a 400° oven 3 to 5 minutes, until hot and crisp.)

CREAMY MUSHROOM FILLING

Makes about 1 cup

1 tablespoon butter
1 shallot, finely chopped
½ pound cultivated or wild mushrooms, finely chopped
½ teaspoon salt
¼ teaspoon freshly ground pepper
1 tablespoon brandy
2 ounces cream cheese (¼ cup)
1 teaspoon fresh thyme leaves or ¼ teaspoon dried
¼ teaspoon concentrated beef-flavored liquid bouillon, such as Bovril

1. In a medium frying pan, melt butter over medium heat. Add shallot and cook until softened but not browned, 1 to 2 minutes. Stir in mushrooms and cook until mushroom liquid is exuded and then evaporates, about 3 minutes. Season with salt and pepper and add brandy. Cook until brandy has nearly cooked away, about 5 minutes, then remove from heat and let cool 10 minutes.

2. In a food processor or blender, combine mushroom mixture, cream cheese, thyme, and beef-flavored liquid bouillon. Process until well blended. If made in advance, cover and refrigerate up to 4 days.

CREAMY PESTO FILLING

Makes about 1 cup

- **2 tablespoons pine nuts (pignoli)**
- **2 cups (loosely packed) fresh basil leaves**
- **¼ cup grated Parmesan cheese**
- **2 ounces cream cheese (¼ cup)**
- **1 large garlic clove, minced**
- **½ teaspoon salt**
- **¼ teaspoon freshly ground pepper**

1. Preheat oven to 325°F. Place pine nuts in an ovenproof pan and bake, stirring once or twice, until just golden brown, 7 to 10 minutes.

2. In a food processor or blender, combine all ingredients and puree until smooth. If made in advance, cover and refrigerate up to 4 days.

129 COCKTAIL POTATO PANCAKES

Prep: 15 minutes Cook: 15 minutes Makes: about 24

- **2 medium baking potatoes**
- **½ small onion**
- **1 egg**
- **1 tablespoon minced fresh marjoram or 1 teaspoon dried**
- **¼ teaspoon salt**
- **⅛ teaspoon freshly ground pepper**
- **1 tablespoon flour**
- **¼ teaspoon baking powder**
- **¼ cup peanut or corn oil**
- **½ cup sour cream**
- **Optional: Caviar, smoked salmon, minced fresh chives, or other herb of choice**

1. In a food processor, grate potatoes and onion and drain in a sieve. In a medium bowl, combine egg, marjoram, salt, and pepper. Beat until well blended. Mix in potatoes, onion, flour, and baking powder.

2. In a large frying pan, warm 2 tablespoons oil over medium heat. Drop tablespoons of potato batter into hot oil and flatten with back of a spoon. Cook, turning once, until golden brown on both sides, about 5 minutes total. Drain on paper towels. Repeat with remaining batter, adding more oil to pan as necessary. (If made in advance, cover and refrigerate up to 2 days. Before serving, arrange in a single layer on a baking sheet and bake in a 450°F oven until heated through, about 5 minutes.)

3. To serve, top each warm pancake with 1 teaspoon sour cream and a dab of caviar or a sprinkling of fresh herbs.

130 PESTO PASTA ROLLS WITH SUN-DRIED TOMATOES

Prep: 15 minutes Cook: 11 to 15 minutes Makes: 12 to 16

½ cup orzo (rice-shaped pasta)
2 egg roll wrappers* (8 inches square)
⅓ cup pesto
1 teaspoon balsamic vinegar
2 scallions, minced
2 tablespoons ricotta or small-curd cottage cheese
½ teaspoon salt
¼ teaspoon pepper
¼ cup chopped oil-packed sun-dried tomatoes or chopped olives

1. In a medium saucepan, cook orzo in boiling salted water until tender, 8 to 10 minutes; drain. Refill saucepan with salted water and bring to a boil.

2. Cook egg roll wrappers in boiling salted water until tender, 3 to 5 minutes. Drain, rinse with cold water, and drain again.

3. In a small bowl, combine orzo, pesto, vinegar, scallions, ricotta cheese, salt, and pepper. Stir until well mixed. Lay egg roll wrappers flat and spread with orzo mixture, leaving ¼-inch margin along far edge of wrapper. Moisten margin with water. Place a thin row of sun-dried tomato down center, gently pressing into orzo. Roll up tightly so that egg roll wrapper wraps around filling, with tomato in center. (If made in advance, wrap tightly in plastic wrap and refrigerate as long as 24 hours.) Use a serrated knife to slice each roll into pieces 1 to 1½ inches thick. To serve, lay pieces flat on a serving plate.

* *Available in Asian markets or in the refrigerated produce or frozen foods section of many supermarkets.*

131 ESCARGOTS IN PASTA SHELLS

Prep: 15 minutes Cook: 10 minutes Makes: 24

These snails won't be slow to go at your party! Escargots can be purchased in cans at the specialty section of your supermarket.

24 escargots (snails)
4 tablespoons butter
4 garlic cloves, minced
24 large sea shell–shaped macaroni
2 sticks (8 ounces) butter, softened
2 shallots, chopped
¼ cup chopped parsley
2 teaspoons Pernod
¼ cup dry white wine
1 cup ground almonds
½ teaspoon salt
¼ teaspoon pepper

1. Preheat oven to 350°F. In a large frying pan, cook escargots in butter with garlic over low heat until heated through, about 4 minutes.

2. In a large pot of boiling salted water, cook pasta shells until tender, about 10 minutes. Drain and arrange on a large baking sheet.

3. In a medium bowl or in a food processor, combine butter, shallots, parsley, Pernod, wine, almonds, salt, and pepper. Blend well. Spoon 1 teaspoon of butter mixture into each shell and fill with 1 escargot. Bake 5 minutes, or until heated through.

---

132 POLENTA AND MUSHROOM TART

Prep: 20 minutes Cook: 40 to 42 minutes Chill: 1 hour
Serves: 8

Serve in wedges with forks as a starter, or cut into bite-size squares to offer as individual appetizers.

3 shallots, chopped
1 tablespoon olive oil
½ pound wild or cultivated mushrooms, thinly sliced
¼ cup medium-dry sherry, such as Amontillado
1 teaspoon fresh lemon juice
1 tablespoon chopped parsley
1½ teaspoons fresh thyme leaves or ½ teaspoon dried
¾ teaspoon salt
⅛ teaspoon freshly ground pepper
2 cups milk
2 cups reduced-sodium chicken broth
1 cup instant polenta or yellow cornmeal
½ cup grated Parmesan cheese
4 tablespoons butter, cut into bits

1. In a large frying pan, cook shallots in olive oil over medium heat until softened but not browned, 1 to 2 minutes. Add mushrooms and cook until mushroom liquid is exuded and then evaporates, about 3 minutes. Add sherry and lemon juice and toss to coat. When sherry has nearly evaporated, remove from heat. Stir in parsley, thyme, ¼ teaspoon salt, and ⅛ teaspoon pepper. Remove mushroom mixture from heat and set aside.

2. Use a 22-inch piece of plastic wrap to line inside of a 9-inch round cake pan, letting excess plastic drape over edges. For garnish, place 1 perfect mushroom slice and a small sprig of thyme in center.

3. In a medium saucepan, combine milk, chicken broth, and remaining ½ teaspoon salt over high heat. When mixture boils, whisk in polenta in a slow steady stream. Reduce heat to medium and cook, stirring, 5 minutes, or until polenta is thickened to consistency of hot cereal. Remove from heat and stir in Parmesan cheese and butter until well blended.

4. Pour half of polenta into prepared pan, taking care not to disturb center mushroom garnish. Using your fingers or a spoon, pat into an even layer. Spread mushroom mixture over polenta, leaving a ½-inch border around edges. Top with remaining polenta, pressing down gently to seal. Cover with excess plastic wrap and let cool. Refrigerate until firm, about 1 hour, or as long as 2 days.

5. Preheat oven to 400°F. Unmold polenta onto a foil- or parchment-lined baking sheet and discard plastic wrap. Bake until heated through and golden around edges, about 30 minutes. Cut into pie-shaped wedges and serve warm.

133 PUFF PASTRY HEARTS WITH CHICKEN LIVER PÂTÉ

Prep: 20 minutes Chill: 1 hour Cook: 10 to 15 minutes Makes: 48

A small napkin-lined basket overflowing with hearts makes an attractive addition to any buffet. For variation, a cheese filling, such as Bourbon Blue Cheese Spread (page 121) or Swiss Simplicity (page 124), could be substituted for the pâté.

1 (17¼-ounce) package frozen puff pastry sheets, thawed as package directs
1 egg yolk
1 tablespoon cream or milk
¼ cup sesame seeds
¾ pound (1½ cups) smooth chicken liver pâté, purchased or homemade (page 140)

1. Unfold pastry sheets onto a clean work surface. Using a 2-inch cookie cutter, cut 24 heart shapes from each sheet. Arrange on a baking sheet, cover well with plastic wrap, and refrigerate until pastry is firm, about 1 hour or as long as overnight.

2. Preheat oven to 400°F. In a small bowl, mix egg yolk with cream until well blended. Quickly brush over hearts and sprinkle with sesame seeds. Bake until pastry is puffed and golden and centers appear cooked, 10 to 15 minutes. Let cool. (If made in advance, store airtight up to 2 days or freeze. Reheat 5 minutes in a 400° oven before filling.)

3. Using your fingers or a small serrated knife, split each heart horizontally and fill with about 1½ teaspoons pâté, then sandwich hearts back together.

134 BAY SCALLOPS IN PUFF PASTRY SHELLS

Prep: 30 minutes Chill: 25 to 30 minutes
Cook: 15 to 20 minutes Makes: 30

Tiny puff pastry shells, known as bouchées, are sold fresh in many bakeries and frozen in some supermarkets. They are also easily made from prepared puff pastry sheets and make very showy receptacles for all sorts of hot and cold fillings. In this version, a quick turn in the oven is just enough time to cook a tiny bay scallop.

1 (17¼-ounce) package frozen puff pastry sheets, thawed as package directs
30 bay scallops (about ¼ pound) or 7 or 8 quartered sea scallops
Saffron Mayonnaise Sauce or Watercress Mayonnaise Sauce (recipes follow)

1. Using a 2-inch biscuit cutter, make 30 puff pastry rounds and arrange 1 inch apart on a foil- or parchment-lined baking sheet. Refrigerate until firm, about 15 minutes.

2. Using a 1-inch biscuit cutter, make a 1-inch indentation in center of each pastry round, being careful not to cut all the way through. Refrigerate until quite firm, 10 to 15 minutes. Preheat oven to 400°F.

3. Bake chilled pastry until puffed and golden brown, 10 to 15 minutes. Let cool on a rack. Using tip of a sharp knife, remove puffed lids and part of soft centers. (If made in advance, store airtight at room temperature up to 2 days. Freeze for longer storage.)

4. Place 1 uncooked scallop in each puff pastry shell and cover with about ¼ teaspoon mayonnaise sauce. Bake 5 minutes, or until sauce is heated through and scallop is just opaque throughout. Serve at once.

SAFFRON MAYONNAISE SAUCE

Makes ¼ cup

¼ teaspoon saffron threads
½ teaspoon fresh lemon juice
¼ cup mayonnaise

In a small bowl with a pestle or back of a spoon, crush saffron threads to a powder. Stir in lemon juice and let stand to soften. Mix in mayonnaise until well blended. If made in advance, cover and refrigerate up to 4 days.

WATERCRESS MAYONNAISE SAUCE

Makes about ⅓ cup

¼ cup mayonnaise
½ teaspoon fresh lemon juice
1 tablespoon minced fresh watercress

In a small bowl, combine mayonnaise and lemon juice. Stir until well blended. Mix in watercress. If made in advance, cover and refrigerate up to 2 days.

135 SHRIMP EXTRAVAGANZA

Prep: 30 minutes   Cook: none   Chill: 1 hour   Serves: 24

This wowzie presentation is one way to appear extravagant as you serve a small army with a miserly ½ pound of shrimp. Pull out all the stops to make this savory as pretty as a wedding cake. A pedestal cake stand makes a perfect serving plate.

CREAM CHEESE BASE

- **2 (8-ounce) packages cream cheese, softened**
- **1 bunch of scallions, chopped**
- **½ cup chopped parsley**
- **2 tablespoons sour cream or mayonnaise**
- **1 tablespoon fresh lemon juice**
- **3 drops of hot pepper sauce**

DECORATIVE BORDER

- **12 ounces cream cheese, softened**
- **¼ cup sour cream or mayonnaise**
- **1 teaspoon lemon juice**
- **⅛ teaspoon salt**

SAUCY TOPPING

- **¾ cup bottled chili sauce**
- **2 tablespoons chopped cilantro or parsley**
- **1 tablespoon prepared white horseradish**
- **1 teaspoon fresh lemon juice**
- **3 drops of hot pepper sauce**

FINAL GARNISH

- **½ pound tiny shelled cooked shrimp**
- **2 teaspoons capers, rinsed and drained**
- **4 thin lemon slices**
- **Grated lemon zest and chopped parsley, cilantro, chives, or dill**
- **Crackers or bread rounds**

1. Use a 16-inch piece of plastic wrap to line the inside of a 7- or 8-inch round cake pan, letting excess plastic drape over edges. Make Cream Cheese Base: In a medium bowl or food processor, combine cream cheese, scallions, parsley, sour cream, lemon juice, and hot sauce. Blend well. Turn into prepared pan, cover with excess plastic wrap, and refrigerate until firm, 1 hour or as long as 2 days. Unmold cream cheese base onto a serving plate and discard plastic wrap.

2. Make Decorative Border: In a medium bowl or in a food processor, combine cream cheese, sour cream, lemon juice, and salt. Blend well. Using a pastry bag fitted with a large decorative tip, pipe a single row of stars or rosettes around top surface diameter of cream cheese base, forming a ledge.

Use remaining mixture in pastry bag to pipe a design around outside of cream cheese base.

3. Make Saucy Topping: In a small bowl, combine chili sauce, cilantro, horseradish, lemon juice, and hot sauce. Mix until well blended. Carefully pour mixture into center of cream cheese base, within confines of cream cheese ledge.

4. Top with shrimp and a scattering of capers. Cut lemon slices in half and arrange with flat edge around outside of cream cheese base. Sprinkle with grated lemon zest and parsley over top. If made in advance, carefully cover with an inverted bowl to avoid disturbing decoration and refrigerate as long as 2 hours. Serve at cool room temperature with crackers and bread rounds.

---

136 SWEET POTATO BABYCAKES

Prep: 20 minutes Cook: 15 minutes Makes: 24 to 30

The snappy taste of ginger complements the natural sweetness of the yam. There is no reason not to make plenty of these, because they can be done in advance and reheated.

1 egg
½ teaspoon fresh lemon juice
½ teaspoon salt
⅛ teaspoon freshly ground pepper
2 tablespoons minced crystallized ginger
1½ tablespoons honey
1 garlic clove, minced
2 medium yams or sweet potatoes (about 1 pound), peeled and grated
1 small onion, grated
1½ teaspoons flour
¼ teaspoon baking powder
¼ to ⅓ cup peanut or corn oil
⅓ cup sour cream
Optional toppings: Minced crystallized ginger, minced chives or scallion green, or a dab of chunky applesauce

1. In a large bowl, combine egg, lemon juice, salt, and pepper. Beat until well blended. Add crystallized ginger, honey, and garlic and mix well. Stir in yams and onion. Sprinkle flour and baking powder over yam mixture, mixing well.

2. In a large frying pan, warm 2 tablespoons oil over medium heat. Drop tablespoons of mixture into hot oil and flatten with back of a spoon. Cook, turning once, until golden brown on both sides, about 5 minutes total. Drain on paper towels. Repeat with remaining yam mixture, adding more oil to pan as necessary. (If made in advance, cover and refrigerate up to 2 days. Before serving, arrange pancakes in a single layer on a baking sheet and bake in a 450°F oven until heated through, about 5 minutes.)

3. To serve, top each warm pancake with ½ teaspoon sour cream and any additional topping, as desired.

137 WILD RICE PANCAKES WITH SMOKED SALMON

Prep: 15 minutes Cook: 37 minutes Makes: 36 to 42

Packaged long grain and wild rice makes this economical.

1 tablespoon butter
1½ teaspoons salt
1 (6-ounce) box Long Grain and Wild Rice
2 eggs
1 tablespoon olive oil
2 tablespoons flour
4 scallions, finely chopped
1½ teaspoons fresh thyme leaves or ½ teaspoon dried
⅛ teaspoon freshly ground pepper
¼ to ⅓ cup peanut or corn oil
1 cup sour cream
3 ounces thinly sliced smoked salmon, cut into strips about 2 inches long and ½ inch wide
Optional toppings: Minced fresh chives, dill, or cilantro; or capers

1. In a medium saucepan, combine butter, salt, and 2⅓ cups water over medium heat. Stir in rice, discarding seasoning packet from box. Bring mixture to a boil. Cover, reduce heat to low, and simmer until rice is tender, about 25 minutes. Drain in a sieve and let cool 5 minutes.

2. In a medium bowl, beat eggs with oil until well blended; mix in flour. Stir in scallions, thyme, and pepper until well mixed. Stir in rice to coat.

3. In a large frying pan, warm 2 tablespoons oil over medium heat. Drop tablespoons of rice mixture into hot oil and flatten with back of a spoon. Cook, turning once, until golden brown on both sides, about 4 minutes total. Drain on paper towels. Repeat with remaining mixture, adding more oil to pan as necessary. (If made in advance, cover and refrigerate up to 2 days.)

4. Serve at room temperature, topped with 1 teaspoon sour cream, a piece of smoked salmon, and any other of the optional garnishes.

138 SUPPLI AL TELEFONO

Prep: 15 minutes Chill: 2 hours Cook: about 25 minutes
Makes: 24

Melted mozzarella strings resemble telephone wires, giving this Italian classic its whimsical name.

1½ tablespoons butter
1 cup Arborio rice
4 cups hot reduced-sodium chicken broth
3 eggs
¼ cup grated Parmesan cheese
1 tablespoon minced parsley
⅛ teaspoon freshly ground pepper
¼ teaspoon grated nutmeg
¼ pound prosciutto, finely chopped
½ cup flour
1 cup fine dry bread crumbs
¼ pound mozzarella cheese, cut into 24 cubes
About 4 cups corn or peanut oil

1. In a medium saucepan, melt butter over medium-low heat. Add rice and cook, stirring, 2 to 3 minutes, until rice is coated with butter and looks opaque. Add 2 cups of broth and cook, stirring, until stock is almost absorbed, 5 to 6 minutes. Add 1 more cup stock and cook until almost absorbed, 4 to 5 minutes. Continue to add remainder of broth gradually and cook, stirring, until rice is tender but still firm and liquid forms a thick sauce, about 10 to 15 minutes longer. Remove from heat and let cool to lukewarm.

2. In a large bowl, beat 1 egg until blended. Add rice along with cheese, parsley, pepper, nutmeg, and prosciutto. Blend well. Cover and refrigerate at least 1 hour until chilled.

3. In a small bowl, beat remaining 2 eggs with 2 teaspoons water. Place flour and bread crumbs in 2 separate shallow dishes.

4. With floured hands, scoop up a heaping tablespoon of rice mixture in palm of your hand. Place a cube of mozzarella in center. Pack another heaping tablespoon of rice mixture over cheese and form into a compact ball about 1½ inches in diameter. Roll ball in flour and shake off excess. Roll ball in beaten egg, coat with bread crumbs, and set on a baking sheet. Repeat with remaining rice and cheese. Cover with plastic wrap and refrigerate 2 hours.

5. In a deep fryer or a large heavy saucepan, pour in oil to a depth of 3 inches and heat to 375°F on a deep-frying thermometer. Add rice balls in batches without crowding and deep-fry, turning occasionally, until golden brown, 3 to 5 minutes. Remove with a skimmer or slotted spoon and drain on paper towels. Keep warm while frying remaining balls. Serve at once.

139 TORTA RUSTICA

Prep: 20 minutes Cook: 40 minutes Rise: 4 hours Serves: 8 to 10

Serve wedges of this hearty rustic appetizer and wait for the compliments to begin.

- **1 (¼-ounce) envelope active dry yeast**
- **¼ cup warm water (105° to 115°)**
- **1 tablespoon sugar**
- **2 cups flour**
- **1 stick (4 ounces) butter, softened**
- **2 whole eggs**
- **½ teaspoon salt**
- **1 medium onion, chopped**
- **½ pound mushrooms, sliced**
- **2 tablespoons olive oil**
- **1 tablespoon heavy cream**
- **1 egg yolk**
- **2 cups diced cooked ham (about ½ pound)**
- **½ pound sliced provolone cheese**
- **1 (7-ounce) jar roasted red bell peppers, cut into thin strips**
- **1 (9-ounce) package frozen artichoke hearts, thawed, drained, and coarsely chopped**

1. In a medium bowl, dissolve yeast in warm water; stir in sugar. Add flour, butter, whole eggs, and salt. Beat with an electric mixer about 5 minutes, until dough is smooth; it will be sticky. Cover and refrigerate at least 4 hours or as long as 24.

2. Preheat oven to 375°F. In a large frying pan, cook onion and mushrooms in olive oil over medium heat until onions are softened but not browned and mushrooms are tender, about 5 minutes.

3. On a floured work surface, roll or pat two-thirds of dough into a 13- to 14-inch circle. Press dough evenly into a greased 8-inch springform pan to cover bottom and sides. In a small bowl, beat cream and egg yolk until well blended; brush lightly over dough; reserve excess for glaze.

4. Fill dough-lined pan in layers in following order: ham, half of cheese, mushrooms and onions, remaining cheese, pepper strips, and chopped artichoke hearts.

5. Roll or pat out remaining third of dough into an 8-inch circle; brush with reserved glaze. Place dough glazed-side down over filling. Press edges together to seal, tucking them under. Slash center for a steam vent and brush top with remaining glaze.

6. Bake until torta is heated through inside and golden brown outside, about 35 minutes. Loosen torta from pan with a flexible spatula. If made in advance, let stand uncovered at room temperature up to 2 hours. Cut into wedges and serve warm or at room temperature.

140 CHARD-STUFFED PROSCIUTTO

Prep: 10 minutes Cook: 2 to 3 minutes Makes: about 18

You may choose to serve these with utensils, as they tend to be a bit messy to eat out of hand. Either way, we assure you that the results will be nothing short of delicious. If chard is unavailable, use other bitter greens, such as escarole, spinach, or mustard greens.

3 tablespoons extra-virgin olive oil
1 bunch of red or green Swiss chard leaves, coarsely chopped (about 6 cups)
3 large garlic cloves, minced
2 tablespoons balsamic vinegar
¼ teaspoon salt
⅛ teaspoon freshly ground pepper
½ pound thinly sliced prosciutto or ham (about 18 slices)

1. In a large nonreactive frying pan, heat olive oil over medium heat. Add greens and cook, tossing, until wilted, 1 to 2 minutes. Stir in garlic, vinegar, salt, and pepper. Cook until greens are just tender, about 1 minute. Remove from heat.

2. Lay prosciutto slices flat. Place a generous tablespoon of greens at one end of each slice and roll into a tight cylinder, taking care that a bit of green protrudes from each open end. Serve at room temperature or slightly chilled.

Chapter 5

Strictly Southwestern

Whether you're sipping a margarita or a diet soda, zesty flavors perk up the taste buds and make for lively conversation—the perfect combination for party food. That's why we decided to give this Mexican-inspired cooking a chapter of its own. When you want to create an event that's a complete fiesta, or if you'd just like to add a Latin accent to a general assortment of appetizers and hors d'oeuvres, this is the place to look.

Here you'll find the lively flavors of the American Southwest, where the food is as packed with taste as it is with color. Ingredients like chiles, avocados, cilantro, and lime add snap to simple recipes. There is a selection of guacamole dips and nachos, along with salsas galore. Salsas are highly flavored, low-fat sauces that double as dips. They are usually seen next to a basket of corn tortilla chips, but most are delightful dunks for vegetables, boiled shrimp, and grilled kebabs as well.

For easy entertaining there are recipes like Quickie Con Queso Dip, Bean-a-Mole, and Chilaquiles. To make a splash, pass a platter of Blue Quesadillas with Fresh Pear Salsa or Chicken Empanadas. Whichever dish you choose from this chapter, your guests are sure to cry *"Olé!"*

---

141 GUACAMOLE

Prep: 10 minutes Cook: none Makes: 1½ cups

1 large ripe avocado
1 tablespoon grated onion
1 fresh jalapeño pepper, peeled, seeded, and finely chopped
2 teaspoons lime juice
½ teaspoon ground cumin
½ teaspoon salt
1 small tomato, peeled, seeded, and chopped

1. Using a sharp knife, cut avocado in half; remove pit and peel. Quickly dunk each avocado half in a bowl of cold water to prevent darkening. Drain well.

2. In a small bowl, use the tines of a fork to mash avocado, leaving some texture. Blend in onion, jalapeño pepper, lime juice, cumin, and salt. Stir in tomato. Serve immediately, or cover tightly with plastic wrap touching the surface of dip to prevent darkening and store in the refrigerator up to 4 hours.

142 NEW MEXICO GUACAMOLE

Prep: 10 minutes Cook: none Makes: 2 cups

The best avocados are those with thick black, nubby skins. Keep them at room temperature. When they are ready to use, they will be soft as a ripe peach.

2 large ripe avocados
½ teaspoon salt
4 teaspoons fresh lime juice
2 scallions, thinly sliced
1 medium tomato, peeled and finely diced
1 garlic clove, minced
2 tablespoons minced jalapeño pepper
1 tablespoon minced cilantro

1. Using a sharp knife, cut avocado in half; remove pit and peel. Quickly dunk each avocado half in a bowl of cold water to prevent darkening. Drain well.

2. In a medium bowl, use tines of a fork to mash avocado, leaving some texture. Add salt and lime juice a little at a time, to taste, until well mixed. Blend in scallions, tomato, garlic, jalapeño pepper, and cilantro. Serve immediately or cover with plastic wrap directly on surface of guacamole to prevent darkening and refrigerate.

143 SWEET PEA GUACAMOLE

Prep: 10 minutes Cook: none Makes: about 3 cups

When ripe avocados are unavailable, you'll be quite pleased with the results produced by this surprise ingredient.

2 (10-ounce) packages frozen peas, thawed and drained
⅓ cup sour cream
3 scallions, chopped
2 fresh jalapeño or other small green chile peppers, seeded and minced
2 tablespoons fresh lime or lemon juice
1 tablespoon olive oil
2 garlic cloves, minced
1 teaspoon salt
½ teaspoon ground cumin
⅛ teaspoon cayenne
⅓ cup chopped fresh cilantro (optional)

In a food processor or blender, combine peas, sour cream, scallions, jalapeño peppers, lime juice, olive oil, garlic, salt, cumin, cayenne, and cilantro. Process, turning machine quickly on and off, until ingredients are well blended but still somewhat coarse in texture. Serve immediately, or store in an airtight container in refrigerator for up to 3 days.

144 BEAN-A-MOLE

Prep: 10 minutes Cook: none Makes: 2½ cups

This recipe was named by our friend David Brown, who enjoyed its similarity to guacamole.

- **2 (15-ounce) cans pinto beans, drained**
- **1 (4-ounce) can diced green chiles**
- **2 scallions, chopped**
- **2 tablespoons olive oil**
- **1 tablespoon lime or lemon juice**
- **2 garlic cloves, minced**
- **½ teaspoon salt**
- **½ teaspoon chili powder**
- **¼ teaspoon ground cumin**
- **Tortilla chips or crackers**

In a food processor, combine pinto beans, chiles, scallions, olive oil, lime juice, garlic, salt, chili powder, and cumin. Mix until well blended and beans are slightly mashed but still maintain some texture. If made in advance, cover and refrigerate. Serve with tortilla chips or crackers.

145 BEEFY GUACAMOLE

Prep: 10 minutes Cook: 9 to 11 minutes Makes: 3 cups

This hearty dip can also be spooned into warm tortillas for a somewhat messy but very delicious appetizer.

- **1 small onion, chopped**
- **1 tablespoon vegetable oil**
- **1 pound ground round (85% lean)**
- **1 teaspoon salt**
- **4 ripe medium avocados (about 2 pounds)**
- **1 cup sour cream**
- **½ cup mayonnaise**
- **1 (4-ounce) can diced green chiles**
- **2 tablespoons fresh lime or lemon juice**
- **1 teaspoon hot pepper sauce**
- **¾ teaspoon ground cumin**
- **Sprigs of fresh cilantro or chopped fresh tomato**

1. In a large skillet, cook onion in oil over medium-high heat until just softened, about 3 minutes. Add ground round and season with salt. Cook, stirring and breaking meat into uniform chunks, until meat is lightly browned and just cooked through, 6 to 8 minutes. Drain well and let cool.

2. Using a sharp knife, cut avocados in half; remove pits and peel. Quickly dunk each avocado half in a bowl of cold water to prevent darkening. Drain well.

3. In a medium bowl, use the tines of a fork to mash avocados. Add sour cream, mayonnaise, chiles, lime juice, hot sauce, and cumin. Stir until well blended. Stir in beef and onion mixture. Garnish with sprigs of fresh cilantro or chopped fresh tomato. Serve at once.

146 CHEESY CHILI DIP

Prep: 2 minutes Cook: 10 minutes Makes: 3 cups

1 (15-ounce) can chili without beans
1 (8-ounce) package Mexican-style pasteurized process cheese spread, cut into bits
Tortilla chips

In a medium saucepan, combine chili and cheese spread. Cook over low heat, stirring frequently, until cheese has melted and mixture is heated through, about 10 minutes. Serve warm with tortilla chips.

147 QUICKIE CON QUESO DIP

Prep: 5 minutes Cook: 5 to 7 minutes Makes: 3 cups

Here's an instant "out-of-the-pantry" pleaser that's perfect with tortilla chips.

1 (7-ounce) can green chile salsa
1 (4-ounce) can chopped green chiles
4 cups shredded sharp Cheddar cheese (about 1 pound)

In a medium saucepan, combine salsa, chiles, and cheese. Cook over low heat, stirring frequently, until cheese is melted, 5 to 7 minutes.

148 PIÑATA DIP

Prep: 5 minutes Cook: none Makes: 2½ cups Serves: 6

Guacamole with a twist.

5 slices of bacon
2 cups sour cream
1 teaspoon seasoned salt
1½ teaspoons chili powder
1 medium avocado, chopped
1 medium tomato, peeled and chopped

1. In a large frying pan, cook bacon over medium heat until crisp, 5 to 7 minutes. Drain well on paper towels, then finely chop or crumble.

2. In a medium bowl, combine sour cream, seasoned salt, and chili powder. Fold in bacon, avocado, and tomato.

149 SPICY JÍCAMA STICKS

Prep: 10 minutes   Cook: none   Makes: about 24

Although jícama has Mexican origins, it is being seen in more and more supermarkets across America. It is a large, brown-skinned, bulbous root vegetable with crisp white meat and a flavor that resembles that of a fresh water chestnut.

1 pound jícama
¼ cup fresh lime juice
1 tablespoon chopped fresh cilantro (optional)
2 tablespoons chili powder

1. Peel jícama, rinse with cold water, and pat dry. Cut into ¼- to ⅜-inch-thick slices, then cut crosswise into pieces about ½ inch wide.

2. Set 2 small bowls on a platter. Combine lime juice and cilantro in one bowl; place chili powder in the other. Surround with jícama sticks. Have guests dip jícama first in lime juice, then in chili powder.

150 NACHOS

Prep: 10 minutes   Cook: 5 to 7 minutes   Makes: 24

One of the quickest and easiest appetizers is also one of our favorites. This version is made in minutes and is always a hit.

24 large tortilla chips
½ pound Monterey Jack cheese, cut into 24 cubes
3 jalapeño peppers, fresh or pickled, sliced
4 scallions, minced
½ cup sour cream

1. Preheat oven to 400°F. Arrange tortilla chips on a large baking sheet in a single layer. Top each chip with a cheese cube, then with a slice of jalapeño pepper. Sprinkle with scallions.

2. Bake 5 to 7 minutes, until cheese is bubbly. Before serving, top each nacho with 1 teaspoon sour cream.

151 NACHOS GRANDES

Prep: 10 minutes Cook: 7 to 10 minutes Makes: 24

1 pound chorizo or hot Italian sausages
24 large tortilla chips, 3 to 4 inches in diameter
1 (15-ounce) can plain or spicy refried beans
4 fresh or pickled jalapeño peppers, thinly sliced
½ pound Monterey Jack cheese, cut into 24 cubes
1 cup guacamole, purchased or homemade (page 87)
1 cup sour cream
1 (2¼-ounce) can sliced ripe olives

1. Crumble chorizo with your fingers. In a large frying pan, cook crumbled chorizo over medium-high heat, stirring occasionally, until meat is lightly browned. Remove with slotted spoon and set aside.

2. Preheat oven to 400°F. Arrange tortilla chips on a baking sheet and top with 1 heaping tablespoon each refried beans and chorizo. Top each with a slice of jalapeño pepper and a cheese cube.

3. Bake 7 to 10 minutes, until beans are heated through and cheese has melted. Before serving, top each nacho with 1½ tablespoons each guacamole, sour cream, and sliced olives.

152 MACHO NACHOS

Prep: 15 minutes Cook: 20 to 25 minutes Serves: 8 to 10

1 (8-ounce) bag tortilla chips (about 6 cups), plus more for serving
1 tablespoon vegetable oil
1 pound ground round (85% lean)
1 (1¼-ounce) package taco seasoning mix
1 (16-ounce) can refried beans
1 cup shredded Monterey Jack cheese (about 4 ounces)
1 (4-ounce) can diced green chiles
1 cup shredded Cheddar cheese (about 4 ounces)
¾ cup salsa, purchased or homemade (page 94)
½ cup sour cream
1 (2¼-ounce) can sliced ripe olives
¼ cup thinly sliced scallions
¼ cup chopped fresh cilantro (optional)

1. Mound 6 cups tortilla chips in a large, shallow ovenproof serving dish, such as a 10-inch pie plate. Preheat oven to 400°F.

2. In a large frying pan, heat oil over medium-high heat. Add ground round and cook, stirring to break up lumps of meat, until nicely browned and just cooked through, 7 to 10 minutes. Pour off fat and stir in taco seasoning mix until well blended.

3. In a medium bowl, combine refried beans, Monterey Jack cheese, and chiles. Stir until well blended. Spoon bean mixture over chips and top with meat and Cheddar cheese.

4. Bake until cheeses melt and beans are heated through, 20 to 25 minutes. Remove from oven and quickly drizzle salsa over top. Dollop with sour cream and sprinkle on sliced olives, scallions, and cilantro. Serve warm with additional tortilla chips for dipping.

153 TACO PARFAIT

Prep: 25 minutes Cook: 10 to 15 minutes Chill: 2 hours
Serves: 12 to 16

Our friend Sheila Belitkus layers these zesty ingredients in a springform pan to make an impressive presentation.

- **½ cup chopped onion**
- **1 tablespoon vegetable oil**
- **1 pound ground round (85% lean)**
- **1½ teaspoons salt**
- **2 garlic cloves, minced**
- **1 (4-ounce) can diced green chiles**
- **2 cups sour cream**
- **1 (1¼-ounce) package taco seasoning mix**
- **⅛ teaspoon hot pepper sauce**
- **1 (16-ounce) can plain or Mexican-style refried beans**
- **¾ cup guacamole, purchased or homemade (page 87)**
- **1 cup shredded Cheddar or Monterey Jack cheese (about 4 ounces)**
- **2 medium tomatoes, chopped**
- **½ cup sliced scallions**
- **1 (2¼-ounce) can sliced ripe olives**
- **Tortilla chips**

1. In a large frying pan, cook onion in oil over medium-high heat until softened but not browned, 3 to 5 minutes. Add ground round, salt, and garlic. Cook, stirring to break up lumps of meat, until beef is nicely browned and just cooked through, 7 to 10 minutes. Using a slotted spoon, transfer mixture to a large bowl and stir in chiles.

2. In a small bowl, combine sour cream and taco seasoning mix. Stir until well blended. In another bowl, mix hot sauce into refried beans.

3. Spread beans over bottom of an 8-inch springform pan or plate. Top with meat mixture, then a layer each of seasoned sour cream and guacamole. Cover with plastic wrap, pressing directly onto surface of guacamole. Refrigerate until well chilled, at least 2 hours or as long as 2 days. Just before serving, remove plastic wrap and carefully release sides of springform pan. Top taco parfait with cheese, tomatoes, scallions, and olives. Serve with a small knife to spread parfait on tortilla chips.

154 CHILAQUILES

Prep: 10 minutes Cook: 30 minutes Serves: 6

This tortilla pie requires small plates and forks for eating. For a more substantial appetizer or light meal, add a layer of 4 to 6 ounces shredded cooked chicken.

- **4 (6-inch) corn tortillas**
- **½ cup sour cream**
- **2 cups salsa, purchased or homemade (page 94)**
- **1½ cups shredded Monterey Jack cheese (about 6 ounces)**
- **½ cup chicken broth**

1. Preheat oven to 350°F. Place 1 tortilla in an oiled 7- or 8-inch round shallow baking dish, such as a ceramic quiche or pie plate. Top with 2 heaping tablespoons sour cream, a heaping ½ cup salsa, ⅓ cup cheese, and another tortilla. Repeat layers, ending with the fourth tortilla. Drizzle chicken broth over all and top with remaining ½ cup cheese.

2. Place on a baking sheet and cook until cheese has melted and layers are heated through, about 30 minutes. Cut into 6 pie-shaped wedges and serve warm.

155 SARAH'S SALSA

Prep: 15 minutes Cook: none Chill: overnight Makes: 3 cups

The combination of canned and fresh tomatoes and chiles makes for an interesting salsa.

- **1 (16-ounce) can whole tomatoes, drained and coarsely chopped**
- **1 small tomato, peeled, seeded, and chopped**
- **1 (4-ounce) can diced green chiles**
- **⅓ cup minced fresh Anaheim chile peppers**
- **1 jalapeño or serrano chile pepper, minced**
- **¼ cup minced red onion**
- **2 scallions, minced**
- **2 tablespoons red wine vinegar**
- **2 tablespoons minced cilantro or parsley**
- **1 teaspoon coarse salt**
- **2 teaspoons fresh lime juice**
- **1 large garlic clove, minced**
- **¼ teaspoon ground cumin**
- **⅛ teaspoon sugar**
- **5 drops of hot pepper sauce**
- **Pinch of oregano**

1. In a medium bowl, combine canned tomatoes, fresh tomato, canned chiles, fresh Anaheim chiles, jalapeño pepper, red onion, scallions, vinegar, cilantro, salt, lime juice, garlic, cumin, sugar, hot sauce, and oregano. Stir gently until well mixed.

2. Cover and refrigerate overnight, or as long as 2 days. Serve at room temperature.

156 FIERY RED SALSA

Prep: 5 minutes Cook: none Makes: 1 cup

This salsa is not for the fainthearted. Add more hot red pepper if you dare.

- **1 cup chopped tomatoes**
- **½ to 1 teaspoon crushed hot red pepper, or more to taste**
- **1 teaspoon fresh lime juice**
- **1 teaspoon cider vinegar**
- **1 garlic clove, minced**
- **½ teaspoon ground cumin**
- **¼ teaspoon ground oregano**

In a small bowl, combine tomatoes, hot pepper, lime juice, vinegar, garlic, cumin, and oregano. Stir to mix. Serve immediately, or cover and refrigerate up to 2 days.

157 SALSA VERDE CON CREMA

Prep: 10 minutes Cook: none Chill: 1 hour Makes: 2 cups

An excellent "go with" for Beer-Boiled Shrimp (page 111).

- **1 cup salsa verde, bottled or homemade (page 96)**
- **½ cup sour cream**
- **½ cup mayonnaise**
- **1 tablespoon fresh lime juice**
- **2 teaspoons minced jalapeño or serrano chile**
- **2 teaspoons minced cilantro or parsley**
- **½ teaspoon salt**

In a small bowl, combine salsa verde, sour cream, mayonnaise, lime juice, chile, cilantro, and salt. Stir until well mixed. Cover and refrigerate 1 hour or as long as 2 days. Serve at room temperature.

158 SALSA FRESCA

Prep: 5 minutes Cook: none Chill: 1 hour Makes: 1½ cups

Delicious with all types of chips or vegetables.

- **2 large ripe tomatoes, peeled, seeded, and chopped**
- **½ cup chopped red onion**
- **1 garlic clove, minced**
- **¼ cup minced fresh hot chiles, such as jalapeño or serrano, stems and seeds removed**
- **¾ teaspoon salt**

1. In a medium bowl combine tomatoes, red onion, garlic, chiles, and salt. Stir until well mixed.

2. Cover and refrigerate 1 hour or as long as 1 day before serving.

159 TRADITIONAL SALSA VERDE

Prep: 5 minutes Cook: none Makes: 2 cups

Tomatillos are found in Latin grocery stores and the Latin American food section of many supermarkets.

- **1 (13-ounce) can tomatillos, well drained**
- **¼ cup minced red onion**
- **1 tablespoon minced cilantro**
- **1 fresh serrano or jalapeño chile pepper, stem and seeds removed, chopped**
- **¾ teaspoon salt**

In a blender or food processor, combine tomatillos, red onion, cilantro, chile pepper, and salt. Puree until smooth. Serve immediately or cover and refrigerate up to 2 days.

160 SALSA VERDE

Prep: 10 minutes Cook: 20 minutes Makes: 2 cups

Unlike most salsas, this one freezes well.

- **1 tablespoon olive oil**
- **½ cup chopped onion**
- **2 tablespoons flour**
- **1 (16-ounce) can whole tomatoes, coarsely chopped, and their juice**
- **1 (7-ounce) can diced green chiles**
- **1 garlic clove, minced**
- **1 teaspoon salt**
- **¼ teaspoon ground cumin**

1. In a medium saucepan, heat oil over medium heat. Add onion and cook until softened but not browned, 2 to 3 minutes. Stir in flour until well blended. Cook 1 minute longer. Add tomatoes with their juice, chiles, garlic, salt, and cumin.

2. Bring to a boil, reduce heat to low, and simmer, stirring occasionally, until sauce is thickened, about 20 minutes. Let cool before serving. Store in refrigerator up to 3 days, or freeze. Serve at room temperature.

161 SOUTHWESTERN RED CHILI DIP

Prep: 10 minutes Cook: 28 to 38 minutes Makes: 3 cups

This recipe is a basic in Southwestern cooking. It may be used as a dip or as a sauce.

2 tablespoons olive oil
2 tablespoons flour
½ cup chili powder
1 (14½-ounce) can beef broth
½ teaspoon salt
1 garlic clove, minced
¼ teaspoon oregano
⅛ teaspoon ground cumin

1. In a medium saucepan, heat oil over medium heat. Stir in flour and cook, stirring frequently, until mixture is lightly browned, about 3 minutes. Add chili powder, beef broth, salt, garlic, oregano, and cumin, stirring until well mixed. Cook, stirring occasionally, until sauce is smooth and bubbly, about 5 minutes.

2. Reduce heat to low and simmer, stirring occasionally, until flavors are fully developed, 20 to 30 minutes. Serve warm or let cool, cover, and refrigerate up to 3 days.

162 BABY BEAN BURRITOS

Prep: 15 minutes Cook: 10 to 15 minutes Makes: 24

If you love spicy foods, you'll find these irresistible. They're also a bit messy to eat, so be sure to provide lots of napkins.

12 (6-inch) flour tortillas
1 medium onion, chopped
1 tablespoon vegetable oil
2 garlic cloves, minced
1 or 2 fresh jalapeño peppers, seeded and minced
1 (16-ounce) can plain or Mexican-style refried beans
1 cup shredded Monterey Jack cheese (about 4 ounces)
½ teaspoon ground cumin
⅓ cup chopped cilantro (optional)
Sour cream and salsa

1. Preheat oven to 325°F. Stack tortillas and cut in half. Wrap tortilla stack in foil and heat until warmed through, 10 to 15 minutes.

2. Meanwhile, in a large frying pan, cook onion in oil over medium-high heat until softened but not browned, 2 to 3 minutes. Add garlic and jalapeño peppers and cook until garlic is just fragrant, about 30 seconds. Reduce heat to low and stir in refried beans, Monterey Jack cheese, and cumin until well blended. Continue cooking, stirring occasionally, until heated through, 5 to 7 minutes longer.

3. Spread about 1½ tablespoons bean mixture on each tortilla half and roll up jelly-roll fashion. Arrange on a serving plate and sprinkle with cilantro. Serve warm with sour cream and salsa.

163 MEXICALI YOGURT SPREAD

Prep: 10 minutes Cook: none Makes: 1½ cups to serve 4 to 6

Serve this spicy dip with a colorful assortment of bell pepper strips, cucumber rounds, radishes, and jícama sticks.

1¼ cups Yogurt Cheese (page 19)
1 (4-ounce) can chopped green chiles
3 tablespoons chopped fresh cilantro
1 tablespoon olive oil
1 garlic clove, minced
½ teaspoon ground cumin
½ teaspoon salt
⅛ teaspoon cayenne

In a medium bowl, combine yogurt cheese, chiles, cilantro, olive oil, garlic, cumin, salt, and cayenne. Stir until well blended. If made in advance, cover and refrigerate up to 2 days.

164 MARGARITA KEBABS

Prep: 15 minutes Marinate: 2 hours Cook: 10 to 15 minutes Serves: 4 to 6

1 cup margarita drink mix or 1 cup fresh lime juice mixed with 4 teaspoons sugar and ½ teaspoon salt
1 teaspoon ground coriander
1 garlic clove, minced
1 pound pork tenderloin, cut into 24 (1-inch) cubes
2 tablespoons olive oil
2 teaspoons fresh lime juice
⅛ teaspoon sugar
1 tablespoon minced cilantro or parsley
2 ears corn, quartered
1 large red bell pepper, seeded and cut into 8 (1-inch) squares

1. Combine margarita mix, coriander, and garlic. Pour over pork cubes and marinate 2 hours at room temperature or as long as 24 hours in the refrigerator.

2. If using bamboo skewers, soak 8 of them in water at least 30 minutes to prevent burning. In a small bowl, combine olive oil, lime juice, sugar, and cilantro until well blended. Preheat broiler.

3. Thread 3 pork cubes onto each skewer, alternating with pieces of corn and red bell pepper. Broil about 4 inches from heat, basting with olive oil mixture and turning occasionally, until nicely browned outside yet still juicy inside, about 10 to 15 minutes.

165 BLUE QUESADILLAS WITH FRESH PEAR SALSA

Prep: 15 minutes Chill: 1 hour Cook: 5 to 7 minutes
Makes: 4 (8-inch) quesadillas

These remarkable treats will be the hit of your party.

- **½ pound creamy blue cheese, such as Bavarian Blue or Cambozola**
- **8 (8-inch) flour tortillas**
- **2 tablespoons vegetable oil**
- **Fresh Pear Salsa (recipe follows)**
- **2 tablespoons honey**

1. Freeze cheese until very firm but not frozen, about 1 hour.

2. Preheat oven to 500°F. Brush one side of 4 tortillas with oil and arrange oil-side down on a baking sheet. Cut cheese into ½-inch cubes and distribute about ½ cup over each tortilla. Using a slotted spoon, spread 2 to 3 tablespoons pear salsa over cheese. Top with remaining tortillas and brush with oil. Bake until cheese is melted and tortillas are lightly browned, 5 to 7 minutes.

3. Using a large spatula, transfer quesadillas to a cutting board. Use a pizza wheel or a large sharp knife to cut into pie-shaped wedges. Drizzle with honey and serve with additional pear salsa.

166 FRESH PEAR SALSA

Prep: 15 minutes Cook: none Makes: 2½ cups

Fresh Pear Salsa is best served the same day it is made. It is marvelous with cheeses and with grilled or roasted chicken and pork.

- **2 ripe pears (about 1 pound)**
- **2 dried pear halves, finely chopped**
- **½ cup chopped red onion**
- **¼ cup chopped fresh mint or cilantro**
- **Juice and grated zest of 1 lime**
- **1 tablespoon minced fresh ginger**
- **1 large jalapeño pepper, seeded and minced**
- **¾ teaspoon salt**
- **¼ teaspoon crushed hot red pepper**

Core pears and cut into ½-inch cubes. In a medium bowl, gently toss cubed pears with chopped dried pears, red onion, mint, lime juice and zest, ginger, jalapeño pepper, salt, and hot pepper until well mixed. Cover and refrigerate until serving time.

167 CHICKEN EMPANADAS

Prep: 30 minutes Chill: 1 hour Cook: 30 minutes Makes: 36

Even Yankees love the south-of-the-border flavor in these pastry crescents. They make great passed hot hors d'oeuvres at any party.

- **2 cups flour**
- **6 ounces cream cheese, softened**
- **2 sticks (8 ounces) butter, softened**
- **⅓ cup raisins**
- **⅔ cup minced onion**
- **3 tablespoons vegetable oil**
- **1 pound finely diced raw chicken (about 2 large skinless, boneless chicken breast halves)**
- **3 tablespoons toasted pine nuts (pignoli)**
- **3 tablespoons chopped pimiento-stuffed green olives**
- **1¼ teaspoons salt**
- **¾ teaspoon ground cumin**
- **½ teaspoon crushed hot red pepper**
- **Pinch of cinnamon**
- **1 egg, beaten**

1. In a food processor, combine flour, cream cheese, and butter. Process until mixture forms a ball. Wrap in plastic and chill at least 1 hour or as long as 3 days.

2. In a small saucepan filled with boiling water, cook raisins until softened, about 5 minutes. Drain and set aside. In a large skillet, cook onion in oil over medium heat until softened but not browned, 5 to 7 minutes. Stir in chicken, pine nuts, olives, salt, cumin, hot pepper, cinnamon, and raisins. Cook, stirring often, until chicken is cooked through and no longer pink, about 5 minutes. Remove from heat and let cool.

3. Preheat oven to 350°F. Roll out dough about ⅛ inch thick. Cut into 3-inch circles. Divide filling among pastry rounds, using about 2 teaspoons each, and brush edges with water. Fold rounds in half, forming crescents, and crimp edges with a fork to seal.

4. Arrange empanadas on a greased baking sheet and brush with beaten egg. Bake until golden brown, about 30 minutes.

168 CHILE-CHEESE WON TONS

Prep: 50 minutes Chill: 1 hour Cook: 15 to 20 minutes total
Makes: about 70

Serve these unconventional appetizers by themselves or with any of the guacamole recipes featured at the beginning of this chapter.

- **¾ pound Hot Pepper Jack cheese (Monterey Jack cheese with chile peppers), cut into ½-inch cubes**
- **1 (1-pound) package won ton wrappers***
- **2 to 4 cups peanut or corn oil**

1. In a food processor, chop cheese until finely crumbled.

2. Place one won ton wrapper in palm of your hand with a corner pointing toward you. Using a chopstick or a finger dipped in water, lightly moisten edges of wrapper. Place about 1 teaspoon cheese filling in center and fold corner nearest you over filling, tucking in the point to enclose completely, rolling wrapper to within 1 inch of top corner. Just inside wrapper, on either side of filling, moisten with water and press to seal. Moisten 2 side corners with water, overlap the points slightly, and pinch them together to seal. As each won ton is completed, arrange in a single layer on a large baking sheet or platter and cover with plastic wrap. Repeat with remaining wrappers and filling. Cover and refrigerate 1 hour or as long as 2 days.

3. In a wok or large heavy saucepan, heat 2 inches of oil to 350°F on a deep-frying thermometer over medium-high heat. Cook won tons in batches without crowding, turning occasionally, until crisp and golden, about 2 minutes. Drain on paper towels as you fry the rest. (If made in advance, keep warm in a 250° oven for up to 1 hour. Fried won tons can also be wrapped and refrigerated for up to 2 days. Reheat in a 450° oven until wrappers are once again crisp and sizzling hot, about 5 minutes.) Serve warm.

* *Available in Asian markets and many supermarkets.*

Chapter 6

Starring Shrimp and Other Seafood

For luxury and lightness, there is no substitute for seafood. And when it comes to entertaining, shrimp is always a star. It suits so many different palates, it is so easy to cook, and it is such a treat, even when you stretch to the limit, as we are fond of doing for large parties. While there are some shrimp recipes in other chapters as well, this is where you'll find the big cache or everyone's favorite cocktail food. They're prepared simply in Herbed Shrimp Cocktail, Beer-Boiled Shrimp with Cilantro Cocktail Sauce, and Spicy Marinated Shrimp. They're turned into a savory spread in recipes like Potted Pecan Shrimp and Tequila Shrimp Mousse. And they're made into fabulous hot and cold hors d'oeuvres in, respectively, Joyce's Porcupine Prawns and Crab-Stuffed Shrimp.

Other mollusks and crustaceans featured in this chapter include clams, crabs, lobster, scallops, and oysters. There are a sampling of fish dishes as well, including Samurai Swordfish Kebabs with Sesame Soy Dipping Sauce, Tuna and Caper Pâté, and the classic Seviche.

---

169 CREAMY HOT CRAB DIP

Prep: 15 minutes Cook: 15 minutes Serves: 6 to 8

Serve this with crackers or crisp raw vegetables. A basket of Belgian endive leaves for dipping would make an appropriately elegant accompaniment.

- **1 (8-ounce) package cream cheese, softened**
- **1 tablespoon dry white wine or vermouth**
- **2 tablespoons minced onion**
- **½ teaspoon prepared white horseradish**
- **¼ teaspoon salt**
- **⅛ teaspoon pepper**
- **½ pound lump crab meat, picked over**
- **¼ cup sliced almonds**

1. Preheat oven to 375°F. In a medium bowl, combine cream cheese and wine. Blend well. Mix in onion, horseradish, salt, and pepper. Fold in crab.

2. Transfer mixture to a small shallow baking dish and sprinkle almonds over top. Bake 15 minutes, or until almonds are golden brown and mixture is hot and bubbly.

170 CLAMBAKE IN A CRUST

Prep: 10 minutes Cook: 3 hours Serves: 12 to 16

Here's a cozy way to go clamming on a cold, wintry day. Not only is the long, slow cooking a boon for the busy host or hostess; it is sure to fill the kitchen with wonderful aromas to entice guests as they walk in.

1 large (1½-pound) round or oval loaf of French or Italian bread
3 (6½-ounce) cans chopped clams, liquid reserved
1 pound cream cheese, softened
3 tablespoons dry white wine
2 scallions, chopped
1 teaspoon fresh lemon juice
½ teaspoon salt
½ teaspoon hot pepper sauce
Raw vegetables, for dipping

1. Preheat oven to 250°F. Using a long serrated knife, slice bread in two horizontally to remove upper third. Set top aside. Using a small serrated knife or your hands, remove and reserve center from loaf to form a hollow shell about ½ inch thick. Cut center of bread into bite-size cubes and reserve until serving time.

2. Measure out ¼ cup reserved clam liquid; discard remainder or save for another use. In a medium bowl, combine clam liquid with cream cheese, wine, scallions, lemon juice, salt, and hot sauce. Beat until well blended.

3. Fold clams into cream cheese blend. Pack mixture into bread shell and cover with reserved bread lid. Wrap loaf tightly in aluminum foil.

4. Bake clam-stuffed loaf for 3 hours. Serve hot with reserved bread cubes and assorted raw vegetables for dipping.

171 ENGLISH POTTED KIPPERS

Prep: 10 minutes Cook: none Chill: 1 hour Serves: 6 to 8

Kippered herring, which is a kind of smoked herring, is available in the seafood section of better supermarkets. This spread is a favorite in England. The food processor makes it a snap to prepare. Serve with crackers or pumpernickel bread.

1 pound kippered herring
1 stick (4 ounces) butter, softened
2 tablespoons fresh lemon juice
Dash of hot pepper sauce
Freshly ground black pepper

1. In a medium heatproof bowl, pour boiling water over kippered herring to cover; let stand until just softened, about 5 minutes. Drain kippers and pat dry. Remove skin and bones.

2. In a food processor, combine herring, butter, lemon juice, hot sauce, and pepper. Puree until smooth. Transfer to a crock or bowl. Cover tightly and refrigerate 1 hour or as long as 4 days.

172 EVERYBODY'S FAVORITE CRAB SPREAD

Prep: 15 minutes Cook: none Serves: 8

This yummy concoction has seen its way to a lot of holiday parties! Make sure you invite it to yours.

12 ounces cream cheese, softened
½ cup mayonnaise
2 scallions, chopped
1½ teaspoons Dijon mustard
¾ teaspoon seasoned salt
½ teaspoon prepared white horseradish
¼ teaspoon lemon juice
⅛ teaspoon hot pepper sauce
1 (2-ounce) jar diced pimiento, drained
2 tablespoons chopped parsley
¾ pound lump crab meat, picked over
Crackers or crisp raw vegetables

1. In a medium bowl, combine cream cheese and mayonnaise. Mix until well blended. Stir in scallions, mustard, seasoned salt, horseradish, lemon juice, and hot sauce. Mix until well blended.

2. Fold in pimiento, parsley, and crab. Cover and refrigerate for 2 hours or as long as 2 days. Serve with crackers or crisp raw vegetables.

173 SCALLOP AND SOLE TERRINE

Prep: 15 minutes Cook: 30 minutes Serves: 8

This is a classic French dish made easy with the food processor. We like to serve it with the Watercress Mayonnaise Sauce on page 79.

1 pound scallops
½ pound sole or other white fish
¾ cup heavy cream
½ teaspoon salt
¼ teaspoon freshly ground white pepper
¼ teaspoon paprika
1 egg white

1. Preheat oven to 400°F. In a food processor, puree half of scallops with sole, cream, salt, white pepper, paprika, and egg white. Butter a 9x5x3-inch loaf pan and line bottom with parchment or wax paper.

2. Spread half of fish paste on bottom of pan. Layer with remaining half of scallops. Top with remaining fish paste. Place in a larger pan of hot water that reaches halfway up sides of terrine.

3. Bake 30 minutes, or until firm to the touch. Let stand for about 10 minutes before slicing. Serve warm or chilled.

174 DEVILED CRAB

Prep: 15 minutes Cook: 15 minutes Serves: 8 to 12

This is devilishly good. Serve with your favorite crackers for a bite of heaven.

- **6 tablespoons butter**
- **½ cup chopped green bell pepper**
- **½ cup chopped onion**
- **¼ cup chopped celery**
- **1 tablespoon chopped fresh tarragon or 1 teaspoon dried**
- **1 tablespoon Worcestershire sauce**
- **Dash of hot pepper sauce**
- **1 teaspoon dry mustard**
- **1 teaspoon salt**
- **1 teaspoon freshly ground pepper**
- **6 tablespoons flour**
- **2 cups milk**
- **2 pounds lump crab meat, picked over**
- **1 (2-ounce) jar minced pimiento, drained**
- **½ cup fine dry bread crumbs**

1. In a large skillet, melt 4 tablespoons of butter over medium heat. Add green pepper, onion, celery, tarragon, Worcestershire, hot sauce, mustard, salt, and pepper. Cook, stirring occasionally, until vegetables are softened but not browned, about 5 minutes. Mix in flour and cook, stirring, until light golden, about 2 minutes. Gradually stir in milk. Bring to a boil, stirring often, until mixture thickens, about 5 minutes. Stir crab and pimiento into thickened sauce.

2. Preheat your broiler. Transfer crab mixture to an ovenproof serving dish, sprinkle bread crumbs on top, and dot with remaining 2 tablespoons butter. Broil about 6 inches from heat until crumbs are lightly browned, 3 to 5 minutes.

175 LOBSTER MOUSSE

Prep: 20 minutes Refrigerate: 4 hours Serves: 10 to 12

- **2 envelopes (¼ ounce each) unflavored gelatin**
- **1½ cups mayonnaise**
- **⅓ cup fresh lemon juice**
- **2½ to 3 cups cooked lobster (fresh, frozen, or canned)**
- **1½ cups minced celery**
- **½ cup minced onion**
- **1 teaspoon salt**
- **½ teaspoon white pepper**
- **⅔ cup heavy cream**

1. In a small saucepan, soak gelatin in ½ cup cold water to soften, then cook over low heat, stirring, until dissolved, 1 to 2 minutes. Immediately remove from heat and pour into a medium bowl; let cool slightly. Add mayonnaise to gelatin and blend well. Stir in lemon juice and set aside.

2. In a food processor, combine lobster, celery, onion, salt, and pepper. Puree until smooth. Add to mayonnaise mixture and mix until blended.

3. In a medium bowl, beat cream until stiff. Fold whipped cream into lobster mixture. Pour mousse into an oiled 6-cup mold and refrigerate until well chilled and set, at least 4 hours.

176 SAMURAI SWORDFISH KEBABS

Prep: 10 minutes Marinate: 30 minutes Cook: 5 to 7 minutes
Makes: 32 to 36

For this dish, you'll need about 3 dozen bamboo skewers about 6 inches long. Be sure to soak the skewers in a bowl of water for at least half an hour before using to prevent burning.

2 pounds swordfish, cut ¾ to 1 inch thick
1 tablespoon fresh lemon juice
½ teaspoon salt
½ cup olive oil
1 teaspoon Asian sesame oil*
3 drops Asian hot chili oil*
Sesame Soy Dipping Sauce (recipe follows)
Sprigs of fresh cilantro or parsley, for garnish

1. Cut fish into ¾-inch cubes and arrange in a shallow nonreactive pan. In a small bowl, mix lemon juice with salt. Whisk in olive oil, sesame oil, and chili oil until well blended. Pour marinade over fish, toss to coat, cover with plastic wrap, and marinate at room temperature 30 minutes. Meanwhile, soak skewers in water.

2. Preheat oven to 500°F. Thread one piece of fish onto each skewer about 1 inch from the end and arrange in a single layer on a baking sheet. Bake until fish is lightly browned outside but still juicy inside, 5 to 7 minutes. Arrange warm skewers around a bowl of sesame soy dipping sauce. Garnish with sprigs of fresh cilantro.

* *Available in Asian markets or in the Asian food section of many supermarkets.*

177 SESAME SOY DIPPING SAUCE

Prep: 5 minutes Cook: none Makes: about ⅔ cup

This is a great all-purpose dipping sauce for any Asian-flavored grilled fish, chicken, or meat. It's also good with spring rolls and Chinese dumplings.

½ cup soy sauce
1 tablespoon rice wine vinegar,* preferably red
1½ teaspoons fresh lemon juice
1 teaspoon Asian sesame oil*
2 drops of Asian hot chili oil*
1 scallion, thinly sliced
½ teaspoon grated fresh ginger
Dash of sugar

In a small bowl, combine all ingredients. Stir to blend well.

* *Available in Asian markets or in the Asian food section of many supermarkets.*

178 QUICK CRAB MOUSSE

Prep: 15 minutes Cook: 6 to 8 minutes Chill: 4 hours
Serves: 12 to 16

This is a delicious way to make half a pound of crab feed a crowd. Don't let the long list of ingredients intimidate you; they go together very easily.

1 (¼-ounce) envelope unflavored gelatin
2 (10½-ounce) cans condensed cream of mushroom soup
1 (8-ounce) package cream cheese, softened
½ cup mayonnaise
½ cup sour cream
1 cup chopped celery
½ cup chopped scallions
1 (2-ounce) jar diced pimiento, drained
⅛ teaspoon salt
1 teaspoon lemon juice
⅛ teaspoon hot pepper sauce
½ pound lump crab meat, picked over
¼ cup chopped parsley
Crackers or bread rounds

1. In a small bowl, soften gelatin in 3 tablespoons of cold water.

2. In a medium saucepan over medium-low heat, cook undiluted soup, stirring occasionally, until heated through, 3 to 5 minutes. Stir in cream cheese, a few tablespoons at a time, whisking until well blended, and cook about 3 minutes. Stir in gelatin mixture and remove from heat.

3. Whisk in mayonnaise and sour cream. Stir in celery, scallions, pimiento, salt, lemon juice, and hot sauce. Fold in crab and parsley. Pour mixture into an oiled 6- or 7-cup mold, cover with plastic wrap, and refrigerate until set, about 4 hours or as long as 2 days. Unmold and serve with crackers or bread rounds.

179 LOBSTER PUFFS

Prep: 10 minutes Cook: 10 minutes Makes: 24

Egg whites rather than whole eggs and nonfat dry milk make these luxurious puffs as light as they are delicious.

2 egg whites
¼ cup instant nonfat dry milk
1 cup finely chopped cooked lobster
1 scallion, minced
2 teaspoons chopped parsley
½ teaspoon salt
1 teaspoon grated Parmesan cheese (optional)
⅛ teaspoon cayenne

1. Preheat oven to 375°F. In a medium bowl, beat egg whites until frothy. Gradually add dry milk and beat until stiff but not dry.

2. Fold in lobster, scallion, parsley, salt, Parmesan cheese, and cayenne. Drop tablespoons of mixture onto a greased baking sheet.

3. Bake 10 minutes, or until puffed and lightly browned.

180 POTTED PECAN SHRIMP

Prep: 5 minutes Cook: none Chill: 1 hour Serves: 6 to 8

1 (8-ounce) package cream cheese, softened
2 tablespoons minced celery
2 tablespoons beer
2 teaspoons grated onion
¼ teaspoon Worcestershire sauce
⅛ teaspoon dry mustard
½ cup chopped cooked shelled shrimp (about ¼ pound)
½ cup chopped toasted pecans

1. In a medium bowl, combine cream cheese, celery, beer, onion, Worcestershire, and mustard. Blend well.

2. Stir in shrimp and toasted pecans. Pack into a crock or other serving container, cover, and refrigerate 1 hour or as long as 2 days.

181 SEAFOOD LEEK PÂTÉ

Prep: 15 minutes Cook: none Chill: 3 hours Serves: 12

Leeks are an aromatic member of the onion family, and their subtle flavor enhances seafood. Serve this pâté on small plates with forks or with firm crackers.

6 medium leeks (about 2 pounds)
1¼ pounds cooked shrimp or crab meat
3 hard-boiled eggs
2 tablespoons prepared white horseradish
2 tablespoons Dijon mustard
3 tablespoons fresh lemon juice
1 tablespoon dried dill
1½ teaspoons freshly ground white pepper
1 teaspoon paprika
2 sticks (8 ounces) butter, softened
1 (8-ounce) package cream cheese, softened
½ teaspoon salt
1 tablespoon capers, drained and chopped

1. Trim all but 1 inch of the green ends from leeks. Trim root ends and remove any coarse outer leaves. Place leeks on a cutting board. Using a sharp knife, cut in half lengthwise, leaving attached at root. Wash leeks twice in cold water, or until all sand and grit is removed. In a large pot of boiling water, cook leeks until tender, about 4 minutes. Drain well. Chop 6 leek halves and reserve remaining 6 for later.

2. In a food processor, combine chopped leeks, shrimp, eggs, horseradish, mustard, lemon juice, dill, white pepper, paprika, butter, cream cheese, and salt. Puree until smooth. Mix in capers.

3. Line inside of an 8x4-inch loaf pan with plastic wrap. Separate reserved leek halves into individual leaves and lay over plastic wrap to line loaf pan. Fill with seafood mixture and cover with plastic wrap. Chill until firm, about 3 hours or as long as 2 days. To serve, unmold, remove plastic, and cut into slices about ¾ inch thick.

182 SPICY MARINATED SHRIMP

Prep: 10 minutes Cook: 12 to 18 minutes Marinate: 8 hours Serves: 6 to 8

Cooking shrimp in their shells gives a more intense flavor, and cooking them in beer makes them perfectly delicious. Serve on lettuce leaves as a first course or with toothpicks as an hors d'oeuvre.

- **1 quart flat beer**
- **1½ pounds large shrimp (16 to 20 pieces per pound) in the shell**
- **½ cup sherry vinegar or white wine vinegar**
- **¼ cup Dijon mustard**
- **¼ cup chopped parsley**
- **3 large shallots, chopped**
- **1 garlic clove, minced**
- **2 teaspoons crushed hot red pepper**
- **2 teaspoons salt**
- **¼ teaspoon freshly ground pepper**
- **½ cup extra-virgin olive oil**

1. In a medium nonreactive saucepan, bring beer to a simmer over medium heat.

2. Rinse shrimp under cold running water. Using a slotted spoon, lower about one-sixth of shrimp (¼ pound) into simmering beer. Cook until just pink, loosely curled, and opaque throughout, 2 to 3 minutes. Remove with a slotted spoon and repeat in batches until all shrimp are cooked. When shrimp are cool enough to handle, shell and devein.

3. In a medium bowl, combine vinegar, mustard, parsley, shallots, garlic, hot pepper, salt, and pepper. Whisk until well blended. Whisk in olive oil. Add shrimp and toss to coat well. Cover and refrigerate 8 hours or as long as 24. Drain and serve chilled.

183 HERBED SHRIMP COCKTAIL

Prep: 10 minutes Cook: none Chill: 2 hours Serves: 6 to 8

Fresh herbs add a unique flavor to this shrimp cocktail. This is wonderful spooned into leaves of Belgian endive for a light appetizer.

- **8 ounces tiny shelled cooked shrimp (about 1⅔ cups)**
- **¼ cup olive oil**
- **¼ cup fresh lemon juice**
- **¼ cup thinly sliced scallions**
- **1½ teaspoons chopped fresh oregano or ½ teaspoon dried**
- **1½ teaspoons chopped fresh basil or ½ teaspoon dried**
- **½ cup chopped celery**
- **1 cup shredded lettuce**

1. In a medium bowl, combine shrimp, oil, lemon juice, scallions, oregano, and basil. Cover and refrigerate at least 2 hours or overnight.

2. Drain, reserving marinade. Combine celery with shrimp until well mixed and serve on a bed of shredded lettuce. Drizzle reserved marinade over shrimp.

184 BEER-BOILED SHRIMP WITH CILANTRO COCKTAIL SAUCE

Prep: 2 minutes Cook: 12 to 18 minutes Serves: 6 to 8

Here's a little twist on tradition. Dark beer gives a deliciously different taste to this recipe.

1 quart flat beer, preferably dark
1½ pounds large shrimp (16 to 20 pieces per pound) in the shell
Fresh lemon wedges
Cilantro Cocktail Sauce (recipe follows)

1. In a medium nonreactive saucepan, bring beer to a simmer over medium heat.

2. Rinse shrimp under cold running water. Using a slotted spoon, lower about one-sixth of shrimp (¼ pound) into simmering beer. Cook until just pink, loosely curled, and opaque throughout, 2 to 3 minutes. Remove with a slotted spoon and repeat in batches until all shrimp are cooked.

3. When shrimp are cool enough to handle, shell and devein. If made in advance, cover and refrigerate up to 24 hours. Serve chilled or at room temperature with fresh lemon wedges and a bowl of cilantro cocktail sauce for dipping.

185 CILANTRO COCKTAIL SAUCE

Prep: 10 minutes Cook: none Makes: about 2 cups

1½ cups ketchup or chili sauce
⅓ cup chopped cilantro or parsley
3 scallions, chopped
1½ tablespoons fresh lemon juice
1½ tablespoons prepared white horseradish
3 drops of hot pepper sauce

In a small bowl, combine ketchup, cilantro, scallions, lemon juice, horseradish, and hot sauce. Stir until well blended. If made in advance, cover and refrigerate up to 24 hours.

186 PICKLED OYSTERS

Prep: 15 minutes Cook: 13 to 15 minutes Chill: 4 hours Serves: 8

To turn this into an easy-to-make hors d'oeuvre, ask your fishmonger to shuck the oysters for you, but be sure to tell him to reserve the liquor, the flavorful juices from inside the shells.

- **2 pints oysters, shucked, liquor reserved**
- **⅔ cup champagne vinegar or other white wine vinegar**
- **2 tablespoons whole allspice berries**
- **1 tablespoon whole cloves**
- **2 dried hot red peppers**

1. In a medium nonreactive saucepan, bring oyster liquor to a boil over medium-high heat. Skim foam from surface. Lower heat to a bare simmer and add oysters. Poach until oysters plump and edges begin to curl, 3 to 5 minutes. Remove with a slotted spoon and place in a large glass or ceramic container.

2. Strain oyster cooking juices through a sieve lined with damp cheesecloth and return to saucepan. Add vinegar, allspice, cloves, and hot peppers. Simmer 10 minutes. Let cool, then strain pickling liquid over oysters and refrigerate 4 hours or as long as 1 week.

187 JOYCE'S PORCUPINE PRAWNS

Prep: 15 minutes Cook: 2 minutes Makes: 20 to 25

Our friend Joyce Jue, an internationally recognized authority on Asian cuisines, has a special flair for appetizers. This tantalizing treatment gives shrimp a puffed and crunchy exterior, with protruding bits of noodle that resemble the spines of a porcupine.

- **1 pound large shrimp, shelled and deveined, with tails intact**
- **1 ounce Chinese rice stick noodles (also known as rice vermicelli or py mei fun)**
- **2 to 4 cups peanut or corn oil**
- **½ teaspoon salt**
- **¼ cup flour**
- **2 eggs, lightly beaten**
- **Lemon wedges**

1. Pat shrimp dry. Chop or break rice stick noodles into pieces about ¼ inch long. Fill a wok or large heavy saucepan with 2 inches of oil and heat over medium-high heat until oil reaches 375°F on a deep-frying thermometer.

2. Season shrimp with salt; then dredge lightly in flour, shaking off excess. Dip shrimp in beaten egg and then roll in broken rice stick noodles. Deep-fry in batches without crowding, turning once, until crisp and golden, about 2 minutes. Drain well on paper towels and serve immediately with lemon wedges.

188 BAKED CHINESE SHRIMP TOAST

Prep: 15 minutes Cook: 10 minutes Makes: 32

Traditionally, shrimp toast is deep-fried just before serving. We think you'll be pleased with both the flavor and the convenience of this method.

2 scallions, chopped
1 tablespoon chopped water chestnuts
1½ teaspoons chopped fresh ginger
1½ teaspoons cornstarch
1 garlic clove, crushed through a press
½ teaspoon salt
⅛ teaspoon sugar
Dash of cayenne
1 egg white
1½ teaspoons dry vermouth or sherry
½ pound medium-size raw shrimp, shelled and deveined
8 thin slices of firm-textured white bread
4 tablespoons butter, softened
2 tablespoons chopped cilantro or parsley

1. Preheat oven to 375°F. In a food processor, combine scallions, water chestnuts, ginger, cornstarch, garlic, salt, sugar, and cayenne. Pulse on and off several times until well mixed. Add egg white and vermouth and process until egg white is slightly foamy, 3 to 5 seconds. Add shrimp and pulse on and off until mixture has formed a paste yet shrimp still retain some texture.

2. Remove crusts from bread. Lightly butter both sides of each bread slice. Spread shrimp mixture over 1 side of each slice, then cut diagonally into 4 triangles. Arrange triangles shrimp-side up on a baking sheet. (If made in advance, cover and refrigerate up to 8 hours.)

3. Bake until shrimp topping has just turned pink and bread is lightly toasted, about 10 minutes. Garnish with chopped cilantro and serve at once.

189 CRAB-STUFFED SHRIMP

Prep: 10 minutes Cook: 2 to 3 minutes Makes: 24

24 large shrimp in the shell
1 cup crab meat (½ pound), picked over
⅓ cup mayonnaise
2 teaspoons minced chives
¼ teaspoon curry powder
1 teaspoon fresh lemon juice
¼ teaspoon salt
¼ teaspoon freshly ground pepper

1. In a large pot of boiling salted water, cook shrimp over medium-high heat until just pink and loosely curled, 2 to 3 minutes. Drain and let cool. Remove shells, leaving tails intact. Make a deep slit along the back of each shrimp and remove vein.

2. In a medium bowl, combine crab meat, mayonnaise, chives, curry powder, lemon juice, salt, and pepper. Stuff shrimp with crab mixture and arrange on a platter.

190 TANGY SKEWERED SHRIMP

Prep: 15 minutes Marinate: 2 hours Cook: 1 to 2 minutes
Serves: 6 to 8

Bottled salad dressing can be a boon for the busy cook. Lighten up even more by using a low-calorie brand.

1 pound medium shrimp, shelled and deveined
1½ cups French or Italian salad dressing, bottled or homemade

1. In a medium bowl, combine shrimp and salad dressing until well mixed. Cover and refrigerate, stirring occasionally, 2 hours. Meanwhile, soak 12 to 16 wooden skewers in water for at least 30 minutes to prevent burning.

2. Preheat oven to 425°F. Drain shrimp from marinade and thread 2 on each skewer. Arrange in a single layer on a baking sheet and bake in upper third of oven until shrimp are pink, loosely curled, and opaque throughout, 1 to 2 minutes.

191 TUNA AND CAPER PÂTÉ

Prep: 15 minutes Cook: none Serves: 10 to 12

1 (8-ounce) package cream cheese, softened
2 hard-boiled eggs, coarsely chopped
⅓ cup chopped parsley
2 tablespoons fresh lemon juice
2 tablespoons dry white wine or vermouth
1 teaspoon Dijon mustard
¼ teaspoon salt
¼ teaspoon freshly ground pepper
1 (12½-ounce) can tuna, drained
1 (4¼-ounce) can chopped olives
¼ cup capers, rinsed and drained
2 tablespoons chopped celery
2 tablespoons chopped onion
Cocktail rye or crackers

1. In a food processor, combine cream cheese, hard-boiled eggs, parsley, lemon juice, wine, mustard, salt, and pepper. Process until well blended.

2. Add tuna, olives, half the capers, the celery, and onion. Using an on-off motion, process until well mixed. Garnish with remaining capers and serve with cocktail rye or crackers.

192 MACKEREL PÂTÉ

Prep: 5 minutes Cook: none Serves: 6 to 8

- **1 (8-ounce) package cream cheese, softened**
- **1 (6½-ounce) can oil-packed mackerel**
- **⅓ cup chopped parsley**
- **¼ cup chopped onion**
- **3 tablespoons fresh lemon juice**
- **2 tablespoons butter, softened**
- **1 tablespoon Dijon mustard**
- **¼ teaspoon freshly ground pepper**
- **⅛ teaspoon hot pepper sauce**
- **⅛ teaspoon salt**

In a food processor, combine cream cheese, mackerel, parsley, onion, lemon juice, butter, mustard, pepper, hot sauce, and salt. Puree until smooth. If made in advance, cover and refrigerate up to 3 days.

193 BUTTERY SHRIMP PÂTÉ

Prep: 5 minutes Cook: none Serves: 6 to 8

Pack this savory mixture into a small bowl or crock and serve with your favorite crackers.

- **1 stick (4 ounces) butter, softened**
- **4 ounces cream cheese, softened**
- **1 teaspoon dried dill weed**
- **½ teaspoon dry sherry or lemon juice**
- **½ pound tiny shelled cooked shrimp**

In a medium bowl or in a food processor, combine butter, cream cheese, dill, and sherry. Blend well. Fold in shrimp. If made in advance, cover and refrigerate up to 2 days.

194 ANGELS ON HORSEBACK

Prep: 10 minutes Cook: 10 minutes Makes: 24

This is a traditional oyster appetizer that is always a hit.

- **12 bacon slices, halved crosswise**
- **1 pint small shucked oysters, drained well**
- **½ teaspoon salt**
- **⅛ teaspoon pepper**
- **⅛ teaspoon paprika**
- **2 tablespoons chopped parsley**

1. Preheat oven to 450°F. On a clean work surface, lay out bacon slices and top each with an oyster. Season oysters with salt, pepper, paprika, and parsley. Roll bacon around oysters and fasten with wooden toothpicks.

2. Arrange oysters on a rack in a shallow baking pan and cook until bacon is crisp, about 10 minutes.

195 SIMPLY SALMON MOUSSE

Prep: 15 minutes Cook: none Chill: 4 hours Serves: 12 to 16

Serve this mild mousse with dark pumpernickel bread and cucumber slices.

- **1 (¼-ounce) envelope unflavored gelatin**
- **¼ cup cold dry white wine or water**
- **½ cup boiling water**
- **¼ cup mayonnaise**
- **¼ cup sour cream**
- **1 tablespoon fresh lemon juice**
- **1 tablespoon minced onion**
- **1 teaspoon salt**
- **¼ teaspoon paprika**
- **⅛ teaspoon hot pepper sauce**
- **1 (15-ounce) can salmon, skin and bones removed, flaked**
- **1 cup heavy cream**

1. In a large heatproof bowl, soften gelatin in cold wine. Slowly stir in boiling water until gelatin dissolves. Let cool to room temperature.

2. Whisk in mayonnaise, sour cream, lemon juice, onion, salt, paprika, and hot sauce until well blended. Refrigerate until mixture begins to thicken, about 20 minutes. Mix in salmon.

3. In another large bowl, whip cream until soft peaks form. Fold whipped cream into salmon mixture, one-third at a time, until well blended. Pour mixture into an oiled 5- or 6-cup mold. Cover and refrigerate until firm, at least 4 hours or as long as 2 days. Unmold onto a serving plate and serve chilled.

196 MOLDED SHRIMP PASTEL

Prep: 15 minutes Cook: none Chill: 4 hours Serves: 10 to 12

- **1 (¼-ounce) envelope unflavored gelatin**
- **¾ cup dry white wine**
- **½ pound cooked shrimp**
- **1 tablespoon chopped onion**
- **1 teaspoon fresh lemon juice**
- **¼ teaspoon prepared white horseradish**
- **¼ teaspoon salt**
- **Dash of cayenne**
- **1 cup mayonnaise**
- **Crackers or bread rounds**

1. In a small bowl, soften gelatin in ¼ cup cold water. In a small saucepan, warm wine over low heat. Stir in gelatin mixture until dissolved, remove from heat, and let cool.

2. In a food processor or blender, combine shrimp, onion, lemon juice, horseradish, salt, and cayenne. Puree until smooth. Add mayonnaise and process until well blended.

3. Stir in gelatin mixture until well blended and pour into oiled 3-cup mold. Cover and refrigerate until firm, at least 4 hours or as long as 2 days. Unmold onto a serving plate and serve chilled with crackers or bread rounds.

197 HERRING MOUSSE

Prep: 15 minutes Cook: 3 minutes Chill: 4 hours Serves: 12 to 16

- **1 (¼-ounce) envelope unflavored gelatin**
- **¾ cup half-and-half**
- **1 (12-ounce) jar herring fillets in sour cream**
- **1 (2-ounce) jar sliced pimiento, drained**
- **2 teaspoons Dijon mustard**
- **2 teaspoons prepared white horseradish**
- **⅓ cup thinly sliced scallions**
- **¼ cup chopped pimiento-stuffed green olives**
- **1 cup sour cream**
- **½ cup mayonnaise**
- **1 tablespoon lemon juice**

1. In a small heatproof bowl, sprinkle gelatin over half-and-half and let stand 5 minutes to soften. Set over boiling water and heat until gelatin dissolves, about 3 minutes. Let cool.

2. Reserve 2 pieces of herring for garnish. In a food processor, combine remaining herring in sour cream and puree until smooth. Add gelatin mixture and process until well blended.

3. Transfer herring mixture to a large bowl and stir in pimiento, mustard, horseradish, scallions, and olives. Fold in sour cream, mayonnaise, and lemon juice. Turn into an oiled 6-cup mold and refrigerate until firm, about 4 hours or overnight. To serve, unmold and garnish with reserved herring.

198 OYSTER BEIGNETS

Prep: 15 minutes Cook: 5 to 6 minutes Makes: 48

Serve these with your favorite cocktail or tartar sauce. Jarred oysters work well in this recipe.

- **1 cup flour**
- **½ teaspoon sugar**
- **4 tablespoons butter**
- **1 cup milk**
- **4 eggs**
- **1 (8- to 10-ounce) jar oysters, drained and chopped**
- **2 to 4 cups peanut or corn oil**

1. Combine flour and sugar in a small bowl and set aside. In a small saucepan, combine butter and milk. Place over low heat until butter melts, 3 to 5 minutes. Vigorously stir in flour mixture until it forms a ball and leaves sides of the pan, about 2 minutes. Remove from heat.

2. Add eggs, one at a time, beating thoroughly after each addition. Continue beating until a stiff shiny batter is formed. Add oysters to batter and mix well.

3. In a wok or large heavy saucepan, heat oil to 350°F on a deep-frying thermometer over medium heat. Drop mixture by teaspoonfuls into hot oil, a few at a time, and fry until beignets are golden brown, 5 to 6 minutes. Drain and serve hot or warm.

199 TEQUILA SHRIMP MOUSSE

Prep: 20 minutes Cook: 13 minutes Chill: 2 hours Serves: 12

- **2 (¼-ounce) envelopes unflavored gelatin**
- **1 (14½-ounce) can chicken broth**
- **½ cup tequila**
- **1½ teaspoons chopped fresh basil or ½ teaspoon dried**
- **1½ teaspoons chopped fresh dill or ½ teaspoon dried**
- **¼ teaspoon celery seeds, crushed**
- **⅛ teaspoon hot pepper sauce**
- **¼ cup fresh lime juice**
- **1 cup sour cream**
- **½ cup mayonnaise**
- **½ pound tiny shelled cooked shrimp**
- **½ cup finely chopped celery**
- **¼ cup chopped pimiento-stuffed green olives**
- **1 tablespoon chopped parsley**

1. In a small bowl, soften gelatin in ½ cup cold water. Warm over low heat until gelatin is dissolved.

2. In a medium saucepan, combine chicken broth, tequila, basil, dill, celery seeds, and hot sauce. Bring to a simmer over medium heat. Stir in softened gelatin until well blended. Stir in lime juice and pour into a medium bowl. Refrigerate until gelatin thickens slightly, about 10 minutes.

3. In a small bowl, combine sour cream and mayonnaise. Blend well. Fold into gelatin mixture. Fold in shrimp, celery, olives, and parsley. Turn into an oiled 5-cup mold and refrigerate until firm, about 2 hours, or as long as 2 days. Unmold onto a serving plate.

200 SEVICHE

Prep: 15 minutes Cook: none Chill: 5 hours Serves: 8

Remember—the lime juice cooks the fish.

- **1½ pounds firm-textured white fish, such as halibut, rockfish, or red snapper**
- **1½ to 2 cups fresh lime juice**
- **1 cup olive oil**
- **1 cup orange juice, preferably fresh**
- **1 to 2 fresh hot red or green chiles, seeded and slivered**
- **1 small onion, thinly sliced**
- **1 garlic clove, minced**
- **Salt and freshly ground pepper**

1. Remove skin and bones from fish and cut into ½-inch cubes. Place fish in a small bowl and add enough lime juice to cover. (It is extremely important that lime juice covers all of the fish. Add more if necessary.) Cover with plastic wrap and refrigerate 3 hours.

2. In a small bowl, combine olive oil, orange juice, chiles, onion, and garlic. Add to fish and stir well to mix. Cover and refrigerate 2 more hours or as long as 2 days. Season with salt and pepper before serving.

Chapter 7

From the Cheese Board

Cheese is one of the most popular cocktail foods for several reasons: there's little or no labor involved in preparation; it is best served at room temperature; and it is easily garnished with little more than a cluster of grapes.

Fortunately for today's savvy host and hostess, noble cheeses also lend themselves to fancier presentations, making us appear as though we'd spent a full day hard at work in the kitchen. One whirlwind tour of your supermarket can provide enough accompaniments to draw raves. Try this for your next party and see what we mean:

On a large wooden board, uncoil an Armenian string cheese into its many lacy ropes. Arrange 2 or 3 other cheeses on the board as well, striving for a variety of flavors, shapes, and textures that provide visual as well as edible stimulation. Fit in small bowls of brine- or oil-cured olives—with a tiny ramekin for their pits on the side—salted almonds or walnut halves, fresh or dried fruits, and assorted breads and crackers. Tuck in sprigs of fresh herbs, or fresh grape or other nontoxic leaves from your garden. This edible still life goes together in minutes, involves absolutely no cooking, and looks spectacular.

Another option is to serve several varieties of one type of cheese, such as Cheddar from England, Ireland, Vermont, Wisconsin, and Washington, for a taste comparison. Accompany the cheese with an assortment of breads, crackers, apples, pears, and grapes.

When you want to provide your own personal touch to cheeses, first look through this chapter. A wheel of creamy Brie always looks lavish, but wait until your guests taste Brie Stuffed with Pesto! Your reputation as a gourmet cook will be set for life. Smartly flavored cheeses are easily turned into interesting and attractive spreads, mousses, and savory "cakes."

As cheeses tend to be quite filling, we prefer not to serve them prior to dinner; save them to steal center stage at your cocktail buffet.

201 PESTO TORTA

Prep: 20 minutes Cook: none Chill: 1 hour Serves: 8 to 10

This stunning appetizer with its green stripes of pesto is always a favorite with our guests. Serve with a small knife for spreading on crostini, baguette slices, or crackers.

2 tablespoons pine nuts (pignoli)
1 (8-ounce) package cream cheese, softened
2 sticks (8 ounces) unsalted butter, softened
1 cup pesto, purchased or homemade (page 159)
Sprig of fresh basil or parsley

1. Preheat oven to 325°F. Place pine nuts in a small ovenproof pan and bake, shaking once or twice, until just golden, 7 to 10 minutes. Let cool.

2. Cut a double thickness of cheesecloth 12 inches square; moisten with water and wring dry. Smoothly line the inside of a 3-cup bowl or terrine with the cheesecloth, letting excess drape over edges.

3. In a food processor, combine cream cheese and butter. Process until well blended. Use a rubber spatula to pack enough of mixture into prepared mold to make a layer ¾ to 1 inch thick. Top with 2 to 3 tablespoons pesto, extending it evenly to sides of mold. Repeat layers, ending with cheese, until mold is filled.

4. Fold ends of cheesecloth over torta, pressing down gently. Refrigerate until firm, about 1 hour. Invert onto a serving plate and discard cheesecloth. Serve immediately or cover with plastic wrap and refrigerate up to 3 days. Sprinkle pine nuts over top and garnish with sprigs of basil.

202 CRUSTY CAMEMBERT WITH CRANBERRY SALSA

Prep: 5 minutes Cook: 5 minutes Serves: 6 to 8

1 (8-ounce) wheel of Camembert or Brie, well chilled
2 tablespoons flour
1 egg, beaten
1 cup fresh bread crumbs
2 tablespoons butter
Cranberry Salsa (recipe follows)

1. Dredge whole cheese in flour and then in egg until all sides are well coated. Cover completely with bread crumbs.

2. In a small skillet, melt butter over medium heat. Add cheese and cook, carefully turning once, until crust is golden brown and crusty on both sides, about 5 minutes total. Transfer to a serving plate and surround cheese with Cranberry Salsa. Serve with a small knife for spreading a bit of cheese and salsa on unsalted crackers or baguette slices.

CRANBERRY SALSA

Makes: 1¾ cups

- **1½ cups fresh or frozen cranberries**
- **⅓ cup sugar**
- **2 scallions, chopped**
- **¼ cup chopped fresh mint or cilantro**
- **Juice and grated zest of 1 lime**
- **1 jalapeño pepper, seeded and minced**
- **2 teaspoons chopped fresh ginger**
- **⅛ teaspoon salt**

In a food processor, combine cranberries, sugar, scallions, mint, lime juice and zest, jalapeño pepper, ginger, and salt. Pulse on and off until mixture is uniformly chopped yet still maintains some texture. Cover and refrigerate 2 hours, or as long as 8 hours, to let flavors blend.

---

203 BOURBON BLUE CHEESE SPREAD

Prep: 10 minutes Cook: none Chill: 24 hours Serves: 8 to 12

- **1 (8-ounce) package cream cheese, softened**
- **4 ounces blue cheese, softened**
- **5 tablespoons butter, softened**
- **1 garlic clove, crushed**
- **Dash of hot pepper sauce**
- **Dash of Worcestershire sauce**
- **¼ teaspoon salt**
- **¼ teaspoon pepper**
- **3 tablespoons Kentucky bourbon**

In a medium bowl or food processor, combine cream cheese, blue cheese, and butter. Blend well. Add garlic, hot sauce, Worcestershire, salt, pepper, and bourbon. Mix well. Cover and refrigerate at least 24 hours or as long as 1 week.

---

204 BRIE MELT

Prep: 3 minutes Cook: 3 to 5 minutes Serves: 6

It doesn't get any easier than this. Keep a wheel or two of Brie in your freezer, so you'll always be prepared to make this lovely appetizer.

- **1 tablespoon butter, softened**
- **1 (8-ounce) wheel of Brie cheese**
- **¼ cup slivered almonds**
- **Crackers or baguette slices**

1. Preheat broiler. Spread butter on top of cheese right over white rind. Place in a flameproof serving dish. Broil 4 to 6 inches from heat until bubbly, 3 to 5 minutes.

2. Top with nuts and broil until nuts are barely golden, about 2 minutes longer. Serve at once, with crackers and baguette slices.

205 SOUTHERN BLUE CHEESE BALL WITH CHOPPED PECANS

Prep: 10 minutes Cook: none Chill: overnight Serves: 8 to 12

Another wonderful way to show off one of the South's favorite nuts. Serve with crackers or celery sticks.

12 ounces cream cheese, softened
6 ounces blue cheese, softened
2 tablespoons grated onion
1 teaspoon Worcestershire sauce
½ cup minced parsley
½ cup finely chopped pecans

1. In a medium bowl, or a food processor, combine cream cheese, blue cheese, onion, and Worcestershire sauce. Mix until well blended.

2. Stir in parsley and ¼ cup of pecans. Shape into a ball, wrap in plastic wrap, and refrigerate overnight.

3. About 1 hour before serving, roll ball in remaining ¼ cup pecans. Serve at room temperature.

206 GINGERED ALMOND CHEESE BALL

Prep: 10 minutes Cook: none Chill: 24 hours Serves: 16 to 18

Prepare this cheese ball at least one day ahead so the flavors will have time to mellow and blend.

3 (8-ounce) packages cream cheese, softened
1 cup stem ginger in syrup,* drained and coarsely chopped
1 (6-ounce) can salted roasted almonds, chopped
Unsalted crackers or celery sticks

1. In a medium bowl or in a food processor, combine cream cheese and ginger. Mix until well blended. Shape into a 4½-inch ball or 2 smaller balls and wrap tightly in plastic wrap. Refrigerate 24 hours or as long as 3 days.

2. Remove plastic wrap and roll cheese ball(s) in chopped almonds until well coated. Serve with unsalted crackers or celery sticks.

* *Available in Asian markets and many gourmet food departments.*

207 HERBED MOZZARELLA APPETIZER

Prep: 10 minutes Cook: none Marinate: 12 hours Serves: 6 to 8

If your local delicatessen or cheese shop sells fresh whole-milk mozzarella, by all means use it in this recipe. The difference in flavor and texture is worth the price.

- **¾ pound mozzarella cheese, preferably fresh**
- **½ cup extra-virgin olive oil**
- **2 tablespoons chopped mixed fresh herbs, such as basil and parsley, or 2 teaspoons dried**
- **1 small garlic clove, minced**
- **¼ to ½ teaspoon crushed hot red pepper**
- **¼ teaspoon salt**
- **¼ teaspoon freshly ground black pepper**
- **Oil-cured olives, sun-dried tomato halves or roasted red pepper strips, and Crostini (page 151)**

1. Drain cheese, if necessary, and cut into ½-inch cubes. In a medium bowl, combine cheese, olive oil, herbs, garlic, hot pepper, salt, and black pepper. Toss gently to coat. Cover and refrigerate, stirring occasionally, at least 12 hours or as long as 3 days.

2. To serve, let cheese return to room temperature. Using a slotted spoon, mound cheese in center of a serving platter and surround with olives, tomatoes or peppers, and crostini. Serve with cocktail forks or toothpicks.

208 FRUITED CHEESE BALL

Prep: 15 minutes Cook: none Serves: 12

This is a perfect make-ahead appetizer for fall get-togethers. It is hearty enough for a tailgate picnic, elegant enough for your best party. Serve with water crackers, wheat crackers, or wheatmeal biscuits.

- **1 (8-ounce) package cream cheese, softened**
- **½ pound Cheddar cheese, shredded (about 2 cups)**
- **2 tablespoons honey**
- **2 tablespoons medium-dry sherry**
- **1 teaspoon curry powder**
- **2 scallions, chopped**
- **¼ cup chopped dried apricots (about 2 ounces)**
- **¼ cup chopped dried apples (about 2 ounces)**
- **2 tablespoons currants or coarsely chopped raisins**
- **2 tablespoons chopped dates**
- **½ cup chopped nuts, such as pistachios**

1. In a medium bowl or in a food processor, combine cream cheese, Cheddar cheese, honey, sherry, and curry. Blend until well mixed. Mix in scallions, apricots, apples, currants, and dates.

2. Form into 1 or 2 balls or logs and roll in chopped nuts. Wrap tightly in plastic wrap and refrigerate at least 2 hours, or as long as 4 days before serving.

209 BLUE CHEESE BALLS
Prep: 20 minutes Cook: none Makes: 48

Here thin pretzel sticks are used as edible toothpicks. Of course, you can use the wooden kind if you prefer.

8 ounces blue cheese
1 (8-ounce) package cream cheese, softened
1 tablespoon brandy
Dash of cayenne
¼ cup chopped parsley
48 thin pretzel sticks

1. In a medium bowl, combine blue cheese, cream cheese, brandy, and cayenne. Blend until well mixed.

2. Use 2 teaspoons of cheese mixture to form balls about ¾ inch in diameter. Refrigerate, well covered, for 2 hours or as long as 3 days.

3. To serve, roll blue cheese balls in chopped parsley and spear with a pretzel.

210 CALIFORNIA CHEESE LACE
Prep: 5 minutes Cook: 5 to 7 minutes Cool: 2 minutes Makes: 80

This ultimate cheese wafer is nothing but cheese itself. Allow plenty of these per person, as they are as easy to munch as potato chips.

Vegetable cooking spray
8 ounces Monterey Jack cheese, cut into ½-inch squares ¼ inch thick

1. Preheat oven to 350°F. Spray one or more baking sheets with vegetable cooking spray. Arrange squares of cheese on baking sheet, allowing a 2-inch border around edges of pan as well as between each square.

2. Bake until cheese is melted and bubbly, 5 to 7 minutes. Let cool on baking sheet until just set, about 2 minutes, then use a wire spatula to remove them to a wire rack to cool and harden. Serve at room temperature.

211 SWISS SIMPLICITY
Prep: 5 minutes Cook: none Makes: 2 cups

½ pound Swiss cheese, shredded (about 2 cups)
½ cup mayonnaise
½ teaspoon Dijon mustard
1 tablespoon chopped parsley
Crackers or cocktail rye bread

1. In a medium bowl, blend Swiss cheese, mayonnaise, and mustard until well blended. Pack into a crock or serving bowl, cover, and refrigerate at least 2 hours or as long as 3 days.

2. To serve, let return to room temperature and top with parsley. Serve with crackers or cocktail rye bread.

212 BRIE STUFFED WITH PESTO

Prep: 10 minutes Chill: 30 minutes to 1 hour
Cook: 8 to 10 minutes Serves: 24 to 30

It is easier to slice through a wheel of ripe cheese when it is well chilled.

- **1 (8½-inch) wheel of Brie cheese (about 2 pounds)**
- **½ cup pesto, purchased or homemade (page 159)**
- **2 tablespoons pine nuts (pignoli)**
- **Crackers or baguette slices**
- **Fresh basil sprigs**

1. Freeze Brie until just firm but not frozen, about 1 hour. Preheat oven to 325°F. With a long sharp knife, split Brie horizontally in half. Spread pesto in an even layer over cut side of bottom half to about ¼ inch from edge. Set top of Brie in place and press gently to sandwich layers.

2. Spread pine nuts in a shallow pan and bake, shaking pan once or twice, until lightly browned, 7 to 10 minutes. Sprinkle toasted pine nuts over top of Brie, pressing them in gently. Serve at room temperature with crackers or baguette slices. Garnish with fresh basil.

213 SPICED BRIE TART

Prep: 10 minutes Cook: 45 minutes Serves: 12

This rich and glorious tart should be cut into very thin slices.

- **1 unbaked (8-inch) tart or pie shell**
- **½ pound Brie cheese**
- **2 tablespoons light cream or milk**
- **2 eggs, beaten**
- **1½ teaspoons sugar**
- **1 teaspoon ground ginger**
- **Dash of grated nutmeg**

1. Preheat oven to 425°F. Prick pastry with a fork, then press a sheet of foil directly onto pie shell. Bake for 6 minutes, remove foil, and bake until just golden, about 4 minutes longer. Remove pastry shell from oven. Reduce oven temperature to 375°.

2. In a medium saucepan, melt Brie with cream over low heat until smooth, about 5 minutes. Remove from heat and let cool briefly.

3. Add eggs, sugar, ginger, and nutmeg to cheese mixture and stir until well blended. Pour mixture into pastry shell and bake until lightly browned and puffy, about 30 minutes. Serve warm or at room temperature.

214 SALSA AND GOAT CHEESE BOMBE

Prep: 20 minutes Cook: 6 to 10 minutes Chill: 4 hours Serves: 12

Vegetable cooking spray
2 (¼-ounce) envelopes unflavored gelatin
¼ cup plain or spicy tomato juice
1 (16-ounce) jar salsa
¼ cup chopped cilantro or parsley
¼ cup heavy cream or milk
1 (8-ounce) package cream cheese, softened
4 ounces soft, mild goat cheese
Fresh cilantro sprigs
Corn-flavored or other crackers

1. Coat inside of a 4-cup glass or plastic mold with vegetable cooking spray and place in freezer. In a small heatproof bowl, soften 1 envelope gelatin in tomato juice. Place bowl over simmering water until gelatin dissolves, 3 to 5 minutes. Let cool 5 minutes.

2. In a medium bowl, combine salsa and chopped cilantro. Stir in gelatin mixture until well blended. Pour into prepared mold and refrigerate until set, about 2 hours.

3. In a small heatproof bowl, soften remaining gelatin in cream. Place bowl over simmering water until gelatin dissolves, 3 to 5 minutes. In a medium bowl, combine cream cheese and goat cheese. Blend until well mixed. Stir in gelatin mixture until well blended.

4. Carefully pack cheese mixture over jelled salsa, cover, and refrigerate until set, at least 4 hours or as long as 2 days. Unmold onto a serving plate and garnish with cilantro sprigs. Serve with crackers.

215 BEER CHEESE

Prep: 10 minutes Cook: none Chill: 4 hours Serves: 12 to 16

The better the beer, the better the cheese. Serve with crackers or cocktail rye rounds.

4 cups shredded sharp Cheddar cheese (about 1 pound)
4 cups shredded Monterey Jack cheese (about 1 pound)
3 garlic cloves, crushed through a press
3 tablespoons chili sauce
1 teaspoon salt
1 teaspoon dry mustard
Dash of hot pepper sauce
1 cup beer

1. In a food processor, combine Cheddar, Monterey Jack, garlic, chili sauce, salt, mustard, and hot sauce.

2. With machine on, slowly add beer and process until mixture is smooth. Transfer to a crock or bowl, cover, and refrigerate at least 4 hours to let flavors mellow.

A DIFFERENT KIND OF CAKE

Dessert lovers have long enjoyed creamy sweetened cheesecakes. Savory cheesecakes are made according to many of the same principles and draw just as many raves as their sweeter cousins. Savory cheesecakes are also a fine way to combine the flavors of your favorite cheeses into one show-stopping cocktail treat for a crowd.

Serve on a lettuce-lined pedestal plate, or place directly on a large wooden cutting board, surrounded by dried fruits such as peaches and apricots, a scattering of toasted walnut or pecan halves, slices of fresh apple or pear, and clusters of fresh watercress. Accompany with a basket of crackers or baguette slices for spreading. Savory cheesecakes are quite rich, so cut into thin wedges to be eaten with a fork, or serve with a small knife for spreading.

---

216 GOAT CHEESE CAKE

Prep: 15 minutes Cook: 1½ hours
Serves: 12 to 16

Serve this savory cheesecake with water wafers or any other cracker of your choice. The irresistible tang of the goat cheese will make this a party favorite with your guests.

- **2 tablespoons butter, softened**
- **¼ cup fine fresh bread crumbs**
- **4 medium leeks**
- **½ pound pancetta or bacon, finely chopped**
- **¼ cup olive oil**
- **1 pound 6 ounces soft white goat cheese, such as Montrachet**
- **4 large eggs**
- **½ cup crème fraîche or sour cream**
- **½ teaspoon salt**
- **¼ teaspoon pepper**

1. Preheat oven to 325°F. Wrap outside of an 8-inch springform pan tightly in aluminium foil. Grease inside with softened butter and coat with bread crumbs.

2. Trim all but 1 inch of green ends from leeks. Trim root ends and remove any coarse outer leaves. Place leeks on a cutting board and cut in half lengthwise. Wash cut leeks twice in cold water, or until all sand and grit are removed. Drain and pat dry. Cut leeks crosswise into ½-inch pieces.

3. In a large frying pan, cook pancetta in olive oil over medium heat until lightly golden, 2 to 3 minutes. Add leeks and cook until softened and slightly translucent, 2 to 3 minutes longer. Remove from heat.

4. In a large bowl, combine goat cheese, eggs, and crème fraîche. Blend well. Stir in pancetta, leeks, salt, and pepper. Pour mixture into prepared pan and set in a larger pan filled with enough hot water to reach halfway up sides of springform. Bake 1½ hours, or until center is firm. Let cool completely. If made in advance, refrigerate, well covered, up to 2 days. Unmold and serve at room temperature.

217 FOUR-CHEESE CAKE

Prep: 10 minutes Cook: none Chill: 4 hours Serves: 12 to 16

Molding this delicious spread in a quiche pan gives it a decorative fluted edge. Tip: To prevent apple slices from darkening, dip them in lemon juice.

- **3 (8-ounce) packages cream cheese, softened**
- **2 tablespoons sour cream**
- **8 ounces chopped pecans (about 2 cups)**
- **4 ounces Valembert or Camembert cheese**
- **4 ounces Gruyère or Swiss cheese, finely shredded**
- **4 ounces blue cheese**
- **½ cup chopped parsley**
- **Red and green apple slices**

1. Line inside of a 9½-inch quiche pan with a sheet of aluminum foil, pressing in against fluted edges. In a small bowl, combine 1 package of cream cheese with sour cream and blend well. Spread over bottom of quiche pan. Top with chopped pecans.

2. In a medium bowl or in a food processor, combine Valembert, Gruyère, blue cheese, and remaining 2 packages cream cheese. Beat or process until well blended. Carefully spread over pecans.

3. Cover with plastic wrap and refrigerate at least 4 hours or as long as 3 days. Remove plastic wrap and invert cake onto a serving plate. Peel off foil and top with chopped parsley. Arrange apple slices around cheesecake.

218 BLUE CHEESE CAKE

Prep: 20 minutes Cook: 2 hours 50 minutes Chill: 2 hours Serves: 12 to 16

- **1 tablespoon butter, softened**
- **⅓ cup fine fresh bread crumbs**
- **¼ cup grated Parmesan cheese**
- **3½ (8-ounce) packages cream cheese, softened**
- **4 eggs**
- **⅓ cup heavy cream**
- **½ pound bacon, chopped**
- **1 medium onion, minced**
- **½ pound blue cheese, crumbled (about 2 cups)**
- **¼ teaspoon freshly ground pepper**
- **¼ teaspoon hot pepper sauce**

1. Preheat oven to 300°F. Grease an 8-inch springform pan with 1 tablespoon softened butter. Wrap outside of pan tightly in aluminum foil. In a small bowl, combine bread crumbs and Parmesan cheese; toss to mix. Coat bottom and sides of springform with Parmesan crumbs.

2. In a medium bowl, combine cream cheese, eggs, and cream. Beat until well blended.

3. In a large frying pan, cook bacon over medium heat until crisp, about 5 minutes. Remove with a slotted spoon and drain well on paper towels. Pour off all but 2 tablespoons fat from pan. Add onion to bacon fat and cook until softened but not browned, 3 to 5 minutes. Add to cream cheese mixture. Add blue cheese, bacon, pepper, and hot sauce and blend well. Turn cheese mixture into prepared springform pan and place in a larger roasting pan. Add enough hot water to roasting pan to reach halfway up sides of springform.

4. Bake 1¾ hours; do not open oven door. Turn off oven and let cheesecake remain in water in oven 1 hour longer.

5. Carefully lift springform out of water and let cool on a wire rack. Cover and refrigerate at least 2 hours or as long as 2 days. To serve, run a knife around edge of pan and remove side of springform.

219 ROQUEFORT MOUSSE

Prep: 20 minutes Cook: 5 minutes Chill: 2 hours Serves: 10 to 12

Light, yet full of flavor, this spread makes a perfect addition to a make-ahead summer buffet. Serve with thin water wafers, as a strongly flavored cracker will overwhelm the soufflé.

- **½ teaspoon unflavored gelatin**
- **3 egg yolks**
- **¾ cup plus 3 tablespoons heavy cream**
- **6 ounces Roquefort cheese**
- **¼ teaspoon Dijon mustard**
- **¼ teaspoon salt**
- **⅛ teaspoon freshly ground white pepper**
- **2 egg whites***

1. In a medium heatproof bowl, soften gelatin in 2 tablespoons cold water. Place bowl over a pan of simmering water until gelatin dissolves, about 2 minutes.

2. In a medium saucepan, beat egg yolks and 3 tablespoons cream over low heat until hot and just beginning to thicken to a creamy consistency, about 3 minutes; do not boil or egg yolks will curdle. Stir egg yolk mixture into softened gelatin. Set aside.

3. Force Roquefort through a sieve, then whisk into egg yolk mixture. Season with mustard, salt, and white pepper.

4. In a clean medium bowl, beat ¾ cup cream until soft peaks form. In another bowl, beat egg whites until stiff but not dry. Fold whipped cream into Roquefort base until well blended, then fold in beaten egg whites. Transfer to an oiled 3-cup mold and refrigerate until set, 2 hours or as long as 2 days, before unmolding.

220 CHÈVRE MOUSSE

Prep: 20 minutes Cook: 6 minutes Chill: 2 hours Serves: 12

Chèvre is French for goat cheese and English for delicious! Serve this wonderful appetizer with crackers for a buffet table or as a first course mounded onto small serving plates.

3 eggs,* separated
1 cup heavy cream
1 (11-ounce) package mild goat cheese, such as Montrachet, crumbled
1 (¼-ounce) envelope unflavored gelatin
¼ teaspoon salt
½ teaspoon freshly ground white pepper

1. In a medium nonreactive saucepan, whisk egg yolks with ¼ cup of cream until blended. Set over low heat and cook, whisking, until hot and creamy, about 3 minutes; do not boil or egg yolks will curdle. Add cheese and cook, whisking, until melted and smooth, about 1 minute.

2. In a small heatproof bowl, soften gelatin in 2 tablespoons cold water, then dissolve over a small pot of hot water. Whisk dissolved gelatin, salt, and white pepper into cheese mixture.

3. In another medium bowl beat remaining ¾ cup cream until thick. In a large bowl, beat egg whites until stiff peaks form.

4. Fold whipped cream into cheese mixture, then fold in beaten egg whites until well blended. Pour mixture into an oiled 4-cup mold and refrigerate until set, at least 2 hours or as long as 2 days.

* **CAUTION:** *Because of the possible threat of salmonella—a bacteria that causes food poisoning—from raw eggs, U.S. Government officials recommend that the very young, the elderly, pregnant women, and people with serious illnesses or weakened immune systems not eat raw or lightly cooked eggs. Keep this in mind and consume raw or lightly cooked eggs at your own risk.*

Chapter 8

Nuts, Olives, and Other Nibbles

Nutty nibbles, crunchy munchies, and, oh yes, of course, olives have their own place at any cocktail party or casual evening's entertainment—not to speak of in front of the VCR. Before a sit-down dinner, many accomplished cooks prefer to serve just a tasty tidbit to tantalize the tongue while sparing the appetite for the main event. At a large cocktail party, small bowls of interesting olives, nuts, and other snacks are the punctuation marks that any smart host or hostess sets out around the room.

In little more time than it would normally take to rip open a bag of pretzels or potato chips, you can whip up a batch of Rosemary Toasted Walnuts, Parmesan Popcorn, or Garlicky Olives with Orange and Cumin. Almost all these recipes can be prepared ahead, and many keep well in covered containers at room temperature, which makes them great gifts from the kitchen, perfect to bring to someone else's party.

221 BESS'S UNBELIEVABLE CHEESE CRISPS

Prep: 15 minutes Cook: 10 to 12 minutes Makes: 72

Bess keeps these in the freezer and reheats them in the microwave as she needs them. Be sure the cereal is fresh; otherwise, it won't provide the desired crunch.

4 cups shredded sharp Cheddar or Jalapeño Jack cheese (1 pound)
2 cups flour
2 cups fresh crisp rice cereal, such as Rice Krispies
2 teaspoons sugar
½ teaspoon salt
⅛ teaspoon cayenne
⅛ teaspoon dry mustard
2 sticks (8 ounces) butter or margarine, melted
Dash of Worcestershire sauce

1. Preheat oven to 350°F. In a large bowl, combine cheese, flour, rice cereal, sugar, salt, cayenne, mustard, melted butter, and Worcestershire. Toss until well blended. (Mixing with your hands actually works best.)

2. Form mixture into 1-inch balls and arrange about 1 inch apart on an ungreased baking sheet. Use the tines of a fork to form a criss-cross pattern while pressing balls into disks ¼ to ⅜ inch thick.

3. Bake until edges are golden brown, 10 to 12 minutes. Serve warm or at room temperature.

222 BANANA CHIPS

Prep: 5 minutes Cook: 30 minutes Makes: about 4 cups

Don't monkey around with these! Make a lot.

- **4 green-tipped bananas**
- **¼ cup flour**
- **2 cups vegetable oil**
- **Salt**

1. Peel bananas and thinly slice about ⅛ inch thick. Dredge slices in flour to coat lightly.

2. In a wok or large heavy saucepan, heat oil to 375°F on a deep-frying thermometer. Add banana slices in batches without crowding and fry 3 minutes, or until golden brown. Drain chips on paper towels and sprinkle with salt to taste.

PARMESAN POPCORN

Prep: 5 minutes Cook: 3 to 6 minutes Serves: 4 to 6

- **⅓ cup unpopped popcorn**
- **2 tablespoons butter or olive oil**
- **¼ teaspoon onion powder**
- **¼ teaspoon garlic powder**
- **2 tablespoons grated Parmesan cheese**

1. Pop the corn as package directs.

2. Meanwhile, in a small saucepan, combine butter, onion powder, and garlic powder. Place over medium heat until butter is just melted.

3. As soon as popcorn is done, transfer to a large bowl. Drizzle seasoned butter over popcorn and toss to coat evenly. Immediately sprinkle on Parmesan cheese and toss until mixed and melted.

224 PEKING PECANS

Prep: 5 minutes Cook: 8 to 10 minutes Makes: 4 cups

This has been a favorite cocktail nibble in our homes for years.

- **6 tablespoons butter**
- **1 pound pecan halves (about 4 cups)**
- **2 tablespoons soy sauce**
- **2 teaspoons salt**
- **Freshly ground pepper**

1. Preheat oven to 300°F. Put butter in a large baking pan and set in oven until melted. Add pecans and toss to coat. Bake 8 to 10 minutes, until nuts just start to brown.

2. Let cool for a minute or two, then toss with soy sauce, salt, and pepper to taste until well mixed. Serve slightly warm or at room temperature.

225 PECAN-WICHES

Prep: 15 minutes Cook: 7 to 10 minutes Makes: 24

Toasting nuts releases their natural oils to make them not only crispier but more aromatic.

48 pecan halves

2 tablespoons cream cheese, blue cheese, or Cheddar cheese spread

1. Preheat oven to 350°F. Arrange pecan halves in a single layer on a baking sheet and bake until fragrant and lightly browned, 7 to 10 minutes. Let cool completely.

2. Spread ¼ teaspoon cheese on flat side of 1 pecan half; top with another pecan to make a tiny sandwich. Refrigerate, well covered, up to 2 days if made in advance. Serve at room temperature.

226 MEXICAN PEANUTS

Prep: 10 minutes Cook: 3 minutes Makes: 2 pounds

These nuts improve with standing. Just don't try to eat the chilies; they are for flavoring only.

4 garlic cloves, minced
2 tablespoons olive oil
1 teaspoon crushed hot red pepper
½ teaspoon ground cumin
2 pounds dry-roasted peanuts
1 teaspoon coarse (kosher) salt
1 teaspoon chili powder

1. In a large frying pan, cook garlic in olive oil over moderate heat for 1 minute. Add hot pepper and cumin.

2. Mix in peanuts and cook, stirring, 2 minutes. Sprinkle with coarse salt and chili powder. Mix well and store in a covered jar or tin.

227 GINGERED PEANUTS

Prep: 2 minutes Cook: none Makes: 1½ cups

If ginger lovers are expected, you'd better double the recipe. This sweet-salty-hot flavor combination is a real winner.

1 (6½-ounce) can salted Spanish peanuts

1 (2½-ounce) jar crystallized ginger, chopped (about ½ cup)

In a small bowl, toss peanuts with crystallized ginger until well mixed. Store airtight.

228 ROSEMARY TOASTED WALNUTS

Prep: 10 minutes Cook: 15 to 20 minutes Makes: 4 cups

A little bit of fresh rosemary often goes a long way, but don't be scared off by the quantity here. This lively combination of flavors works beautifully. For variation, pecans make a delicious substitute for walnuts.

2 tablespoons unsalted butter
2 tablespoons walnut oil or olive oil
1 pound walnut halves (about 4 cups)
⅓ cup chopped fresh rosemary or 2 tablespoons dried, crumbled
1 tablespoon coarse (kosher) salt
1 teaspoon paprika
⅛ teaspoon cayenne

1. Preheat oven to 325°F. Combine butter and oil in a large roasting pan and heat in oven until butter has melted, about 3 minutes. Add nuts and stir to coat well. Spread in a single layer.

2. Sprinkle rosemary, salt, paprika, and cayenne over nuts. Bake 15 to 20 minutes, shaking and stirring several times, until golden brown and fragrant. Drain on paper towels. Serve warm or at room temperature. Store in an airtight container.

229 ASIAN GLAZED PECANS

Prep: 10 minutes Cook: 10 minutes Makes: 2 cups

The Chinese technique of peeling the inner skin from the nuts removes any trace of bitterness.

2 cups pecan halves (about 8 ounces)
2 cups boiling water
½ cup sugar
1½ teaspoons vegetable oil
2 teaspoons coarse (kosher) salt

1. Line a jelly-roll pan with foil or parchment paper. Preheat oven to 325°F. Put pecans in a medium heatproof bowl. Cover with boiling water and let steep 3 minutes. Drain nuts well and pat dry, rubbing away any dark skin that can be easily removed.

2. In a medium bowl, combine warm nuts with sugar, oil, and salt. Toss until well mixed. Spread out pecans in a single layer on prepared baking sheet and bake until shiny and golden, about 10 minutes. Let cool and store airtight.

230 WARM HERBED OLIVES

Prep: 5 minutes Cook: 4 to 6 minutes Serves: 4

There's something very comforting in the simplicity of this aromatic appetizer. We like serving it from a shallow earthenware bowl, with creamy goat cheese and crusty bread on the side for mopping up the oil.

¼ cup extra-virgin olive oil
3 garlic cloves, thinly sliced
2 sprigs of fresh thyme, or ½ teaspoon dried
1 cup drained kalamata olives or ½ cup niçoise olives

1. In a small saucepan, combine olive oil, garlic, and thyme. Cook over low heat until garlic is fragrant, 2 to 3 minutes.

2. Add olives and continue cooking until heated through, 2 to 3 minutes longer. Transfer to a serving bowl and serve warm, not hot.

231 NUTTY SPANISH OLIVES

Prep: 15 minutes Cook: 10 minutes Makes: 16

16 medium pimiento-stuffed olives (about ½ cup)
½ cup sliced almonds
1 (3-ounce) package cream cheese, softened

1. Preheat oven to 325°F. Drain olives and pat dry with paper towels.

2. Spread almonds in a single layer on a jelly-roll pan and bake until lightly browned, about 10 minutes. Let cool, then coarsely chop.

3. For each olive, pinch off about 1 teaspoon cream cheese. Mold around olives to cover. Roll in chopped nuts.

232 CURRIED APPLE SLICES

Prep: 5 minutes Cook: none Makes: 12

1 tablespoon lemon juice
¼ teaspoon curry powder
Dash of cayenne
1 medium Golden Delicious apple

1. In a small bowl, combine lemon juice, curry, and cayenne. Stir to blend well.

2. Cut apple in half and remove core. Cut each half into 6 wedges. Dip apple slices into curried lemon juice, letting excess liquid drain off. Serve immediately.

233 GARLICKY OLIVES WITH ORANGE AND CUMIN

Prep: 10 minutes Cook: none Marinate: 48 hours
Makes: about 2 cups

Be sure to warn your guests that these olives have not been pitted. It's a nice touch to put a small dish near the olives where your guests can deposit their pits.

2 (7½-ounce) cans tree-ripened olives
¼ cup extra-virgin olive oil
10 garlic cloves, peeled and smashed
Zest of 1 orange, cut into large strips
1 teaspoon sherry vinegar or white wine vinegar
1 teaspoon cumin seeds, crushed
2 small dried hot red peppers
1 bay leaf

1. Drain olives and crush each one gently with flat side of a large knife to bruise.

2. In a large jar with a tight-fitting lid, combine olives, olive oil, garlic, orange zest, vinegar, cumin seeds, dried hot peppers, and bay leaf. Cover and refrigerate, shaking jar occasionally to distribute marinade, for 48 hours or as long as 2 weeks. Let return to room temperature before serving.

234 SESAME WON TON CRISPS

Prep: 10 minutes Cook: 6 to 8 minutes Makes: 48

Won ton wrappers are usually sold in 1-pound packages, which contain anywhere from 80 to 140, depending upon thickness. Uncooked wrappers keep well in the freezer.

2 tablespoons soy sauce
1 tablespoon Asian sesame oil
24 won ton wrappers (about 3 inches square)*
2 tablespoons sesame seeds

1. Preheat oven to 350°F. In a small bowl, mix soy sauce with sesame oil.

2. Stack won ton wrappers and cut in half diagonally with a large sharp knife to make triangular pieces. Line a baking sheet with foil to facilitate cleanup. Arrange wrappers in a single layer so edges are not touching. Brush with soy mixture and sprinkle with sesame seeds.

3. Bake until lightly golden and crisp, 6 to 8 minutes. Remove to a wire rack. Serve immediately or store airtight for up to 3 days.

* *Available in Asian markets or the refrigerated foods/produce section of many supermarkets.*

235 SPICED WON TON CRISPS

Prep: 10 minutes Cook: 6 to 8 minutes Makes: 48

For a less traditional approach, won ton wrappers can be wrinkled up and baked in that shape. Just scrunch them in your hand and place on a baking sheet prior to brushing and cooking.

24 won ton wrappers (about 3 inches square)*
¼ cup olive oil or melted butter
Chili powder or curry powder

1. Preheat oven to 350°F. Stack won ton wrappers and cut in half diagonally with a large sharp knife to make triangular pieces.

2. Line a baking sheet with foil to facilitate cleanup. Arrange wrappers in a single layer so edges are not touching. Brush with olive oil and sprinkle lightly with chili powder or curry.

3. Bake until lightly golden and crisp, 6 to 8 minutes. Let cool on a wire rack. Serve immediately or store airtight for up to 3 days.

* *Available in Asian markets or the refrigerated foods/produce section of many supermarkets.*

236 PARMESAN WON TON CRISPS

Prep: 10 minutes Cook: 6 to 8 minutes Makes: 48

Using premade won ton wrappers allows you to produce a batch—or two—of irresistible nibbles easily in no time.

24 won ton wrappers (about 3 inches square)*
¼ cup olive oil or melted butter
3 tablespoons grated Parmesan cheese

1. Preheat oven to 350°F. Stack won ton wrappers and cut in half diagonally with a large sharp knife to make triangular pieces.

2. Line a baking sheet with foil to facilitate cleanup. Arrange wrappers in a single layer so edges are not touching. Brush with olive oil and sprinkle with Parmesan cheese.

3. Bake until light golden and crisp, 6 to 8 minutes. Let cool on a wire rack. Serve immediately or store airtight for up to 3 days.

* *Available in Asian markets or the refrigerated foods/produce section of many supermarkets.*

Chapter 9

Pâtés, Mousses, and Terrines

The French have a genius for turning humble meats into beautiful appetizers that not only taste terrific but also feed a large group, profit from advance preparation, and are easily transported and a snap to garnish. Pâté is nothing more than meatloaf with a French accent, often with a pork base. Don't worry about needing special equipment for these very special hors d'oeuvres. Though lidded terrines and shiny metal pâté molds are lovely to look at and fun to own, the loaf pans already in your cupboard will work just as well.

For a hearty appetizer created to complement a full-bodied wine, serve our rustic Country Terrine with the slightly sour gherkins called cornichons, a bowl of brine-cured olives, a crock of coarse mustard, and crusty slices of French bread.

Delicate mousses made from chicken, chicken livers, or duck, from the classics to the quickies, have an ethereal quality that keeps us coming back for more. Even guests who are reluctant to try something different will be drawn to the Herb-Flecked Chicken Mousse sliced or piped onto tender lettuce leaves or spread on small bread slices. Add a touch of humor to chicken-based pâtés and mousses like this one by cutting out bread slices with a chick-shaped cookie cutter. (For fish- and shellfish-based pâtés and mousses, see Chapter 5.)

If you suffer from the all-too-common fear of unmolding, seek out covered plastic gelatin molds sold through housewares home parties, as they are absolutely foolproof. The beautiful decorative metal molds which many people use to garnish the walls of their kitchens can be rendered easy-to-unmold in the following manner: Generously spray or brush the inside of the mold with oil and place in the freezer to set while you make the mousse. Fill and refrigerate as the recipe directs. When ready to serve, use your fingers to gently press in the edges to release the mousse. Then place a serving plate upside down over the mold and invert. If the mousse is still resistant, place a hot towel over the mold for a minute or two to break the seal. You're now ready to entertain in the French style. *Bon appétit!*

237 CHOPPED CHICKEN LIVERS ITALIANO

Prep: 25 minutes Cook: 5 minutes Chill: 30 minutes
Serves: 6 to 8

This robust spread is unbelievably good. For proper texture, be sure to mix with a fork, as indicated in the recipe.

- **1 pound chicken livers, trimmed**
- **2 tablespoons butter**
- **2 tablespoons olive oil**
- **¼ cup minced onion**
- **⅓ cup dry Marsala or sherry**
- **2 to 3 tablespoons anchovy paste**
- **1 (3-ounce) jar capers, drained**
- **Coarsely ground fresh black pepper**
- **Crackers, bread rounds, or Crostini (page 151)**

1. Rinse chicken livers and pat dry. In a large skillet, melt butter in olive oil over medium heat. Add livers and onion and cook, stirring occasionally, until onion is softened but not browned and livers are still slightly pink inside, about 5 minutes. Increase heat to high and pour in Marsala. When all but 1 tablespoon of wine has evaporated, remove from heat and transfer entire mixture to a medium bowl. Let cool for 10 minutes.

2. Using tines of a fork, mix in anchovy paste and then capers, coarsely crushing chicken livers in the process. Season generously with pepper to taste. Cover and refrigerate 30 minutes or as long as 2 days. Serve at cool room temperature with crackers, bread rounds, or crostini.

238 CHICKEN LIVER PÂTÉ WITH CURRANTS

Prep: 30 minutes Cook: 8 to 11 minutes Serves: 8 to 12

This delicious show-stopper actually benefits by being made a day in advance. The flavors deepen and mellow when allowed to stand overnight. Serve with crackers or bread rounds.

- **1 pound chicken livers, trimmed**
- **2 sticks (8 ounces) butter, softened**
- **1 small onion, coarsely chopped**
- **1 large garlic clove, minced**
- **¼ teaspoon grated nutmeg**
- **¼ teaspoon salt**
- **⅛ teaspoon freshly ground pepper**
- **⅛ teaspoon quatre épices or ground allspice**
- **¼ cup brandy**
- **¼ cup port**
- **½ cup currants or coarsely chopped raisins**
- **1 tablespoon chopped fresh thyme leaves or 1 teaspoon dried**
- **Port Aspic (optional; recipe follows)**

1. Rinse chicken livers and pat dry. In a large skillet, melt 4 tablespoons of butter over medium heat. Add onion and cook until softened but not browned, 2 to 3 minutes. Add garlic and cook until just fragrant, about 30 seconds. Using a slotted spoon, transfer onion and garlic to a food processor.

2. Add 4 more tablespoons butter to same skillet; melt over medium-high heat. Add chicken livers and cook, tossing occasionally, until browned outside yet still juicy and slightly pink inside, about 5 minutes. Season with nutmeg, salt, pepper, and quatre épices. Transfer chicken livers and cooking juices and butter remaining in pan to processor. Return pan to heat and add brandy and port. Bring to a boil, scraping up any browned bits from bottom of pan. Stir in currants and remove pan from heat.

3. Add thyme and remaining 1 stick butter, cut into bits, to food processor. Process until mixture is smooth. Mix in currants and warm liquid from skillet until just blended. Pack mixture into a 3- to 4-cup terrine or serving bowl; smooth top. Pour port aspic over pâté. Refrigerate until aspic is set and pâté is well chilled, at least 2 hours or up to 2 days. Serve chilled.

---

239 PORT ASPIC

Prep: 10 minutes Cook: 5 to 7 minutes Chill: 2¼ to 3 hours
Makes: about ½ cup

This shimmering, ruby-colored aspic was the inspiration of California restaurateur Narsai David. It has a wonderful flavor and can be used to dress up any meat or chicken mousse or pâté.

1 teaspoon unflavored gelatin
½ cup ruby port
1 tablespoon sugar
1½ tablespoons red wine vinegar
¼ teaspoon dried tarragon

1. In a small bowl, soften gelatin in port. In a small saucepan over medium heat, combine sugar and 1 tablespoon water. Bring to a boil, stirring to dissolve sugar. Cook until sugar melts and begins to caramelize, 3 to 5 minutes. Immediately remove from heat and stir in port mixture (be careful—it may spatter) until well blended. Return saucepan to low heat. Add vinegar and tarragon and simmer until fragrant, about 2 minutes.

2. Strain mixture through a fine sieve into a shallow heatproof dish and let cool until only slightly syrupy, 10 to 15 minutes. Spoon or pour aspic over pâté and refrigerate until completely set, 2 to 3 hours.

240 CURRIED LIVER PÂTÉ

Prep: 15 minutes Cook: 48 to 64 minutes Chill: 24 hours Serves: 6 to 8

With her kind permission, we blatantly stole this from Marlene Levinson, a noted San Francisco food authority, who is most generous with her recipes. Be sure to make this a day ahead, as the flavors improve overnight.

1 medium onion, chopped
1 stick (4 ounces) butter
½ pound chicken livers, trimmed and coarsely chopped
1 garlic clove, minced
1 teaspoon curry powder
¼ cup dry sherry
¼ teaspoon ground allspice
¼ teaspoon salt
¼ teaspoon freshly ground pepper
1½ tablespoons flour
1 egg

1. Preheat oven to 325°F. In a large frying pan, cook onion in butter over medium heat until softened but not browned, 2 to 3 minutes. Add chicken livers, garlic, curry powder, sherry, allspice, salt, pepper, and flour, and cook, stirring, 1 minute longer. Reduce heat to low, cover, and cook 15 minutes, or until livers are no longer pink. Uncover, remove from heat, and let cool 5 minutes.

2. In a blender or food processor, combine liver mixture and egg. Puree until smooth. Place mixture in a 2½- to 3-cup ovenproof crock or pâté mold and cover tightly with foil.

3. Set in a larger pan filled with enough hot water to reach halfway up sides of crock. Bake 30 to 45 minutes, or until pâté is firm in the center. Let cool, then refrigerate for 24 hours to develop flavors.

241 PISTACHIO CHICKEN LIVER PÂTÉ

Prep: 20 minutes Cook: 10 minutes Chill: 6 hours Serves: 8 to 12

1½ pounds chicken livers
1½ sticks (6 ounces) butter, softened
3 tablespoons vegetable oil or rendered chicken fat
2 medium onions, coarsely chopped
2 green cooking apples, peeled, cored, and sliced
½ cup brandy
½ cup pistachio nuts, shelled and coarsely chopped
2 tablespoons fresh lemon juice
½ teaspoon salt
¼ teaspoon pepper
⅛ teaspoon grated nutmeg

1. Rinse chicken livers and dry between layers of paper towels. If livers are large, cut into pieces.

2. In a large frying pan, melt ½ stick butter in oil over medium heat. Add onions and apples and cook, stirring occasionally, until onions are golden brown, 5 to 7 minutes. Using a slotted spoon, transfer onions and apples to a food processor. Melt another ½ stick of butter in pan. Add chicken livers and cook over medium heat until browned outside but still pink in centers, about 3 minutes. Remove livers from pan and add to cooked onions and apples in processor.

3. Pour brandy into frying pan and bring to a boil, scraping up any browned bits from bottom of pan with a wooden spoon. Pour into processor and puree until smooth. Add remaining butter and process until well blended.

4. Transfer mixture to a large bowl and stir in chopped pistachio nuts, lemon juice, salt, pepper, and nutmeg. Turn into a 4-cup serving bowl or a lightly greased mold and cover tightly with plastic wrap. Refrigerate 6 hours or as long as 3 days before serving.

---

242 CURRIED BEEF PÂTÉ

Prep: 15 minutes Cook: none Chill: overnight Serves: 12 to 16

Here is a way to turn lowly leftovers into the hit of the party.

- **½ cup golden raisins**
- **½ cup dry sherry**
- **1 medium onion, coarsely chopped**
- **2 garlic cloves, minced**
- **1 stick (¼ pound) butter**
- **2 cups diced lean leftover braised brisket or pot roast, cut into ½-inch pieces (about 1 pound)**
- **1 cup mango chutney**
- **¼ cup heavy cream**
- **3 tablespoons curry powder**
- **1½ teaspoons ground cumin**
- **1 teaspoon sugar**
- **2 tablespoons fresh lemon juice**
- **½ teaspoon salt**
- **¼ teaspoon pepper**
- **½ cup chopped chives**
- **½ cup chopped walnuts**

1. In a small saucepan, cook raisins in sherry over low heat for 5 minutes to soften. Remove from heat and let cool.

2. In a medium frying pan, cook onion and garlic in 4 tablespoons butter over medium heat until soft and golden, about 5 minutes.

3. In a food processor, process beef until finely ground. Add chutney and process until smooth. Add cream, curry powder, cumin, sugar, lemon juice, salt, and pepper and blend well. Add remaining 4 tablespoons butter and sherry from raisins, reserving raisins. Process on and off three times to blend.

4. Turn beef mixture into a bowl and stir in raisins, onion, chives, and walnuts. Pack mixture into a 4-cup crock. Cover and refrigerate overnight. Serve chilled.

243 PORK RILLETTES

Prep: 20 minutes Cook: 4 hours Serves: 20 to 24

Lonnie makes this savory spread for her annual Christmas Eve buffet, always hoping there will be leftovers. (Better luck next year, Lonnie.) Serve with plenty of crusty French bread.

1 pound lean salt pork
1 pound bacon
1 pound boneless pork shoulder
3 carrots, peeled
2 whole cloves
3 bay leaves
½ cup chopped shallots or onion
2 garlic cloves, minced
½ teaspoon freshly ground pepper

1. Cut salt pork, bacon, pork shoulder, and carrots into 3-inch pieces. Tie cloves and bay leaves in a cheesecloth bag. In a large heavy saucepan, combine salt pork, bacon, pork shoulder, carrots, spice bag, shallots, garlic, pepper, and ¼ cup water. Cover and cook over low heat, stirring occasionally, until meat is falling apart, about 4 hours. If liquid evaporates and meat begins to stick to pan during cooking, add more water.

2. Drain mixture, reserving liquid. Pick out and discard spice bag. Using two forks or a potato masher, shred mixture until it retains some texture, yet appears creamy. If mixture seems dry, add reserved liquid, 1 tablespoon at a time. Pack into a decorative crock. Serve immediately, or cover and refrigerate up to 5 days. Serve at room temperature.

244 CHOPPED CHICKEN LIVERS

Prep: 25 minutes Cook: 10 to 17 minutes Serves: 6

For best flavor, combine all of the ingredients while still a bit warm from cooking. Serve this classic spread with crackers, matzoh, toast, or rye bread.

1 pound chicken livers, trimmed
1 stick (4 ounces) butter, or ½ cup rendered chicken fat or vegetable oil
2 onions, finely chopped
3 or 4 hard-boiled eggs, chopped
1 teaspoon salt
½ teaspoon freshly ground pepper

1. Rinse livers under cold water and pat dry. In a large frying pan, cook livers in 4 tablespoons of the butter over medium-high heat until nicely browned outside but still pink inside, about 5 minutes. Remove with a slotted spoon and set aside.

2. In same pan, melt remaining butter. Add onions, reduce heat to medium, and cook until golden brown, 5 to 7 minutes.

3. In a large bowl, combine chicken livers with onions, any pan juices, hard-boiled eggs, salt, and pepper. Mash with a fork until well blended. If made in advance, cover and refrigerate up to 2 days.

245 METTWURST PÂTÉ

Prep: 5 minutes Cook: none Chill: 2 hours Serves: 8

In this case, the wurst is the best! Try this flavorful spread on crackers or party rye.

½ pound mettwurst, teewurst, or Polish sausage
½ cup cottage cheese
⅓ cup chopped walnuts
¼ cup crumbled blue cheese
2 tablespoons chopped parsley

1. In a food processor, combine mettwurst, cottage cheese, walnuts, and blue cheese. Process until smooth. Using an on-off motion, blend in parsley.

2. Pack into a 2-cup serving bowl or oiled mold. Cover and refrigerate 2 hours or as long as 3 days.

246 PÂTÉ DE CAMPAGNE

Prep: 20 minutes Cook: 1¾ to 2 hours Chill: 2 hours Serves: 12

Here is an authentic French pâté. Ask your butcher to order the caul fat for you in advance.

1 cup chopped onion
3 tablespoons butter
½ cup cognac or brandy
1 pound ground pork
1 pound ground veal
2 eggs, lightly beaten
2 teaspoons salt
1 teaspoon freshly ground pepper
¼ teaspoon cinnamon
¼ teaspoon grated nutmeg
¼ teaspoon ground cloves
1 pound caul fat or pork fatback

1. Preheat oven to 350°F. In a large frying pan, cook onion in butter over medium heat until softened but not browned, about 3 minutes. Add cognac and boil until liquid is reduced by half. Scrape into a large bowl.

2. Add pork, veal, eggs, salt, pepper, cinnamon, nutmeg, and cloves to bowl. Blend until well mixed.

3. Line a 2-quart terrine or loaf pan with caul fat or fatback. Pack meat mixture into pan, covering with overlapping fat; then cover tightly with aluminum foil. Set in a large pan of hot water that reaches halfway up sides of terrine.

4. Bake 1¾ to 2 hours, until a metal skewer inserted into center for 30 seconds is hot to the touch when withdrawn, or when an instant-reading thermometer inserted into center registers 165°. Remove terrine from its water bath. Evenly distribute 1 to 2 pounds of weight, such as cans of food, on top of foil to pack down meat mixture. Let cool, then refrigerate 2 hours or as long as 1 week before serving.

247 DUCK LIVER TERRINE

Prep: 20 minutes Cook: 50 to 60 minutes Serves: 8

Asian markets are a good source for duck livers. This rich and creamy classic is delicious on baguette slices.

4 marrow bones (cut about 1 inch long)
1 pound duck livers, rinsed and trimmed
2 egg yolks
1 small garlic clove, chopped
¼ teaspoon grated nutmeg
2 teaspoons salt
½ teaspoon pepper
2 cups milk
½ cup crème fraîche*
3 eggs

1. Dip marrow bones in warm water to loosen marrow. Scoop marrow from bones and soak in cold water for 2 hours. Pat dry and chop coarsely.

2. Preheat oven to 350°F. In a food processor, combine livers, marrow, egg yolks, garlic, nutmeg, salt, and pepper. Puree until smooth. With machine on, add milk and crème fraîche. Add eggs one at a time, processing until well blended.

3. Strain liver puree through a sieve into a medium bowl; then pour into a buttered shallow 4-cup mold. Cover mold with foil and place in oven in a larger pan filled with enough hot water to reach halfway up the sides of mold. Lower oven temperature to 250° and bake 50 to 60 minutes, until firm. Remove from oven and let stand in water bath for 10 to 15 minutes, then remove to a rack to cool. Serve warm or chilled.

* *Available in many cheese and specialty shops.*

248 HERB-FLECKED CHICKEN MOUSSE

Prep: 30 minutes Cook: 40 minutes Chill: 4 hours
Serves: 16 to 20

Although this makes a fabulous spread for crackers, bread rounds, and cucumber slices, it can also be sliced into individual servings. For a light appetizer serve a slice of this mousse on a radicchio or lettuce leaf and garnish with chopped fresh chives.

2 whole chicken breasts on the bone (about 2 pounds total)
½ cup coarsely chopped fresh herbs, such as chervil, chives, basil, and Italian parsley
1 teaspoon salt
⅛ teaspoon white pepper
2 (¼-ounce) envelopes unflavored gelatin
½ cup dry white wine or vermouth, chilled
2 cups chicken broth, heated
½ cup mayonnaise
1 cup heavy cream, chilled

1. In a large saucepan, cover chicken breasts with cold water and bring to a simmer over medium heat. Simmer 10 minutes. Cover, remove from heat, and let stand until chicken is cooked through but still juicy, about 30 minutes. Discard skin and bones. Cut chicken into chunks.

2. In a food processor, combine chicken, herbs, salt, and pepper. Process until chicken and herbs are finely chopped.

3. In a small bowl, soften gelatin in wine; then stir mixture into warm chicken broth. With food processor on, gradually add gelatin mixture to chicken and process until smooth. Transfer to a large bowl and refrigerate until cool, 10 to 15 minutes. Stir in mayonnaise.

4. In a large bowl, whip heavy cream until soft peaks form. Using a rubber spatula, fold one-third of whipped cream into chicken mixture. Fold in remaining whipped cream. Transfer mousse to an oiled 6-cup mold or serving bowl and refrigerate until set, about 4 hours, or as long as 2 days.

---

249 COUNTRY TERRINE

Prep: 30 minutes Cook: 1¼ to 1½ hours Chill: 2 hours
Serves: 12 to 16

Weighting down the cooked mixture removes moisture to give a firmer texture. Serve this hearty appetizer with crusty bread, Dijon mustard, and the tiny French-style sour pickles called cornichons.

¾ pound sliced bacon
1 medium onion, chopped
1 tablespoon butter
1 pound ground pork
½ pound ground veal
½ pound chicken livers, rinsed, trimmed, and chopped
2 garlic cloves, minced
¼ teaspoon ground allspice
Pinch of ground cloves
Pinch of grated nutmeg
2 eggs, beaten
½ cup heavy cream
2 tablespoons brandy
½ cup shelled pistachios
1 teaspoon salt
½ teaspoon pepper
4 ounces sliced cooked ham, cut into strips
1 bay leaf

1. Preheat oven to 350°F. Line a 2-quart terrine or loaf pan with most of the bacon, reserving a few slices for top.

2. In a medium frying pan, cook onion in butter over medium heat until softened but not browned, about 4 minutes. Scrape into a large bowl. Add pork, veal, chicken livers, garlic, allspice, cloves, nutmeg, eggs, cream, brandy, pistachios, salt, and pepper. Stir together until well mixed.

3. Spread half of meat mixture in bacon-lined terrine. Layer ham strips over meat. Fill terrine with remaining meat mixture and cover with reserved bacon slices. Place bay leaf on top and cover with lid or heavy-duty aluminum foil.

4. Set terrine in a pan of boiling water that reaches halfway up the sides of terrine. Bake 1¼ to 1½ hours, until a metal skewer inserted into center for 30 seconds is hot to the touch when withdrawn, or when an instant-reading thermometer inserted into center registers 165°. Remove terrine from its water bath. Evenly distribute 1 to 2 pounds of weight, such as cans of food, on top of foil to pack down meat mixture. Let cool, then refrigerate 2 hours or as long as 1 week before serving.

250 QUICK CURRIED CHICKEN PÂTÉ

Prep: 5 minutes Cook: none Serves: 6

A good reason to make sure you have leftover chicken. Great on Beaten Biscuits (page 204), but equally good packed in a decorative crock and served with crackers or apple slices.

1¼ cups chopped cooked chicken
1 stick (4 ounces) butter, cut into bits
¼ medium Delicious apple, peeled
1 shallot, coarsely chopped
1 teaspoon fresh lemon juice
½ teaspoon salt
½ teaspoon curry powder
Freshly ground pepper

1. In a food processor, combine chicken, butter, apple, shallot, lemon juice, salt, curry powder, and pepper. Puree until smooth.

2. Pack mixture into a serving crock. If made in advance, cover and refrigerate up to 2 days.

251 NUTTY MUSHROOM PÂTÉ

Prep: 20 minutes Cook: 10 to 12 minutes Chill: 2 hours Serves: 4

Serve this rich and woodsy-tasting vegetarian pâté with crackers or baguette slices and no one will miss the meat.

½ cup coarsely chopped walnuts or almonds
4 tablespoons butter
¼ cup chopped shallots
½ pound mushrooms, coarsely chopped
1 (3-ounce) package cream cheese, softened
2 tablespoons chopped parsley
1 tablespoon brandy
1½ teaspoons fresh thyme leaves or ½ teaspoon dried
⅛ teaspoon salt
Dash of cayenne

1. Preheat oven to 325°F. Spread walnuts on a baking sheet and bake until fragrant and lightly browned, 10 to 12 minutes.

2. In a large frying pan, melt butter over medium heat. Stir in shallots and cook until softened but not browned, 2 to 3 minutes. Add mushrooms and cook, stirring occasionally, until mushroom liquid has exuded and evaporated, 7 to 10 minutes.

3. In a blender or food processor, combine nuts, mushroom mixture, cream cheese, parsley, brandy, thyme, salt, and cayenne. Process until mushrooms and nuts are finely minced. Cover and refrigerate at least 2 hours or as long as 2 days. Serve at room temperature.

Chapter 10

Pizzas, Canapés, and Sandwiches

This chapter shows just what you can do with a slice of toast, a loaf of bread, or a bit of dough. We are fairly sure that the Earl of Sandwich would be delighted with the evolution of his masterpiece. We touch upon a few bite-size sandwiches, open faced and otherwise, hot and cold, that are always a welcome addition at cocktail time. Beef and Rosemary Crostini and colorful Aram Sandwiches are a far cry from the limp little tea sandwiches served in years gone by. And it would be downright un-American to overlook the fun of Mini Burgers and Hot Puppies.

Be sure to try the irresistible pizzas—Pesto and Mozzarella or Onion and Artichoke—made with frozen bread dough. Nobody will mistake these for pies from the local pizza parlor. To make it easier on busy cooks, there are also "instant" English muffin–based Spicy Pizza Bites.

For upper-crust appetizers, there are ideas like Roquefort Rounds with Fresh Thyme, Crab and Parmesan Toasts, and Creamy Pistachio Bites. For down-home eating, there is even a bite-sized version of the deli sandwich with our little Reuben Puffs.

---

252 CHEESY ANCHOVY CLOUDS

Prep: 15 minutes Cook: 4 to 6 minutes Makes: 24

12 thin slices of firm-textured white bread
18 anchovy fillets
6 thin slices of fontina cheese
6 thin slices of mortadella
Freshly ground black pepper
¾ cup olive oil
4 eggs
⅓ cup cream
¼ cup grated Parmesan cheese

1. Remove crusts from bread. On each of 6 bread slices, place 3 anchovy fillets and 1 slice of fontina cheese. Fold each slice of mortadella in half and place on top. Season with pepper and cover with remaining bread slices.

2. In a large frying pan, heat olive oil over low heat. In a medium shallow bowl, beat eggs with cream and Parmesan cheese until well blended. Dip each sandwich into egg batter. Carefully immerse sandwiches into hot oil and fry, turning once, until golden brown, about 2 to 3 minutes per side.

3. Drain on paper towels. Cut each sandwich into quarters and arrange on a serving platter. Serve hot.

253 CROSTINI

Prep: 5 minutes Cook: 5 to 7 minutes Makes: 24

These little toasts are a welcome change from crackers. They can be topped with almost any savory spread or pâté, Mushroom Duxelles (page 63), or something as simple as chopped ripe tomatoes and a drizzle of extra-virgin olive oil.

- **24 slices of narrow French bread (baguette), cut ¼ to ⅜ inch thick**
- **¼ cup extra-virgin olive oil**

Preheat oven to 400°F. Arrange bread slices on a baking sheet and brush with oil. Bake until lightly toasted and golden brown, 5 to 7 minutes. Let cool. Store airtight.

254 GARLICKY ARTICHOKE CROSTINI

Prep: 15 minutes Cook: 10 to 17 minutes Makes: 24

- **24 slices of baguette (narrow French bread), cut ¼ to ⅜ inch thick**
- **¼ cup extra-virgin olive oil**
- **3 garlic cloves—2 halved, 1 crushed through a press**
- **1 (6-ounce) jar marinated artichoke hearts, drained and chopped**
- **1 cup shredded mozzarella cheese (4 ounces)**
- **2 teaspoons chopped fresh marjoram or oregano or ½ teaspoon dried**
- **¼ teaspoon pepper**
- **⅓ cup grated Parmesan cheese**

1. Preheat oven to 400°F. Arrange bread slices on a baking sheet and brush with oil. Bake until lightly toasted and golden brown, 5 to 7 minutes.

2. When cool enough to handle, rub browned side with cut garlic cloves, grating against rough surface to distribute flavor. Set crostini aside. Reduce oven temperature to 350°F.

3. In a small bowl, combine artichoke hearts, crushed garlic, mozzarella cheese, marjoram, and pepper. Mix until well blended. Spread 1 heaping teaspoon artichoke mixture over each crostini and sprinkle Parmesan cheese on top. Bake until cheese has melted and topping is bubbly, 5 to 10 minutes. Serve warm.

255 BEEF AND ROSEMARY CROSTINI

Prep: 10 minutes Cook: 13 to 17 minutes Chill: 1 hour Makes: 24

24 slices of baguette (narrow French bread), cut 1/4 to 3/8 inch thick
1/4 cup olive oil
3/4 pound beef fillet cut from the narrow end (1 to 1 1/2 inches in diameter)
Salt and freshly ground pepper
1/3 cup Olive Aïoli (page 22)
Chopped fresh rosemary

1. Preheat oven to 400°F. Arrange bread slices in a single layer on a baking sheet and brush with oil. Bake until lightly toasted and golden brown, 5 to 7 minutes. Let cool, then store airtight.

2. Preheat your broiler. Generously season meat with salt and pepper and cook, turning once, 4 to 6 inches from heat until nicely browned outside but still rare and juicy inside, 8 to 10 minutes total. Let cool. Refrigerate, well wrapped, until meat is firm to the touch, 1 hour or as long as overnight. Trim away fat and slice thinly across the grain.

3. Arrange crostini on a clean work surface. Spread each with about 1/2 teaspoon olive aïoli, then a slice of beef, another dab of aïoli, and a pinch of chopped rosemary. Season with salt and freshly ground pepper and serve.

256 GARLIC CROSTINI

Prep: 10 minutes Cook: 5 to 7 minutes Makes: 24

24 slices of narrow French bread (baguette), cut 1/4 to 3/8 inch thick
1/4 cup extra-virgin olive oil
2 garlic cloves, halved

1. Preheat oven to 400°F. Arrange bread slices in a single layer on a baking sheet and brush with oil. Bake until lightly toasted and golden brown, 5 to 7 minutes.

2. When cool enough to handle, rub browned side with cut side of garlic cloves, grating against rough surface to distribute flavor. Let cool. Store airtight.

257 CRAB AND PARMESAN TOASTS

Prep: 10 minutes Cook: 5 to 7 minutes Makes: 36

- **½ pound crab meat**
- **1¼ cups mayonnaise**
- **1 cup freshly grated Parmesan cheese**
- **2 tablespoons chopped fresh chives or scallions**
- **1 teaspoon fresh lemon juice**
- **⅛ teaspoon freshly ground white pepper**
- **2 sun-dried tomato halves, minced (optional)**
- **36 baguette or other bread slices, cut about ⅜ inch thick**

1. Preheat oven to 400°F. Pick through crab and discard any bits of shell or cartilage.

2. In a medium bowl, combine mayonnaise, Parmesan cheese, chives, lemon juice, and pepper. Mix until well blended. Fold in sun-dried tomatoes and crab.

3. Lay baguette slices in a single layer on a baking sheet and spread each evenly with about 1 tablespoon of crab mixture. Bake until golden brown and bubbly, 5 to 7 minutes. Serve warm.

258 EGGS-TRA-ORDINARY CHEESE TOASTS

Prep: 10 minutes Cook: 13 to 17 minutes Makes: 24

The French term for bite-size morsels is "amuse-gueule," as they are said to amuse the mouth. These simple appetizers amuse the eye also, as they resemble tiny fried eggs.

- **8 slices firm-textured white bread**
- **1 (3-ounce) package cream cheese, softened**
- **1 tablespoon cream or milk**
- **½ teaspoon onion juice**
- **Dash of salt**
- **¼ pound sharp Cheddar cheese**
- **Freshly ground black pepper**

1. Preheat oven to 375°F. Using a 2-inch biscuit cutter, cut 3 rounds from each slice of bread. (Reserve scraps for other uses, such as bread crumbs.) Arrange bread crumbs on a baking sheet and bake until lightly browned, 5 to 7 minutes. Let cool.

2. In a small bowl, combine cream cheese, cream, onion juice, and salt. Blend well. Spread mixture over untoasted sides of bread.

3. Cut Cheddar into 24 (¼-inch) cubes and place 1 cube in center of each round. Sprinkle lightly with pepper. Bake until Cheddar has just melted, resembling an egg yolk, 8 to 10 minutes. Serve warm.

259 MINI BURGERS

Prep: 15 minutes Cook: 20 to 25 minutes Makes: 48

Few can resist the essence of Americana cooking: perfect little hamburgers and fries. Save time by ordering miniature hamburger buns from your local baker.

1 pound ground chuck (80% lean)
¼ cup Worcestershire sauce
12 slices of American cheese (optional)
¼ cup ketchup
2 tablespoons mustard
2 tablespoons mayonnaise
1 tablespoon pickle relish, finely minced
48 Mini Hamburger Buns (recipe follows)
Packaged shoestring potatoes, for garnish

1. Preheat oven to 450°F. Line a jelly-roll pan with foil to facilitate cleanup. Pinch off 1 tablespoon of meat at a time and form into balls. Arrange 1½ inches apart on prepared baking sheet and flatten into 2-inch patties. Brush with Worcestershire sauce.

2. Bake until burgers are just browned, about 5 minutes. Let cool. Lower oven temperature to 400°.

3. If making cheeseburgers, use a 1½-inch biscuit cutter to cut 4 rounds from each cheese slice. Place cheese directly on cooked meat patties.

4. Slice buns three-quarters through. Using a small spatula, place meat patties (with or without cheese) in buns. In a small bowl, combine ketchup, mustard, mayonnaise, and relish. Stir until well mixed. Spoon or pipe about ½ teaspoon sauce onto each patty.

5. Arrange burgers in buns on a baking sheet and cover with foil. (If made in advance, refrigerate as long as 24 hours.) Bake, uncovered, until burgers are heated through and cheese has melted, about 15 minutes. Serve on a platter with shoestring potatoes to resemble French fries.

260 MINI HAMBURGER BUNS

Prep: 15 minutes Rise: 15 minutes Cook: 15 minutes Makes: 48

1 pound frozen white bread dough, thawed
1 egg
1 tablespoon cream or milk
¼ cup sesame or poppy seeds

1. Preheat oven to 350°F. Pinch off 2 teaspoons dough at a time and form into 1-inch balls. Arrange 1½ inches apart on a greased baking sheet: flatten gently to resemble hamburger buns. Let rise in a warm place until almost doubled in size, about 15 minutes.

2. In a small bowl, combine egg and cream until well blended. Brush over dough and gently flatten once again. Sprinkle seeds over buns and bake until golden brown and cooked through, about 15 minutes. Let cool. Store airtight up to 2 days or freeze.

261 HOT PUPPIES

Prep: 15 minutes Cook: 15 minutes Makes: 48

- **48 Mini Hot Dog Buns (recipe follows)**
- **¼ cup mustard**
- **¼ cup mayonnaise**
- **1 tablespoon pickle relish, finely minced**
- **3 (5.3-ounce) packages little wieners**

1. Preheat oven to 400°F. Slice buns three-quarters through. In a small bowl, combine mustard, mayonnaise, and pickle relish. Stir until well mixed. Spoon or pipe about ½ teaspoon sauce into each bun. Blot wieners dry with paper towels and place inside buns.

2. Arrange puppies on a baking sheet and cover with foil. (If made in advance, refrigerate as long as 24 hours.) Bake, covered, until hot dogs are heated through, about 15 minutes.

262 MINI HOT DOG BUNS

Prep: 15 minutes Rise: 15 minutes Cook: 15 minutes Makes: 48

- **1 pound frozen white bread dough, thawed**
- **1 egg**
- **1 tablespoon cream or milk**

1. Preheat oven to 350°F. Pinch off 2 teaspoons dough at a time and form into ½-inch cylinders. Arrange 1½ inches apart on a greased baking sheet; flatten gently to resemble hot dog buns. Let rise in a warm place until almost doubled in size, about 15 minutes.

2. In a small bowl, beat egg and cream until well blended. Brush over dough; flatten gently once again. Bake until buns are golden brown and baked through, about 15 minutes. Let cool. Store in an airtight tin up to 2 days or freeze.

263 MINI MONTE CRISTO SANDWICHES

Prep: 10 minutes Cook: 10 minutes Makes: 24

Plump, golden Monte Cristos were all the rage years ago. This lighter rendition makes a very tasty appetizer sure to evoke nostalgia.

- **12 thin slices of firm-textured white bread**
- **6 slices of ham**
- **6 slices of Swiss cheese**
- **6 slices of turkey breast**
- **3 eggs**
- **3 tablespoons milk**
- **¼ teaspoon salt**
- **Oil or melted butter**

1. Lay 6 bread slices flat and top each with a ham slice, a cheese slice, and a turkey slice. Top with remaining bread slices.

2. In a large shallow baking dish, beat eggs with milk and salt until blended. Arrange sandwiches in dish in a single layer, turning once or twice, until bread has absorbed all of egg mixture, about 2 minutes per side.

3. Lightly oil a nonstick griddle or fry pan and place over medium heat until hot but not smoking, about 1 minute. Fry sandwiches in batches, turning once, until golden brown, about 2 minutes per side.

4. Transfer to a cutting board, remove and discard crusts, and cut sandwiches into quarters. Serve immediately, or, if made in advance, arrange sandwich quarters on a baking sheet, cover, and refrigerate. Reheat in a 400°F oven until cheese has melted, about 10 minutes.

264 CREAMY MUSHROOM TOASTS

Prep: 15 minutes Cook: 20 to 22 minutes Makes: 24

For no-fuss entertaining, the topping for these toasts can be made one or two days in advance and kept well covered in the refrigerator.

- **2 tablespoons butter**
- **¼ pound mushrooms, finely chopped**
- **1 teaspoon soy or Worcestershire sauce**
- **1 (3-ounce) package cream cheese, softened**
- **1 tablespoon chopped fresh chives or parsley**
- **6 slices firm-textured white bread, crusts removed**

1. Preheat oven to 400°F. In a medium skillet, melt butter over medium heat. Add mushrooms and cook until lightly browned, 5 to 7 minutes. Remove from heat. Immediately stir in soy sauce and add cream cheese, 1 tablespoon at a time, until well blended. Mix in chives.

2. Arrange bread slices in a single layer on a baking sheet. Bake until lightly toasted on top, about 5 minutes.

3. Spread mushroom mixture evenly over untoasted sides of bread. Bake until hot and bubbly, about 10 minutes. Cut each bread slice into 4 squares or triangles. Serve warm.

265 PAN BASQUAISE

Prep: 20 minutes Cook: 30 minutes Makes: 36

This crusty open-faced sandwich is a favorite appetizer in many tapas bars in Spain's Basque country.

- **4 large red bell peppers**
- **5 tablespoons olive oil**
- **1 (6-ounce) can tuna, drained**
- **¼ cup chopped parsley**
- **2 tablespoons red wine vinegar**
- **3 garlic cloves, minced**
- **½ teaspoon salt**
- **¼ teaspoon freshly ground pepper**
- **2 (8-ounce) baguettes (long, narrow French bread)**
- **4 hard-boiled eggs, sliced**
- **½ pound kalamata olives, pitted and coarsely chopped**

1. Preheat oven to 475°F. Set peppers on a baking sheet and brush with 1 tablespoon olive oil to coat lightly. Bake, turning once or twice, for 20 minutes, or until skins begin to blister.

2. Place peppers in a brown paper or plastic bag to steam for 10 minutes. Pull skins from peppers. Remove stems, seeds, and membranes. Cut peppers into thin slices.

3. In a large frying pan, cook peppers in remaining ¼ cup olive oil over medium heat until softened but not browned, about 2 minutes. Stir in tuna, 2 tablespoons parsley, vinegar, garlic, salt, and pepper, and cook, stirring, until vinegar evaporates, about 2 minutes longer. Remove from heat and let cool. (If made in advance, cover and refrigerate up to 3 days. Return to room temperature before proceeding.)

4. Cut bread into slices 1 inch thick and arrange in a single layer on a baking sheet. Bake until just golden brown around edges, 5 to 7 minutes. Let cool.

5. Spread about 2 tablespoons tuna mixture evenly over each piece of bread. Top with an egg slice, chopped olives, and remaining parsley. Serve at room temperature.

266 PARMESAN PUFFS

Prep: 5 minutes Cook: 10 minutes Makes: 28

- **7 slices of white or wheat bread**
- **1 cup mayonnaise**
- **½ cup grated Parmesan cheese**
- **½ cup chopped scallions or onion**
- **Paprika**

1. Preheat oven to 425°F. Remove crusts from bread and lay bread flat on a clean work surface.

2. In a small bowl, combine mayonnaise, Parmesan cheese, and scallions. Spread about ¼ cup cheese mixture over each bread slice, sprinkle with paprika, and cut into quarters. Arrange on a baking sheet and bake until bubbly hot and golden, about 10 minutes.

267 CURRIED OLIVE TOASTS

Prep: 10 minutes   Cook: 10 minutes   Makes: 30

People never seem to tire of this wonderful combination of flavors and textures. Ease of preparation makes it a total winner.

1 cup shredded Cheddar cheese (about 4 ounces)
1 cup mayonnaise
⅓ cup chopped scallions
1 (4½-ounce) can chopped olives
1 tablespoon curry powder
30 baguette or other French or Italian bread slices

1. Preheat oven to 400°F. In a small bowl, combine Cheddar cheese, mayonnaise, scallions, olives, and curry. Mix until well blended.

2. Arrange baguette slices on a baking sheet and top each with a generous tablespoon of olive mixture. Bake until topping is puffed and golden, about 10 minutes. Serve warm.

268 CHEESY ONION AND MUSHROOM TOASTS

Prep: 10 minutes   Cook: 10 to 14 minutes   Makes: 24

This topping can be made ahead and kept for a week in the refrigerator. The toasts are also great with a salad for a light lunch.

6 slices whole wheat bread, crusts removed
2 tablespoons butter
¼ pound mushrooms, chopped
1 small onion, chopped
1 cup shredded Swiss cheese (about 4 ounces)
½ cup mayonnaise
¼ cup minced parsley
2 teaspoons Dijon mustard
½ teaspoon salt
⅛ teaspoon cayenne
⅓ cup grated Parmesan cheese

1. Preheat broiler. Toast breast slices 4 to 6 inches from heat until lightly browned on top, 2 to 4 minutes.

2. In a large frying pan, melt butter over medium heat. Add mushrooms and onion and cook until softened but not browned, about 5 minutes. Let cool. In a medium bowl, combine mushroom mixture with Swiss cheese, mayonnaise, parsley, mustard, salt, and cayenne. Spread over untoasted sides of bread. Sprinkle Parmesan cheese on top.

3. Broil 4 to 6 inches from heat until golden, about 4 minutes. Cut into quarters and serve.

269 SPICY PIZZA BITES

Prep: 15 minutes Cook: 10 to 15 minutes Makes: 48

These tiny bites pack a lot of flavor. This is always a hit at teen parties.

2 cups shredded Cheddar cheese (about 8 ounces)
1 (8-ounce) can tomato sauce
⅓ cup extra-virgin olive oil
1 (4¼-ounce) can chopped ripe olives
1 (4-ounce) can chopped green chilies
¼ cup chopped scallions
2 garlic cloves, minced
¼ teaspoon salt
⅛ teaspoon crushed hot red pepper
6 English muffins, split in half

1. In a medium bowl, combine Cheddar cheese, tomato sauce, olive oil, chopped olives, chilies, scallions, garlic, salt, and crushed hot pepper. Blend until well mixed. (If made in advance, cover and refrigerate up to 3 days.)

2. Preheat oven to 400°F. Place English muffin halves cut-sides up. Spread a scant ¼ cup cheese mixture over each muffin half. Cut each half into quarters. Arrange on a baking sheet and bake 10 to 15 minutes, until cheese is melted and muffins are lightly toasted.

270 PESTO AND MOZZARELLA PIZZA

Prep: 15 minutes Cook: 15 to 20 minutes Serves: 6 to 8

This rich and fragrant pizza always draws raves.

1 tablespoon olive oil
2 teaspoons cornmeal
1 pound frozen bread dough, thawed
Pesto alla Genovese (page 159)
3 cups shredded mozzarella cheese (about 12 ounces)
2 tablespoons pine nuts (pignoli)
2 tablespoons oil-packed sun-dried tomatoes, chopped (optional)
1 tablespoon Parmesan cheese

1. Preheat oven to 400°F. Oil a baking sheet at least 16 inches long and sprinkle with cornmeal. Use a rolling pin or your hands to spread dough over baking sheet, making a rectangle about 7 by 16 inches.

2. Spread pesto over dough and top with mozzarella, pine nuts, sun-dried tomatoes, and Parmesan. Place baking sheet on lowest shelf in oven (or the floor of a gas oven) and bake until crust is firm and nicely browned, 15 to 20 minutes. Cut into squares and serve warm.

271 PESTO ALLA GENOVESE

Prep: 15 minutes Cook: none Makes: 1½ cups

2 cups packed fresh basil leaves
2 garlic cloves
½ cup grated Parmesan cheese
1½ teaspoons salt
¼ teaspoon freshly ground pepper
½ cup extra-virgin olive oil

In a food processor or blender, combine basil, garlic, Parmesan cheese, salt, and pepper. Process until a coarse paste forms. With machine on, slowly add oil. Use pesto immediately, store in an airtight container in refrigerator for up to 4 days, or freeze.

272 ONION AND ARTICHOKE PIZZA

Prep: 15 minutes Cook: 30 to 40 minutes Serves: 6 to 8

Everyone seems to love pizza, and this subtle yet savvy combination is sophisticated enough for any gathering. Shaping a pizza into a rectangle allows you to cut neat squares for serving.

2 medium onions (about 1 pound), thinly sliced
¼ cup olive oil
2 teaspoons yellow cornmeal
1 (1-pound) loaf frozen white or wheat bread dough, thawed as package directs
1 (9-ounce) package frozen artichoke hearts, thawed and coarsely chopped
1 cup shredded fontina cheese (about 4 ounces)
2 tablespoons grated Parmesan cheese
1 tablespoon chopped fresh oregano or 1 teaspoon dried

1. Preheat oven to 425°F. In a large frying pan, cook onions in 2 tablespoons of olive oil over medium heat, stirring occasionally, until very soft but not browned, 15 to 20 minutes.

2. Lightly oil a 16-inch baking sheet and sprinkle with cornmeal. Use a rolling pin or your hands to spread dough over the sheet, making a rectangle about 7 by 16 inches. Brush dough with 1 tablespoon oil and spread onions evenly over pizza. Top with artichoke hearts, fontina, Parmesan, and oregano. Drizzle remaining 1 tablespoon oil over pizza and bake on lowest shelf (or floor of a gas oven) until crust is firm and nicely browned at edges, 15 to 20 minutes. Cut into serving-size pieces and serve warm.

273 PÂTÉ-STUFFED BAGUETTE SLICES

Prep: 30 minutes Cook: 4 to 5 minutes Chill: 2 hours
Makes: 48 to 60

1 stick (4 ounces) butter, softened
½ pound chicken livers, rinsed and trimmed
1 small tart green apple, peeled, cored, and chopped
2 larger shallots, chopped
¼ cup currants or raisins
2 tablespoons brandy
2 tablespoons tawny or ruby port
½ teaspoon salt
⅛ teaspoon grated nutmeg
⅛ teaspoon freshly ground pepper
⅓ cup shelled pistachios
1 (8-ounce) baguette (narrow French bread), about 2¼ inches in diameter and 24 inches long

1. In a large frying pan, melt 2 tablespoons of the butter over medium-high heat. Add chicken livers and cook, tossing, 2 minutes. Stir in chopped apple and shallots and cook until livers are browned outside but still rosy inside, 2 to 3 minutes longer. Remove from heat and let cool.

2. In a small saucepan, combine currants, brandy, and port. Bring to a simmer over low heat; remove from heat.

3. In food processor, combine chicken liver mixture, salt, nutmeg, and pepper. Process until coarsely chopped. Add remaining 6 tablespoons butter, pistachios, and currants with brandy and port and process until well mixed. If mixture is very soft, refrigerate until firm enough to handle, about 15 minutes.

4. Remove ends from baguette and cut into 3- or 4-inch lengths. Using a coring device or a grapefruit spoon, carefully remove dough centers, leaving a bread shell at least ½ inch thick. (Reserve centers and ends for bread crumbs.) Using a narrow spoon or a pastry bag fitted with a large plain tip, pack pâté into hollow bread, taking care to avoid making air pockets. Wrap each baguette piece in foil and refrigerate until firm, 2 hours or overnight. To serve, use a serrated knife to cut into slices ⅜ to ½ inch thick. Arrange in a single layer on a basket tray or serving platter. Serve at room temperature.

274 SHERRIED PEANUT CANAPÉS

Prep: 15 minutes Cook: 18 to 22 minutes Makes: 32

¼ pound bacon (about 4 slices)
8 slices firm-textured white bread, crusts removed
½ cup peanut butter, at room temperature
1 (3-ounce) package cream cheese, softened
¼ cup medium-dry sherry

1. Preheat oven to 400°F. In a large skillet, cook bacon over medium heat until browned, 5 to 7 minutes. Drain on paper towels and chop finely.

2. Arrange bread slices in a single layer on a baking sheet. Bake until lightly toasted on top, about 5 minutes.

3. In a small bowl, combine peanut butter, cream cheese, and sherry. Mix until well blended. Stir in bacon. Spread mixture evenly over untoasted sides of bread. Bake until hot and bubbly, 8 to 10 minutes. Cut each bread slice into 4 squares or triangles. Serve warm.

275 CILANTRO PESTO TOASTS

Prep: 15 minutes Cook: 13 to 15 minutes Makes: 30

Pesto isn't just for basil anymore! And when mixed with a bit of mayonnaise, it makes a creamy and delicious topping.

2 cups cilantro (about ½ pound), well washed and dried
½ cup flat-leaf Italian parsley
1 large garlic clove
½ cup grated Parmesan cheese
⅓ cup hulled pumpkin seeds (pepitas) or pine nuts (pignoli)
1 tablespoon fresh lime juice or lemon juice
¼ cup extra-virgin olive oil
½ teaspoon salt
¼ teaspoon freshly ground pepper
¼ cup mayonnaise
30 baguette or other small French or Italian bread slices

1. Preheat oven to 350°F. In a food processor or blender, combine cilantro, parsley, garlic, Parmesan cheese, pumpkin seeds, lime juice, olive oil, salt, and pepper. Puree to a coarse paste. Add mayonnaise and blend well. (If made in advance, cover and refrigerate up to 2 days.)

2. Arrange baguette slices on a baking sheet and bake until lightly toasted on top, about 5 minutes. When cool enough to handle, spread untoasted sides of bread with 1 scant tablespoon pesto mixture and bake until hot and bubbly, 8 to 10 minutes. Serve warm.

276 CREAMY PISTACHIO BITES

Prep: 10 minutes Cook: none Makes: 16

16 slices of narrow French bread (baguette), cut ½ inch thick
½ pound soft ripe cheese, such as Bavarian blue, Brie, or Camembert
½ cup coarsely chopped pistachios

Spread each baguette slice with 1 tablespoon cheese. Top with 1½ teaspoons chopped pistachios.

277 REUBEN PUFFS

Prep: 10 minutes Cook: 7 to 10 minutes Makes: 24

Here's a classic deli sandwich turned into a hot canapé. A miniature Reuben sandwich is just the thing to enjoy with an ice-cold drink. These can be assembled as much as a day in advance and kept well covered in the refrigerator until you are ready to bake them.

¼ pound thinly sliced corned beef
2 ounces sliced Swiss cheese, cut into pieces about 2 inches in diameter
24 slices of cocktail rye bread
2 tablespoons melted butter
¼ cup Russian dressing, bottled or homemade
¼ cup drained sauerkraut
Freshly ground black pepper

1. Preheat oven to 400°F. Cut corned beef into 24 rounds about 2 inches in diameter. Cut Swiss cheese into 24 rounds about 2 inches in diameter.

2. Lightly brush both sides of bread rounds with melted butter and arrange in a single layer on a large baking sheet.

3. Spread ½ teaspoon Russian dressing over each bread slice and top with a piece of corned beef. Place ½ teaspoon sauerkraut in center of each sandwich and top with a piece of cheese.

4. Bake until cheese has melted and sandwiches are heated through, 7 to 10 minutes. Sprinkle with freshly ground black pepper before serving.

278 OPEN-FACED SHRIMPWICHES

Prep: 5 minutes Cook: 2 to 4 minutes Makes: 32

Choose your favorite cheese—Swiss, Cheddar, or Monterey Jack—or make a combination of the three. We like to lightly toast the muffins first, but it is not necessary.

1 cup firmly packed shredded cheese (about 4 ounces)
1 cup mayonnaise
¾ cup chopped cooked shrimp (about 5 ounces)
3 scallions, minced
1 teaspoon curry powder
4 English muffins, preferably sourdough, split and lightly toasted if desired

1. Preheat broiler. In a small bowl, combine cheese, mayonnaise, shrimp, scallions, and curry powder. Stir until well blended.

2. Spread mixture evenly over English muffin halves and place on a broiler rack set 4 to 6 inches from heat. Broil until hot and bubbly, 2 to 4 minutes. Cut each English muffin half into quarters and serve hot or warm.

279 ROQUEFORT ROUNDS WITH FRESH THYME

Prep: 15 minutes Cook: 13 to 15 minutes Makes: 24 to 30

24 to 30 slices of narrow French bread (baguette), cut ½ inch thick
¼ cup extra-virgin olive oil
1 (8-ounce) package cream cheese, softened
3 ounces Roquefort or other blue cheese, crumbled (about ¾ cup)
1 teaspoon brandy
1 tablespoon chopped fresh thyme or 1 teaspoon dried
¼ teaspoon freshly ground pepper
Paprika

1. Preheat oven to 400°F. Arrange baguette slices on a baking sheet and brush with oil. Bake until golden, about 5 minutes. Let cool.

2. In a small bowl, combine cream cheese, Roquefort, brandy, thyme, and pepper until well blended. Spread a generous tablespoon of filling over untoasted sides of baguette and sprinkle with paprika.

3. Bake until topping is bubbly and lightly browned, 8 to 10 minutes. Serve warm.

280 ARAM SANDWICHES

Prep: 15 minutes Rest: 45 minutes to 1 hour Cook: none
Chill: 1 hour Makes: about 24

When thin, crisp Armenian crackers (lavash) are moistened with water, they become the base for wonderful pinwheel sandwiches. Large flour tortillas can be used instead of lavash and do not require premoistening. Once you're mastered this technique, experiment with other fillings such as sliced turkey, chicken salad, or curried egg salad.

2 large (15-inch) white or wheat lavash (Armenian cracker bread)*
1 (12-ounce) container whipped cream cheese, softened
1½ tablespoons prepared white horseradish
2 teaspoons dried dill
⅔ to 1 pound thinly sliced roast beef, preferably rare, fat removed
Salt and pepper
1 small head of red leaf lettuce, leaves separated, or 2 cups alfalfa sprouts
1 small English hothouse cucumber, thinly sliced
2 medium tomatoes, thinly sliced

1. Dampen 2 kitchen towels large enough to cover lavash and wring out excess water. Hold 1 cracker under cold running water until thoroughly moistened on both sides, 30 seconds to 1 minute total. Repeat with other cracker. Stack crackers between damp towels and cover with plastic wrap to prevent drying. Let stand until soft and pliable but not soggy, 45 minutes to 1 hour. (Check often, and sprinkle with water if any parts of cracker have dried.)

2. In a small bowl or in food processor, combine cream cheese, horseradish, and dill. Mix until well blended.

3. Lay 1 cracker browned-side up and spread half of dilled cream cheese over top. Arrange a thin layer of roast beef over cheese and season with salt and pepper to taste. Top with half of lettuce leaves, cucumber slices, and tomato. Roll up cracker jelly-roll fashion, gently but firmly to avoid air pockets. Repeat with second cracker and remaining filling. Wrap rolls securely in plastic wrap and refrigerate at least 1 hour or as long as 8 hours.

4. Remove plastic wrap and use a serrated knife to trim ends. Cut rolls into slices about 1 inch thick. Arrange flat on a platter and serve slightly chilled.

* *Available at Middle Eastern delicatessens, specialty food markets, and some supermarkets.*

Chapter 11

New Wave Recipes

That "wave" is the microwave, of course. For appetizers that cook in a flash, every smart cook turns to the microwave oven. And even if it's no longer quite so new, these easy and quick recipes are. With a little advance planning, these "zappetizers" can emerge from your kitchen in record time. Another effort-saving advantage is that when foods are cooked and served in one microwave-safe dish, cleanup is kept to a minimum.

Keep in mind that for successful individual appetizers, it's best to begin with bite-size pieces of uniform size and shape. The microwave can also be a useful tool for rewarming appetizers that have cooled on the buffet. Reheat them in the microwave on High, checking every 30 seconds until heated through.

And remember that microwave ovens are great for defrosting frozen appetizers. There's a whole generation of kids out there whose first cooking experience begins with the microwave. For that reason, this chapter provides plenty of simple snacks for kids of all ages to heat and eat. From Bagel Chips to Enchilada Swirls, these appetizers come together faster than you can say MTV.

281 GOAT CHEESE MARINARA

Prep: 3 minutes Cook: 3 minutes Serves: 6

Ren Rothman, who gave us this recipe, is a creative woman known for serving sensational appetizers with style. Whether spread on crostini or crackers, we guarantee love at first bite with this one.

- **1 (14-ounce) jar marinara sauce**
- **1 (5- to 7-ounce) log of goat cheese, such as Montrachet**
- **1 tablespoon chopped fresh basil (optional)**

1. Pour marinara sauce into a shallow glass or ceramic serving dish.

2. Cut goat cheese into ½-inch rounds and arrange in a single layer over sauce. Top with chopped basil. Microwave on Medium 3 minutes, or until sauce is bubbly-hot and cheese is softened. Serve at once.

282 BLACK BEAN TARTLETS

Prep: 5 minutes Cook: 6 minutes Makes: 20

Canned beans are a boon to the busy cook. With the contrast of the black beans flecked with red onion and green chiles and the white of the sour cream, these make a stunning presentation.

- **½ cup minced red onion**
- **1 tablespoon minced fresh hot green chili**
- **3 garlic cloves, minced**
- **2 tablespoons vegetable oil**
- **1 teaspoon oregano**
- **2 teaspoons chili powder**
- **1 cup canned black beans, rinsed and drained**
- **1½ teaspoons cider vinegar**
- **½ teaspoon salt**
- **⅛ teaspoon pepper**
- **20 purchased 2-inch tartlet shells or Toast Cups (page 29)**
- **⅓ cup sour cream**

1. In medium microwave-safe bowl, combine red onion, green chile, garlic, oil, oregano, and chili powder. Microwave on High 3 minutes.

2. Stir in black beans, vinegar, salt, and pepper. Microwave on High 3 minutes, stirring once. Let cool to room temperature.

3. Shortly before serving, spoon black bean filling into tartlet shells. Garnish each tartlet with about ¾ teaspoon sour cream. Serve at room temperature.

283 BAGEL CHIPS

Prep: 5 minutes Cook: 10 minutes Makes: 24 to 30

These are wonderful for nibbling just by themselves, or with a soft cheese spread or savory topping, such as Smoked Salmon Spread with Scotch and Chives (page 17).

4 bagels
⅓ cup olive oil
Salt (optional)

1. Using a serrated knife, cut bagels horizontally into thin slices about ⅛ inch thick. Brush both sides of slices lightly with oil. Arrange on a microwave roast rack.

2. Microwave on Medium, turning once, about 10 minutes, or until both sides of bagel are crisp. Season, if desired, with salt to taste.

284 CHEERY BEERY FONDUE

Prep: 5 minutes Cook: 14 minutes Makes: 3½ cups

This is a great way to use leftover beer. The sharper the Cheddar cheese, the better in this tangy fondue. Serve with a basket of crusty French, Italian, or sourdough bread cubes and long forks for dipping.

1 tablespoon vegetable oil
1 garlic clove, minced
2 tablespoons flour
¾ cup flat beer
⅛ teaspoon hot pepper sauce
1 tablespoon Dijon mustard
4 cups shredded sharp Cheddar cheese (about 1 pound)

1. In a 2-quart microwave-safe crock or casserole, combine oil and garlic. Microwave on High 90 seconds, or until garlic is tender. Stir in flour until blended with oil, then stir in beer and hot sauce. Microwave on High about 3 minutes, stirring once, until boiling.

2. Stir in mustard and cheese. Microwave on Medium about 10 minutes, stirring every 2 minutes, until cheese is melted and smooth. Transfer to a fondue pot and serve at once.

285 FAST CHILI DIP

Prep: 2 minutes Cook: 2 minutes Makes: 3 cups

Unexpected guests pose no problem when you keep these pantry staples handy. Serve with crunchy tortilla chips. This dip reheats easily.

1 (15-ounce) can chili con carne without beans
1 (8-ounce) jar Cheez Whiz
1 tablespoon taco seasoning (optional)

Place chili, cheese, and taco seasoning in a glass serving dish. Microwave on Medium 2 minutes, until cheese is melted. Stir and serve at once.

286 PUB CHIPS

Prep: 2 minutes Cook: 10 minutes Serves: 1

Here's an appetizer with the tart and salty flavor of classic English fish and chips—without the fish!

1 large baking potato (8 to 10 ounces)
Malt vinegar and salt

1. Scrub potato and dry well. Leaving skin on, slice into ¼-inch rounds.

2. Place slices on a microwave roasting rack. Microwave on High 10 minutes, or until chips begin to brown. Sprinkle with malt vinegar and salt to taste.

287 MICROWAVE CLAM DIP

Prep: 3 minutes Cook: 2½ minutes Makes: 1½ cups

1 (7-ounce) can minced clams
1 cup grated sharp Cheddar cheese
¼ cup minced scallions
Dash of garlic powder
1 teaspoon Worcestershire sauce
1 tablespoon chopped parsley
1 tablespoon chopped ripe olives

1. Drain off and reserve ¼ cup clam juice; discard remainder. Combine all ingredients in 3- to 4-cup glass casserole. Stir well.

2. Microwave on Medium 2½ minutes, stirring occasionally, until hot. Serve at once. To reheat as needed, cover with a paper towel to prevent spattering, and microwave 1 minute or less.

288 EASY EGGPLANT SPREAD

Prep: 5 minutes Cook: 8 minutes Makes: 1½ cups

Make this ahead when you have a few minutes. It will keep for days in the refrigerator.

1 large eggplant
½ teaspoon ground allspice
½ teaspoon garlic salt
½ teaspoon salt
1 tomato, finely chopped
2 teaspoons minced onion
2 tablespoons olive oil
2 teaspoons lemon juice

1. Wash eggplant and cut off green cap. Prick skin in several places with a fork. Place on a microwave-safe paper plate and microwave on High 7 to 8 minutes, turning plate 180° halfway through cooking time. Most of skin will turn from purple to brown and will feel soft. Let cool.

2. Cut eggplant in half. Scoop insides into a food processor bowl; discard peel. Add allspice, garlic salt, salt, tomato, onion, olive oil, and lemon juice. Puree until smooth. Serve chilled with raw vegetables for dipping.

289 CHEESY SPAGHETTI DIP

Prep: 3 minutes Cook: 3 minutes Makes: 2 cups

This one's for the kids. They love this fast fondue-style appetizer. Dippers can range from bread sticks to mini hot dogs to French fries.

¼ pound pasteurized process cheese spread, cubed
½ cup spaghetti sauce
½ cup milk

In a microwave-safe bowl, combine cheese spread, spaghetti sauce, and milk. Microwave on High 3 minutes, stirring after each minute, until heated through and well blended. Serve hot.

290 INSTANT CHEESE FONDUE

Prep: 3 minutes Cook: 3 minutes Makes: 3 cups

Put this fast dip in a fondue pot to keep warm or simply reheat for 30 seconds in the microwave when it cools.

2 cans (10¾ ounces each) Cheddar cheese soup
½ cup dry white wine
1 teaspoon Worcestershire sauce
¼ cup ketchup

1. Put all ingredients in a medium microwave-safe bowl or casserole. Whisk to blend well.

2. Microwave on Medium 3 minutes, stirring often. Whisk until smooth and serve at once.

291 ENCHILADA SWIRLS

Prep: 10 minutes Cook: 2 to 3 minutes Makes: 16

- **1 cup shredded Monterey Jack cheese (about 4 ounces)**
- **1 (4-ounce) can chopped green chiles**
- **1 medium tomato, peeled, seeded, and chopped**
- **½ cup chopped red onion**
- **4 (6-inch) corn tortillas**

1. In a small bowl, combine cheese, chiles, tomato, and red onion. Toss until well mixed.

2. Stack tortillas and wrap in a microwave-safe paper towel. Microwave on High for 30 seconds, or until softened. Remove from paper towel and lay each tortilla flat on a clean work surface. Spread cheese mixture evenly over tortillas. Roll up tortillas jelly-roll fashion and place seam-side down on a microwave-safe platter.

3. Cover enchiladas with a microwave-safe paper towel and microwave on High 2 minutes, or until cheese is melted. Let stand 2 minutes, then cut each enchilada into 4 pieces.

292 CHEESY STUFFED MUSHROOMS

Prep: 5 minutes Cook: 1½ minutes Makes: 16

If you place these under a conventional broiler for a few minutes after they are cooked, they turn a lovely golden brown. If time is of the essence, just serve them after stuffing.

- **16 large mushrooms, 1½ inches in diameter (about ¾ pound)**
- **1½ tablespoons minced scallion**
- **2 teaspoons butter**
- **½ cup grated Parmesan cheese**
- **½ cup small-curd cottage cheese**
- **½ teaspoon Worcestershire sauce**
- **½ teaspoon salt**
- **¼ teaspoon pepper**

1. Trim ends of mushrooms. Pull out mushroom stems and finely chop. Put mushroom caps stem-side up on a microwave-safe glass plate. Sprinkle lightly with 1 teaspoon water. Cover with microwave-safe plastic wrap. Microwave on High 1½ minutes. Drain and pat bottoms dry with paper towels.

2. In a small bowl, combine chopped mushroom stems, scallion, and butter. Cover with microwave-safe plastic wrap. Microwave on High 1 minute. Stir in Parmesan cheese, cottage cheese, Worcestershire, salt, and pepper. Stuff caps with this mixture and serve at room temperature.

293 MUSHROOM TARTLETS

Prep: 5 minutes Cook: 12 minutes Makes: 18

To clean mushrooms, simply wipe with a damp towel. The filling for these tartlets can be made a day ahead.

- **½ pound mushrooms**
- **4 scallions, minced**
- **3 garlic cloves, minced**
- **3 tablespoons butter**
- **¼ cup plus 1½ tablespoons chopped parsley**
- **3 tablespoons dry sherry**
- **¼ teaspoon salt**
- **⅛ teaspoon pepper**
- **18 purchasd 2-inch tartlet shells or Toast Cups (page 29)**

1. Finely chop mushrooms. In medium microwave-safe bowl, place mushrooms, scallions, garlic, and butter. Microwave on High 6 minutes, stirring occasionally.

2. Stir ¼ cup chopped parsley, sherry, salt, and pepper into mushrooms. Microwave on High 6 minutes, stirring occasionally.

3. Shortly before serving, spoon mushroom filling into tartlet shells. Sprinkle remaining 1½ tablespoons parsley over tops. Serve at room temperature.

294 MICROWAVE MIX

Prep: 5 minutes Cook: 9 minutes Makes: 9½ cups

Here is a traditional munchie made easy in the microwave.

- **6 tablespoons butter**
- **4 teaspoons Worcestershire sauce**
- **1 tablespoon garlic salt**
- **1 teaspoon celery salt**
- **1 teaspoon onion salt**
- **2 cups Corn Chex cereal**
- **2 cups Rice Chex cereal**
- **2 cups Cheerios cereal**
- **2 cups thin pretzels**
- **1½ cups mixed nuts**

1. Place butter, Worcestershire, garlic salt, celery salt, and onion salt in a 13x9x2-inch glass baking dish. Microwave on Medium-High 3 minutes, or until butter melts.

2. Add cereals, pretzels, and nuts. Stir to coat thoroughly. Microwave on High 3 minutes. Stir and microwave on High 3 minutes longer. Let cool before serving. Store in an airtight container.

295 SPICED GARBANZOS

Prep: 5 minutes Cook: 20 to 25 minutes Makes: 1 cup to serve 4

- **1 (15-ounce) can chick-peas (garbanzo beans)**
- **¼ teaspoon chili powder**
- **¼ teaspoon ground cumin**
- **¼ teaspoon crushed hot red pepper**
- **¼ teaspoon coarse (kosher) salt**

1. Rinse chick-peas in a sieve under cold running water. Drain well and pat dry. Arrange chick-peas in a single layer on a paper towel on a microwave-safe pie plate; cover with another paper towel. Microwave on High 10 minutes. Turn dish halfway around and continue cooking until crisp, 10 to 15 minutes longer.

2. In a small bowl, combine chick-peas with chili powder, cumin, hot pepper, and salt until well mixed. If made in advance, store airtight up to 3 days.

296 ASHLEY'S NUTTY TREAT

Prep: 5 minutes Cook: 2 minutes Makes: 2 cups

Serve a firm cracker with this nutty favorite. Almonds or walnuts work equally well.

- **1 (8-ounce) package cream cheese**
- **2 tablespoons milk**
- **½ cup sour cream**
- **¼ cup finely chopped green pepper**
- **2 tablespoons minced onion**
- **½ teaspoon garlic salt**
- **¼ teaspoon pepper**
- **1 tablespoon butter**
- **½ cup coarsely chopped pecans**
- **½ teaspoon salt**

1. Put cream cheese in a small microwave-safe casserole suitable for serving. Microwave on Low 45 seconds, or just until softened. Whisk in milk and sour cream. Stir in green pepper, onion, garlic salt, and pepper. Mix well.

2. Place butter in a small microwave-safe bowl. Microwave on Medium 30 seconds to melt. Add nuts and salt. Toss to coat well. Spoon nuts over cheese mixture.

3. Microwave on High 1 minute, or until hot. Serve at once.

297 BEN'S POPEYE TART

Prep: 5 minutes Cook: 13 minutes Serves: 10

This easy tart tastes so good it makes spinach lovers out of teenagers. Use prepackaged and washed spinach to save time.

2 tablespoons butter
¼ teaspoon dried basil
¼ teaspoon dried oregano
½ cup finely chopped onion
2 cups shredded fresh spinach
1 tablespoon flour
1 cup shredded Monterey Jack cheese (about 4 ounces)
1 can (5 ounces) evaporated milk
4 eggs, beaten
Pinch of nutmeg
Pinch of cayenne
1 teaspoon salt

1. Place butter in an 8-inch round glass cake or pie pan. Microwave on Medium-High 30 seconds, or until melted. Add basil, oregano, and onion. Microwave on High 1 minute. Add spinach. Microwave on High 1 minute.

2. In a medium bowl, toss together flour and cheese. Add evaporated milk, egg, nutmeg, cayenne, and salt. Blend well. Stir into spinach mixture. Microwave on Medium 12 minutes, stirring after 6 minutes. Remove from oven. Let stand 10 minutes before serving.

298 NACHO POTATO SLICES

Prep: 5 minutes Cook: 10 minutes Makes: 24

This is a "natural" nacho, which cuts the calories found in the traditional chip version.

2 large baking potatoes (about 1¼ pounds total)
Salt
⅓ cup chopped scallions
1 (4-ounce) can chopped green chiles
½ cup salsa, bottled or homemade
1 (2¼-ounce) can sliced black olives
½ cup shredded Cheddar or Monterey Jack cheese

1. Scrub potatoes, trim ends, and cut into slices ⅜ inch thick. In a microwave-safe dish, arrange potato slices in a single layer. Season lightly with salt. Top with scallions and chiles. Cover with microwave-safe plastic wrap, turning a corner back to allow steam to escape. Microwave on High 8 to 10 minutes, until potatoes are tender.

2. Drizzle salsa over potato slices, then sprinkle with olives and cheese. Microwave uncovered on Medium, 1 minute, or until cheese is melted. Serve hot.

299 HOT SHRIMP APPETIZER

Prep: 5 minutes Cook: 2 minutes Makes: 1½ cups

This will disappear even faster than you can make it. Serve with crackers.

1 cup tiny shelled cooked shrimp, about 8 ounces
3 tablespoons chopped scallions
1 (3-ounce) package cream cheese
½ cup mayonnaise
2 tablespoons chili sauce

1. Reserve a few shrimp and 1 tablespoon chopped scallions for garnish. Place cream cheese in a 2-cup microwave-safe dish. Microwave on high 30 seconds to soften.

2. Stir in mayonnaise, chili sauce, remaining 2 tablespoons chopped scallions, and shrimp. Cover loosely with microwave-safe plastic wrap.

3. Microwave on High 1½ minutes, or until heated through. Garnish with reserved shrimp and scallions. Serve hot.

300 SNAPPY SHRIMP DIP

Prep: 5 minutes Cook: 2 minutes Makes: 1½ cups

1 small garlic clove, minced
1 (10¾-ounce) can shrimp soup
½ pound Swiss cheese, grated
2 tablespoons dry sherry

1. Put garlic, soup, cheese, and sherry into microwave-safe bowl without mixing. Microwave on Medium 1 minute. Stir. Microwave on Medium 1 to 2 minutes longer, until very hot. Serve immediately.

2. If necessary to reheat after being served, cover with a paper towel or wax paper. Microwave on Low 1 to 2 minutes, depending on quantity remaining in bowl.

301 BASIL TOMATO TARTLETS

Prep: 5 minutes Cook: 4 minutes Makes: 20

These are best made with the luscious red tomatoes at the end of summer. Chopped fresh basil makes a wonderful garnish.

- **3 medium tomatoes**
- **3 garlic cloves, minced**
- **1 medium celery rib, minced**
- **2 tablespoons grated Parmesan cheese**
- **1 tablespoon pesto, prepared or homemade (page 159)**
- **½ teaspoon salt**
- **⅛ teaspoon pepper**
- **20 purchased 2-inch tartlet shells or Toast Cups (page 29)**

1. Seed and chop tomatoes. In medium microwave-safe bowl, combine tomatoes, garlic, and celery. Microwave on High a total of 4 minutes, stirring 2 or 3 times.

2. Stir Parmesan cheese, pesto, salt, and pepper into tomato mixture. Let cool. Spoon filling into tartlets. Serve at room temperature.

302 PARMESAN ZUCCHINI STICKS

Prep: 5 minutes Cook: 5 minutes Makes: 24

- **3 medium zucchini (about 1 pound)**
- **½ cup grated Parmesan cheese**
- **½ cup fine dry bread crumbs**
- **½ teaspoon garlic salt**
- **½ teaspoon freshly ground pepper**
- **⅓ cup olive oil**

1. Trim ends of zucchini, then cut into 3-inch lengths. Quarter each piece of zucchini lengthwise.

2. In a medium bowl, combine cheese, bread crumbs, garlic salt, and pepper. Toss to blend well. Pour oil into a shallow dish.

3. Dip zucchini pieces in oil, then roll in cheese mixture to coat. Arrange in a single layer on a microwave-safe plate. Microwave on High 5 minutes, or until crisp-tender.

303 CHRIS'S EASY CHEESY PRETZELS

Prep: 3 minutes Cook: 3 minutes Serves: 4

It doesn't matter what size pretzel you use. All work equally well.

1 package (8 ounces) unsliced process American cheese
½ cup light cream
½ teaspoon hot pepper sauce
8 ounces pretzels
1 tablespoon poppy seeds or toasted sesame seeds

1. Cut cheese into 1-inch cubes. Place in a medium microwave-safe bowl and add cream and hot sauce. Microwave on Medium 2 to 3 minutes, stirring often, until cheese is melted.

2. Dip half of each pretzel into cheese and then sprinkle with seeds. Place on wax paper and let stand until firm, about 5 minutes.

Chapter 12

Dipping Into the Chafing Dish and Fondue Pot

When our mothers married, they probably received silver chafing dishes as wedding gifts. By the time many of us set up our own households, lifestyles had become more casual, and stainless steel and enameled fondue pots were all the rage. (If you don't believe us, check out the garage sales in your neighborhood next Saturday morning.)

Like so many food fads that took the world by storm, a good thing was done to death, until a flicker of fire on a cocktail buffet became the most dreaded cliché. But when you really think about it, what's so wrong about a few friends huddled over a bubbling pot of savory sauce, dipping and dunking and talking the night away? It all depends on what's in the pot.

This chapter offers an assortment of hot dips, sauced meatballs, and melts that will haul your Sterno out of storage. From Sour Cream Beef Bites and Chunky Clam Rarebit to Meatballs in Creamy Mushroom Sauce and Parmesan Fondue with Pesto, there's a dunk here for every sort of dipper.

When setting out a lighted chafing dish or fondue pot, just keep a few tips in mind:

- Set the pot in a strategic place so that it is in no danger of being tipped over and no one has to reach over the flame for another dish.
- Set out plenty of long-handled forks, or small plates and cocktail forks, or the appropriate dipper, such as raw vegetables or bread cubes, on either side of the pot if possible, so more than one person can dip in at once.
- If a dip can become too hot, such as the olive oil and butter–based Bagna Cauda, monitor the flame frequently and warn guests to be careful not to burn their tongues.

304 SPICY TOMATO FONDUE

Prep: 10 minutes Cook: 10 minutes Serves: 8 to 10

Serve this low-calorie fondue with celery sticks or chunks of French bread for dipping.

- **1 (28-ounce) can whole tomatoes**
- **1 tablespoon cornstarch**
- **1 medium onion, chopped**
- **3 tablespoons vegetable oil**
- **1¼ cups chopped green bell peppers**
- **1 tablespoon white wine vinegar**
- **2 teaspoons Worcestershire sauce**
- **1 teaspoon salt**

1. Drain tomatoes, reserving ¼ cup of liquid. Chop tomatoes. In a small bowl, stir cornstarch into reserved tomato liquid.

2. In a medium nonreactive saucepan, cook onion in oil over medium heat until softened but not browned, 3 to 4 minutes. Add chopped tomatoes, bell peppers, vinegar, Worcestershire, salt, and tomato-cornstarch mixture to onion. Bring to a boil and cook, stirring frequently, until slightly thickened, about 5 minutes. Transfer to a small chafing dish or fondue pot.

305 SOUR CREAM BEEF BITES

Prep: 15 minutes Cook: 1½ hours Serves: 8

This tasty answer to "Where's the beef?" has been a favorite of military wives for years.

- **2 pounds boneless beef chuck roast**
- **½ cup flour**
- **¼ cup vegetable oil**
- **2 onions, thinly sliced**
- **½ cup sour cream**
- **¼ cup shredded Cheddar cheese**
- **1 teaspoon salt**
- **½ teaspoon pepper**

1. Cut beef into 1-inch cubes, then roll in flour. In a large frying pan, heat 2 tablespoons oil over medium-high heat. Add half of beef cubes and cook, turning, until browned all over, 5 to 7 minutes. Remove with a slotted spoon and drain on paper towels. Repeat with remaining oil and beef. Pour off all fat, then return beef to pan.

2. In a medium bowl, combine onions, sour cream, cheese, salt, pepper, and ½ cup water; blend well. Pour over beef. Simmer over medium-low heat, covered, until beef is tender, about 1½ hours. Serve in a heated chafing dish with toothpicks.

306 SWEET AND SPICY PUPS

Prep: 5 minutes Cook: 20 minutes Serves: 6 to 8

This simple preparation has delighted people for years—probably because no one can identify the unlikely combination of ingredients.

1 cup currant jelly
⅓ cup mustard
1 pound frankfurters

1. In a small saucepan, cook jelly and mustard over low heat, stirring frequently, until jelly has melted, about 5 minutes.

2. Cut frankfurters into diagonal slices about ½ inch thick. Add to sauce and cook until heated through, about 5 minutes. Transfer to chafing dish and serve with toothpicks.

307 DRUNKEN DOGGIES

Prep: 5 minutes Cook: 35 minutes Serves: 6 to 8

This roundup of ingredients is sure to win the approval of adult hot dog lovers.

1 cup bourbon
½ cup ketchup
½ cup brown sugar
1 pound frankfurters

1. In a medium nonreactive saucepan, combine bourbon, ketchup, and brown sugar. Cook over medium-low heat, stirring frequently, until brown sugar has dissolved and mixture has thickened slightly, about 30 minutes.

2. Cut frankfurters into diagonal slices about ½ inch thick. Add to sauce and cook until heated through, about 5 minutes. Transfer to a chafing dish and serve with toothpicks.

308 CREAMY PIZZA FONDUE

Prep: 10 minutes Cook: 10 to 14 minutes Serves: 12

Especially popular with teenagers. Serve with bread sticks or chunks of Italian bread with long forks.

½ pound ground round (85% lean)
1 small onion, chopped
1 tablespoon melted butter or olive oil
2 (10-ounce) cans pizza sauce
1 tablespoon cornstarch
2 teaspoons dried oregano
½ teaspoon garlic powder
2½ cups shredded Cheddar cheese (about 10 ounces)
1 cup shredded mozzarella cheese (about 4 ounces)

1. In a large frying pan, cook ground beef and onion in butter over medium heat, stirring to break up lumps of meat, until beef is browned and onion is softened, 5 to 7 minutes.

2. In a medium bowl, combine pizza sauce, cornstarch, oregano, and garlic powder. Stir until well mixed. Add to ground beef mixture in pan and cook, stirring occasionally, until mixture thickens and bubbles, 5 to 7 minutes.

3. Reduce heat to low and add cheeses, a third at a time, stirring well after each addition. Transfer to a chafing dish or fondue pot.

309 CREAMY BAGNA CAUDA

Prep: 20 minutes Cook: 8 minutes Serves: 12

A creamy Northern Italian version, sure to become an entertaining favorite. Note that an entire head of garlic goes into this aromatic sauce.

1 medium head of garlic, coarsely chopped
2 sticks (8 ounces) butter
3 (2-ounce) cans flat anchovy fillets, drained and chopped
2 cups light cream
1 cup heavy cream
Assorted raw vegetables and thinly sliced Italian or French bread

1. In a medium saucepan, cook garlic in 1 stick of butter over medium heat until fragrant, about 3 minutes. Add anchovies and reduce heat to low. Cook, stirring, until anchovies dissolve into a paste.

2. Add remaining butter, light cream, and heavy cream. Cook until butter melts and mixture is heated through, about 5 minutes. Pour into a fondue pot.

3. Serve bagna cauda with a basket of raw vegetables and another basket containing bread. Swirl vegetables in sauce, then hold a slice of bread (your edible napkin) under the vegetables to catch any dribbles.

310 CHUNKY CLAM RAREBIT

Prep: 10 minutes Cook: 10 minutes Serves: 8 to 10

The subtle flavor of clams makes this a favorite with shellfish lovers. Serve with crackers or French bread.

- **3 tablespoons butter**
- **½ cup chopped green bell pepper**
- **½ cup chopped mushrooms**
- **3 tablespoons flour**
- **1 (28-ounce) can Italian peeled tomatoes, crushed, with liquid**
- **1 cup milk**
- **2 cups shredded Cheddar cheese (about 8 ounces)**
- **1 tablespoon Dijon mustard**
- **1 teaspoon Worcestershire sauce**
- **2 (6½-ounce) cans minced clams, with liquid**

1. In a large saucepan, melt butter over medium heat. Stir in green pepper and mushrooms and cook until softened but not browned, about 5 minutes.

2. Stir in flour. Cook, stirring, 1 minute. Gradually add tomatoes and their liquid, stirring constantly. Add milk, cheese, mustard, Worcestershire, and clams with liquid and cook, stirring, until heated through and cheese has melted, about 5 minutes. Transfer to a chafing dish or fondue pot.

311 BEEF AND TOMATO FONDUE

Prep: 10 minutes Cook: 10 minutes Serves: 8 to 10

This hearty fondue is great with chunks of French or Italian bread for dipping.

- **1½ pounds ground round (85% lean)**
- **½ cup chopped onion**
- **1 tablespoon vegetable oil**
- **1 (14½-ounce) can whole tomatoes, drained and chopped**
- **2 tablespoons tomato paste**
- **1 tablespoon chopped fresh thyme leaves or 1 teaspoon dried**
- **1 garlic clove, minced**
- **1 teaspoon chili powder**
- **1 teaspoon salt**
- **½ teaspoon ground cumin**
- **¼ teaspoon Worcestershire sauce**
- **⅛ teaspoon hot pepper sauce**

1. In a medium saucepan, cook beef and onion in oil over medium heat, stirring to break up lumps of meat, until beef is no longer pink inside and browned outside, about 5 minutes. Drain off fat.

2. Return pan to heat and stir in tomatoes, tomato paste, thyme, garlic, chili powder, salt, cumin, Worcestershire, and hot sauce. Simmer 5 minutes. Transfer to a chafing dish or fondue pot.

312 SWEET AND SOUR PORK

Prep: 30 minutes Cook: 8 to 10 minutes Serves: 6 to 8

- **1 egg**
- **2 tablespoons dry vermouth or sherry**
- **¼ cup plus 1 tablespoon soy sauce**
- **3 tablespoons flour**
- **2 tablespoons cornstarch**
- **2 to 4 cups peanut or corn oil, plus 3 tablespoons**
- **1 pound lean boneless pork, cut into ¾-inch cubes**
- **3 green bell peppers, cut into ¾-inch squares**
- **1 onion, cut into 8 wedges**
- **1 garlic clove, minced**
- **¼ cup ketchup**
- **2 tablespoons red wine vinegar**
- **⅓ cup (packed) brown sugar**
- **1 teaspoon grated fresh ginger**
- **1 (20-ounce) can pineapple chunks, drained**

1. In a medium bowl, beat egg until smooth. Whisk in 1 tablespoon dry vermouth and 1 tablespoon soy sauce until well blended. Mix in flour and 1 tablespoon cornstarch. In a wok or large saucepan, heat 1 inch of oil to 360°F on a deep-frying thermometer. Toss pork cubes in egg batter and deep-fry, a few at a time, until crisp on the outside and cooked through with no trace of pink in the center, 2 to 3 minutes. Remove with a skimmer or slotted spoon and drain on paper towels.

2. In a wok or large frying pan, heat 3 tablespoons oil. Add bell peppers, onion, and garlic and cook over medium-high heat until softened but not browned, 2 to 3 minutes. Remove with a slotted spoon and set aside. Add ketchup, ¼ cup soy sauce, vinegar, 1 tablespoon vermouth, brown sugar, and ginger to wok and bring to a boil. In a small bowl, combine remaining 1 tablespoon cornstarch with ⅓ cup water. Stir until well blended; stir into sauce mixture. Bring to a boil, stirring constantly, until thickened, about 2 minutes. Stir in pineapple, pork, and reserved vegetables. Transfer to a chafing dish and serve with toothpicks.

313 SONNY'S SLOPPY FONDUE

Prep: 5 minutes Cook: 5 minutes Serves: 8

- **1 (15¼-ounce) can barbecue sauce and beef for Sloppy Joes**
- **½ teaspoon powdered onion**
- **½ teaspoon dried oregano**
- **½ teaspoon pepper**
- **1 cup shredded process American cheese**
- **French bread cubes or crisp raw vegetables**

In a medium saucepan, combine Sloppy Joe mixture, powdered onion, oregano, pepper, and cheese. Cook over low heat, stirring constantly, until cheese melts and mixture is heated through. Transfer to a small chafing dish or fondue pot. Serve with bread cubes or crisp raw vegetables.

314 BAGNA CAUDA

Prep: 5 minutes Cook: 10 minutes Serves: 6 to 8

This Italian "hot bath" is the ideal dunk for raw, blanched or grilled vegetables, bread chunks or bread sticks, and even cooked and peeled shrimp. Anchovy aficionados can dispense with draining them; simply add the entire contents of the anchovy tin to the pot.

- **4 tablespoons butter**
- **¾ cup extra-virgin olive oil**
- **4 large garlic cloves, minced**
- **1 (2-ounce) can flat anchovy fillets, drained (if desired) and chopped**
- **Dash of salt**

1. In a small pot, melt butter in olive oil over medium-low heat.

2. Stir in garlic, anchovies, and salt and cook until garlic is fragrant and anchovies dissolve, about 5 minutes. Transfer to a fondue pot and serve warm, not hot.

315 WELSH RAREBIT FONDUE

Prep: 10 minutes Cook: 5 to 7 minutes Serves: 8 to 10

This silken dipping sauce is great with Crostini (page 150) or bread sticks, cubes of cooked ham, or vegetables such as cauliflower or broccoli. For a heartier fondue, stir in 4 bacon slices, cooked and chopped, and/or 1 large tomato, peeled, seeded, and chopped.

- **1 pound sharp Cheddar cheese, shredded (about 4 cups)**
- **1½ tablespoons cornstarch**
- **½ teaspoon sugar**
- **½ teaspoon dry mustard**
- **1 tablespoon unsalted butter**
- **1 cup flat beer**
- **½ teaspoon Worcestershire sauce**
- **⅛ teaspoon cayenne**

1. In a large bowl, toss cheese with cornstarch, sugar, and mustard until well mixed.

2. In a medium saucepan, melt butter in beer over medium heat. Bring to a boil, reduce heat to low, and gradually stir in cheese mixture, melting each addition before adding more. Stir in Worcestershire and cayenne. Transfer to a fondue pot and serve warm, not hot.

316 MEATBALLS IN CREAMY MUSHROOM SAUCE

Prep: 30 minutes Cook: 11 to 14 minutes Serves: 10 to 12

- **1 small onion, finely chopped**
- **2 teaspoons olive oil or butter**
- **1 garlic clove, minced**
- **1 slice firm-textured white bread, torn into pieces**
- **⅓ cup milk or water**
- **½ pound lean ground pork or turkey**
- **½ pound ground chuck (80% lean)**
- **1 egg, beaten**
- **1½ teaspoons salt**
- **½ teaspoon freshly ground pepper**
- **¼ teaspoon grated nutmeg**
- **Creamy Mushroom Sauce (recipe follows)**

1. Preheat oven to 450°F. In a medium frying pan, cook onion in olive oil over medium heat until softened but not browned, 2 to 3 minutes. Stir in garlic and cook until just fragrant, 30 seconds to 1 minute longer. Let cool. In a small bowl, soak bread in milk to soften.

2. In a large bowl, combine ground pork, ground chuck, sautéed onion and garlic, softened bread with its liquid, egg, salt, pepper, and nutmeg. Blend until well mixed. Form into meatballs about 1 inch in diameter and arrange in a single layer on a greased jelly-roll pan.

3. Bake in the upper third of oven, shaking pan once or twice, until meatballs are nicely browned and cooked through but still juicy, 8 to 10 minutes. (If made in advance, let cool, cover, and refrigerate up to 3 days. Freeze for longer storage.) In a chafing dish, combine meatballs with warm creamy mushroom sauce. Serve with toothpicks or small plates and cocktail forks.

CREAMY MUSHROOM SAUCE

Makes: 2 cups

- **2 tablespoons butter**
- **3 shallots, minced**
- **½ pound cultivated white button or wild mushrooms, whole or halved**
- **2 tablespoons brandy**
- **⅓ cup dry red wine**
- **3 tablespoons heavy cream**
- **1½ cups brown beef gravy, purchased or homemade**
- **1½ teaspoons chopped fresh thyme leaves, or ½ teaspoon dried**
- **Salt and freshly ground pepper**

1. In a large frying pan, melt butter over medium heat. Add shallots and cook until softened but not browned, 1 to 2 minutes. Stir in mushrooms and cook until mushroom liquid is exuded and then evaporates, about 3 to 5 minutes. Add brandy and, standing back, ignite with a long-handled match. When flames subside, add wine and bring to a boil. Continue cooking until liquid reduces by half, 3 to 5 minutes.

2. Whisk in cream and gravy and bring to a boil. Cook until sauce is just thick enough to coat back of a spoon, about 5 minutes. Stir in thyme and season with salt and pepper to taste.

317 PARMESAN FONDUE WITH PESTO

Prep: 5 minutes Cook: 5 minutes Makes: about 4 cups

Using natural cream cheese, found in most delicatessen and cheese shops, makes this divine creation even creamier. Instead of pesto, you may want to try topping the fondue with a bit of chopped scallion or fresh herbs.

- **1 pound natural cream cheese, softened**
- **2 cups light cream**
- **1½ cups freshly grated Parmesan cheese (about 6 ounces)**
- **¼ teaspoon freshly ground white pepper**
- **Dash of salt**
- **⅓ cup pesto, purchased or homemade (page 159)**
- **1 (1-pound) loaf French or Italian bread, cut into 1-inch cubes**
- **Crisp raw vegetables**

1. Melt cream cheese in the top of a medium double boiler set over simmering water. Gradually stir in light cream until mixture is smooth and heated through.

2. Mix in Parmesan cheese, stirring until cheese melts and thickens the sauce. Season with pepper and salt. Transfer to a fondue pot. Swirl pesto on top. Serve with bread cubes and/or crisp raw vegetables for dipping.

318 CREAMY BROCCOLI DIP

Prep: 10 minutes Cook: 3 to 5 minutes Serves: 8

- **2 (8-ounce) packages processed garlic cheese**
- **1 (10½-ounce) can condensed cream of mushroom soup**
- **1 stick (4 ounces) butter, cut into bits**
- **1 small onion, diced**
- **2 tablespoons Worcestershire sauce**
- **Dash of hot pepper sauce**
- **½ teaspoon salt**
- **¼ teaspoon freshly ground pepper**
- **1 (10-ounce) package frozen chopped broccoli, thawed and drained**

1. In a medium saucepan, combine garlic cheese, mushroom soup, butter, onion, Worcestershire sauce, hot sauce, salt, and pepper. Cook over medium heat, stirring, until cheese is melted and mixture is well blended, 3 to 5 minutes.

2. Stir broccoli into cheese mixture. Transfer to a fondue pot for serving.

319 SPICY COCKTAIL MEATBALLS

Prep: 40 minutes Cook: 11 to 14 minutes Makes: 80

As appetizer scholars, we'd love to know who first came up with the idea of creating a sauce from these bizarre ingredients. (And why!) However, it works, and it's a secret recipe treasured by more than one renowned hostess.

- **2 scallions, minced**
- **1 tablespoon olive oil or butter**
- **½ cup fresh bread crumbs**
- **¼ cup milk**
- **1½ pounds ground round (85% lean)**
- **½ pound lean ground pork or turkey**
- **1½ teaspoons salt**
- **1 teaspoon chili powder**
- **¼ teaspoon ground cumin**
- **⅛ teaspoon cayenne**
- **1 (12-ounce) bottle chili sauce**
- **1 (4-ounce) jar grape jelly**
- **2 tablespoons fresh lemon juice**

1. Preheat oven to 450°F. In a small frying pan, cook scallions in olive oil over medium heat until softened but not browned, 1 to 2 minutes; set aside. In a small bowl, soak bread crumbs in milk to soften.

2. In a large bowl, combine ground round, ground pork, sautéed scallions, softened bread crumbs, salt, chili powder, cumin, and cayenne. Blend until well mixed. Form into meatballs about 1 inch in diameter and arrange in a single layer on a greased jelly-roll pan.

3. Bake in upper third of oven, shaking pan once or twice, until meatballs are nicely browned and just cooked through, 8 to 10 minutes. (If made in advance, let cool, cover, and refrigerate up to 3 days. Freeze if desired.)

4. In a small saucepan, combine chili sauce, grape jelly, and lemon juice. Cook over medium heat, stirring occasionally, until heated through, 2 to 3 minutes. Transfer to a chafing dish and add meatballs.

320 LAZY DAY MEATBALLS

Prep: 20 minutes Cook: 35 minutes Chill: overnight Makes: 80

- **2 pounds ground chuck (80% lean)**
- **1 medium onion, grated**
- **2 teaspoons salt**
- **1 teaspoon freshly ground pepper**
- **1 (12-ounce) bottle chili sauce or ketchup**
- **1 (12-ounce) can beer**

1. In a large bowl, combine ground chuck, onion, salt, and pepper. Blend well. Form into meatballs about 1 inch in diameter.

2. In a large saucepan, bring chili sauce and beer to a boil over medium-high heat. Reduce heat to medium-low and gently add uncooked meatballs. Simmer until cooked through, about 20 minutes. Let meatballs cool in sauce. Cover and refrigerate overnight. To serve, skim fat from sauce. Cook over low heat until heated through, about 15 minutes. Serve in a chafing dish with toothpicks.

Chapter 13

All Wrapped Up

Appetizer lovers know that the best things often come in small packages. Whether it's Creamy Mushroom Kisses enveloped in filo dough, Savory Currant and Almond Tartlets in puff pastry, or Just Ducky Won Tons with Cranberry-Ginger Dipping Sauce, tiny gift-wrapped morsels invite curiosity and delight the eye. If you're apprehensive at the prospect of hours of painstaking kitchen labor ahead of you, we have good news: the wrappers are usually purchased ready-made, and nearly all of the recipes in this chapter can be frozen for the future.

Buttery, flaky-light puff pastry is classic cocktail fare from France. It takes hours and hours to prepare. Our recipes rely on the convenient frozen packaged sort now available in supermarkets across the country. Or if you have a bakery in your area that makes good puff pastry, ask if you can purchase sheets of unbaked pastry by the pound, if you want to bake the real thing.

Appetizers wrapped up for the occasion in layer after layer of crispy filo usually mystify people who have never tasted it before; they are sure it must have taken hours to produce such delicate pastry. You, above all people, will know this isn't so. If you prefer to avoid buttering the layers of filo, try brushing them with oil or spraying with vegetable cooking spray. It will not taste quite the same, but it will be lighter and will still make a great appetizer.

321 PIGS IN BLANKETS

Prep: 15 minutes Cook: 8 to 10 minutes Makes: 32

Rare is the child who isn't utterly charmed by this appetizer. Some of us never outgrow the fascination.

1 (10-ounce) can refrigerated flaky biscuits
2 (5.3-ounce) packages cocktail frankfurters
Mustard

1. Preheat oven to 400°F. Separate each biscuit into 2 thinner biscuits and then cut each in half to form 2 semicircles. Fold one semicircle around each cocktail frank, pressing the edges together to seal.

2. Place "pigs," seam-side down, on an ungreased baking sheet. Bake until frankfurters are heated through and biscuits are golden brown, 8 to 10 minutes. Serve with mustard for dipping.

322 PIGS IN COMFORTERS

Prep: 25 minutes Cook: 8 to 10 minutes Makes: 32

This is an upscale version of the preceding recipe, ideal for the budding gourmet.

2 tablespoons mustard
1 tablespoon mayonnaise
1 tablespoon ketchup
1 (10-ounce) can refrigerated flaky biscuits
2 (5.3-ounce) packages cocktail frankfurters
1 egg
3 tablespoons sesame seeds

1. Preheat oven to 400°F. In a small bowl, combine mustard, mayonnaise, and ketchup. Blend well.

2. Separate each biscuit into 2 thinner biscuits and then cut each in half to form 2 semicircles. Spread each semicircle with mustard mixture and top with a cocktail frank. Fold dough around franks, pressing edges together to seal. Place "pigs," seam-side down, on an ungreased baking sheet.

3. In a small bowl, mix egg with 1 tablespoon water until well blended. Brush egg mixture over dough and sprinkle with sesame seeds. Bake until frankfurters are heated through and biscuits are golden brown, 8 to 10 minutes.

323 CRAB AND PORK PINWHEELS

Prep: 30 minutes Chill: 1 hour Cook: 35 minutes Makes: 48

- **1 tablespoon peanut or olive oil**
- **1 pound ground pork**
- **½ cup crab meat (about 4 ounces), picked over**
- **½ teaspoon salt**
- **3 tablespoons minced water chestnuts**
- **2 scallions, minced**
- **2 teaspoons grated fresh ginger**
- **1½ tablespoons soy sauce**
- **1 egg**
- **¼ cup fine dry bread crumbs**
- **Easy Cream Cheese Pastry (recipe follows)**

1. In a large frying pan, heat oil over medium-high heat. Add pork and cook, stirring to break up lumps of meat, until no longer pink, about 5 minutes; drain off fat. Stir in crab, salt, water chestnuts, scallions, ginger, soy sauce, egg, and bread crumbs. Cook, stirring, about 1 minute. Remove from heat and let cool.

2. Divide pastry dough into 4 parts. Roll each piece into a rectangle about 12x9 inches. Cut each rectangle in half lengthwise and spread with cooled filling.

3. Starting from a long end, roll each rectangle tightly, jelly-roll fashion. Moisten edges of dough with water and press to seal. Place rolls on a baking sheet, seam-side down. Cover with plastic wrap and refrigerate 1 hour. Preheat oven to 375°F.

4. Remove plastic wrap and bake rolls until golden brown, 30 to 35 minutes. Let cool before cutting into 1-inch slices with a serrated knife. Arrange cut-side up on a platter; serve warm or cold.

324 EASY CREAM CHEESE PASTRY

Prep: 5 minutes Cook: none Makes: about 1½ pounds

- **2 sticks (½ pound) butter, softened**
- **1 (8-ounce) package cream cheese, softened**
- **2 cups flour**
- **¼ teaspoon salt**
- **Dash of cayenne**

In a medium bowl or in a food processor, blend butter and cream cheese. Mix in flour, salt, and cayenne until well blended. Form into a ball, wrap in plastic wrap, and refrigerate 2 hours, or overnight.

325 FILO SOUFFLÉ ROLLS

Prep: 1 hour Cook: 13 to 17 minutes Makes: about 80

Frozen spinach soufflé makes a light and tasty base for this popular filling. Since these freeze so beautifully, we always make an extra batch to keep on hand.

½ cup finely chopped onion
2 teaspoons olive oil
1 garlic clove, minced
2 (11-ounce) packages frozen spinach soufflé, thawed
1 cup crumbled feta cheese (about 4 ounces)
¼ teaspoon dried dill
⅛ teaspoon grated nutmeg
⅛ teaspoon salt
1½ sticks (6 ounces) unsalted butter, melted
1 (1-pound) package filo pastry, thawed

1. In a medium frying pan, cook onion in olive oil over medium heat until softened but not browned, 3 to 5 minutes. Stir in garlic and cook until just fragrant, about 30 seconds. Transfer mixture to a large bowl. Stir in spinach soufflé, feta cheese, dill, nutmeg, and salt. Mix until well combined.

2. On a flat work surface, unfold filo and cut lengthwise into 6 or 7 strips 2 to 3 inches wide. Cover filo strips with plastic wrap and top with a damp towel to prevent drying.

3. Brush 1 filo strip with butter. Top with a second strip and brush again with butter. Place about 1 teaspoon spinach mixture on short end of strip, about 1 inch from the bottom. Fold bottom edge up to cover filling, then fold in both sides of strip about ¼ inch to form a seal. Beginning at the end containing filling, roll into a neat cylinder. Place filo roll seam-side down on a parchment- or foil-lined baking sheet. Brush with butter and cover with plastic wrap to prevent drying. Repeat with remaining filo and filling. (If made in advance, refrigerate up to 2 days. Freeze for longer storage.)

4. Preheat oven to 350°F. Arrange filo rolls about 1 inch apart on a baking sheet and bake until puffed and barely golden, 10 to 12 minutes. Let cool 5 to 10 minutes before serving.

326 CRABBY BRIE KISSES

Prep: 45 minutes Cook: 12 to 15 minutes Makes: about 48

½ pound Brie, well chilled
½ pound crab meat, picked over
1 tablespoon minced scallions
1 teaspoon fresh lemon juice
¼ teaspoon salt
⅛ teaspoon cayenne
½ pound filo, thawed (10 to 15 sheets)
1 stick (4 ounces) unsalted butter, melted
2 tablespoons pesto (optional)

1. Cut Brie into ½-inch pieces. In a medium bowl, combine Brie, crab meat, scallions, lemon juice, salt, and cayenne. Toss until well mixed.

2. On a clean work surface, unfold filo and cut into 3-inch squares. Cover with plastic wrap and top with a damp towel to prevent drying.

3. Brush 1 filo square with butter. Top with a second square and brush again. Gently ease into a buttered gem-size (1¾-inch) muffin cup. Brush 2 more squares with butter and arrange at a 90-degree angle overlapping the first squares. Place about 1 teaspoon Brie mixture in center and gather up corners of filo, gently twisting to seal. Brush with butter and continue with remaining filo and filling. As each gem-size muffin tin is filled with kisses, cover with plastic wrap to prevent drying. (If made in advance, refrigerate up to 2 days. Freeze for longer storage.)

4. Preheat oven to 350°F. Bake until filling is heated through and pastry is barely golden, 12 to 15 minutes. Use a teaspoon to gently lift kisses from muffin cups. Let cool 5 to 10 minutes before serving. Top each kiss with about ⅛ teaspoon pesto if desired.

---

327 CREAMY MUSHROOM KISSES

Prep: 40 minutes Cook: 12 to 15 minutes Makes: about 48

Filo is the Greek word for leaf, and these crispy, delicate leaves encase some of our all-time favorite appetizers. Look for filo in the refrigerated or freezer section of supermarkets or Middle Eastern delicatessens. Filo comes in 1-pound boxes; leftover dough can be refrigerated or frozen.

- **½ pound filo pastry, thawed (10 to 15 sheets)**
- **1 stick (4 ounces) unsalted butter, melted**
- **1 recipe Mushroom Duxelles (page 63)**

1. On a flat work surface, unfold filo and cut into 3-inch squares. Cover with plastic wrap and top with a damp towel to prevent drying.

2. Brush 1 filo square with butter. Top with a second square and brush again. Gently ease into a buttered gem-size (1¾-inch) muffin cup. Brush 2 more squares with butter and arrange at a 90-degree angle overlapping the first squares. Place about 1 teaspoon mushroom duxelles in center. Gather up corners of filo and gently twist to seal. Brush with butter and continue with remaining filo and filling. As each gem-size muffin tin is filled with kisses, cover with plastic wrap to prevent drying. (If made in advance, refrigerate up to 2 days. Freeze for longer storage.)

3. Preheat oven to 350°F. Bake until filling is heated through and pastry is barely golden, 12 to 15 minutes. Use a teaspoon to gently lift kisses from muffin cups. Let cool 5 to 10 minutes before serving.

328 TRIPLE CHEESE TRIANGLES

Prep: 50 minutes Cook: 10 to 15 minutes Makes: about 80

These *tiropitas* of Greek origin have long been a favorite on the cocktail party circuit. With one taste of the creamy cheese filling tucked inside flaky filo, you'll know why.

- **½ pound feta cheese, crumbled (about 2 cups)**
- **½ pound ricotta cheese (about 1 cup)**
- **1 (8-ounce) package cream cheese, softened**
- **1 egg**
- **⅓ cup chopped parsley**
- **Dash of cayenne**
- **Dash of salt**
- **Dash of grated nutmeg**
- **1 (1-pound) package filo pastry, thawed**
- **1½ sticks (6 ounces) unsalted butter, melted**

1. In a large bowl or food processor, combine feta cheese, ricotta cheese, cream cheese, egg, parsley, cayenne, salt, and nutmeg. Mix until well blended.

2. On a flat work surface, unfold filo and cut lengthwise into 6 or 7 strips 2 to 3 inches wide. Cover filo strips with plastic wrap and top with a damp towel to prevent drying.

3. Brush 1 filo strip with melted butter. Top with a second strip of filo and brush again with butter. Place about 1½ teaspoons cheese mixture on short end of strip, off to 1 corner. Fold 1 corner over to opposite edge, covering filling and making a triangle.Continue folding strip as you would a flag, keeping the triangular shape with each fold. Place filo triangle on a parchment- or foil-lined baking sheet. Brush with butter and cover with plastic wrap to prevent drying. Repeat with remaining filo and filling. (If made in advance, refrigerate up to 8 hours. Freeze for longer storage.)

4. Preheat oven to 350°F. Arrange filo triangles about 1 inch apart on a baking sheet and bake until puffed and barely golden, 10 to 15 minutes. Let cool 5 to 10 minutes before serving.

329 BRIE IN PUFF PASTRY

Prep: 20 minutes Chill: 1 hour Cook: 25 to 30 minutes
Serves: 8 to 12

This very popular appetizer looks as though its assembly required the talents of a French pastry chef, but you'll know better. For larger groups, serve both wheels of cheese. If you're serving only four to six guests, go ahead and save one of the unbaked pastry-wrapped cheeses in the freezer for later.

1 (17¼-ounce) package frozen puff pastry sheets, thawed as package directs
2 (8-ounce) wheels of Brie, well chilled
1 egg yolk
1 tablespoon cream or milk
Fresh apple or pear wedges, or dried apricots or other fruits or sprigs of crisp fresh watercress

1. Unfold 1 sheet of puff pastry onto a lightly floured work surface. Roll out pastry to about ⅛ inch thick and, using a tart pan as a guide, cut into a circle about 11 inches in diameter; reserve scraps for decoration. Place 1 wheel of cheese in center of circle. Fold up pastry to enclose cheese, neatly pleating and pressing pastry down as you go around. When cheese is snugly enclosed, press pastry together, cutting away any excess as necessary. Invert pastry-wrapped Brie seam-side down onto a parchment- or foil-lined baking sheet.

2. Cut decorative shapes from pastry scraps. In a small bowl, beat egg yolk with cream until well blended to make an egg wash. Brush pastry with egg wash and top with pastry scraps, pressing down gently to seal. Brush again with egg wash. Repeat, using second sheet of pastry and remaining wheel of cheese. Refrigerate until firm, about 1 hour. Cover bowl of egg wash and refrigerate until later.

3. Preheat oven to 400°F. Brush cheese once again with egg wash and bake 25 to 30 minutes, until pastry is cooked through, nicely puffed, and golden brown. Use a large wide spatula to transfer cheeses to serving plates. Let cool at least 30 minutes or as long as 4 hours at room temperature before cutting into wedges to serve. Garnish with fresh and/or dried fruits or watercress to eat along with cheese.

330 SAUSAGE AND PARMESAN PUFFS

Prep: 10 minutes Cook: 15 to 20 minutes Chill: 1 hour Makes: 54

Line your baking sheet with a brown grocery bag to absorb any excess grease. Do not use a bag made from recycled paper, though, as they have been treated with chemicals.

1 (17¼-ounce) package frozen puff pastry sheets, thawed as package directs
1 egg
1 tablespoon cream or milk
1 (12-ounce) package fresh pork sausage
⅓ cup grated Parmesan cheese
Poppy or sesame seeds

1. Unfold pastry sheets and cut each into three strips 9¼ by 3¼ inches, using the dough's natural folds as a guideline. In a small bowl, beat egg with cream until well blended. Brush each pastry strip with this glaze.

2. Divide sausage into 6 equal portions and form a roll about ¾ inch in diameter down center length of each pastry strip. Sprinkle Parmesan cheese lightly over sausage rolls. Fold each pastry strip in half lengthwise, as you would close a book, and pinch together. Using tines of a fork, press edges together to seal. Brush with remaining egg glaze and sprinkle with poppy seeds. If pastry is soft, refrigerate until firm. Cut each strip into 9 pieces about 1 inch long. Arrange 1 inch apart (with pastry on top and bottom) on a baking sheet or jelly-roll pan that has been lined with brown paper and refrigerate, well covered, until pastry is firm, about 1 hour or as long as overnight. (For longer storage, freeze and thaw in refrigerator before baking.)

3. Preheat oven to 400°F. Bake until sausage is cooked through and pastry is puffed and golden, 15 to 20 minutes. Serve warm.

331 KIELBASA PUFFS

Prep: 10 minutes Cook: 25 minutes Makes: 24

Serve these with a flavorful coarse-grained mustard for dipping.

1 (17¼-ounce) package frozen puff pastry, thawed as directed on package
2 pounds kielbasa (Polish sausage)

1. Preheat oven to 425°F. Cut sausage into 2 pieces, each about 10 inches long, and peel off casing. Place each piece of sausage on a sheet of puff pastry and wrap tightly to enclose sausages completely; press edges together to seal.

2. Place sausage rolls, seam-side down, on an ungreased baking sheet. Bake 20 to 25 minutes, until golden brown. Let cool slightly, then slice into ¾-inch pieces.

332 NORTH BEACH WON TONS

Prep: 1 hour Chill: 1 hour Cook: 15 to 20 minutes
Makes: about 70

North Beach is where San Francisco's Chinatown meets the old Italian part of the city. Try this cross-cultural appetizer with the Spicy Toasted Almond Dip on page 6.

½ pound fontina cheese, cut into ½-inch cubes
¼ pound Italian salami, coarsely chopped
6 oil-cured or kalamata olives, pitted
1 (1-pound) package won ton wrappers*
2 to 4 cups peanut or corn oil

1. In a food processor, chop cheese until finely crumbled. Add salami and olives and process until well blended.

2. Place 1 won ton wrapper in the palm of your hand with 1 corner pointing toward you. Using a chopstick or finger dipped in water, lightly moisten edges of wrapper. Place about 1 teaspoon filling in center and fold corner nearest you over filling, tucking in the point to enclose completely, rolling wrapper to within 1 inch of top corner. Just inside wrapper, on either side of filling, moisten with water and press to seal. Moisten 2 side corners with water, overlap the points slightly, and pinch them together to seal. As each won ton is completed, arrange in a single layer on a large baking sheet or platter and cover lightly with plastic wrap. Repeat with remaining wrappers and filling. Cover and refrigerate 1 hour or as long as 2 days.

3. In a wok or large heavy saucepan, heat oil to 350°F on a deep-frying thermometer over medium-high heat. Cook won tons a few at a time, turning occasionally, until crisp and golden, about 2 minutes. Drain on paper towels as you fry the rest. (If made in advance, keep warm in a 250° oven up to 1 hour. Fried won tons can also be kept covered in the refrigerator up to 2 days. Reheat in a 450° oven until wrappers are once again crisp and sizzling hot, about 5 minutes.) Serve hot or warm.

* *Available in Asian markets and many supermarkets.*

333 JUST DUCKY WON TONS WITH CRANBERRY-GINGER DIPPING SAUCE

Prep: 1 hour Chill: 1 hour Cook: 15 to 20 minutes
Makes: about 70

If you don't have leftover duck, purchase one cooked from an Asian market or restaurant. If all efforts fail, substitute dark-meat chicken or turkey.

1 tablespoon soy sauce
¼ teaspoon Asian sesame oil*
2 teaspoons chopped fresh cilantro
1 scallion, chopped
1 teaspoon grated orange zest
¼ teaspoon sugar or honey
1½ cups chopped cooked duck (about 1 whole breast)
1 (1-pound) package won ton wrappers*
2 to 4 cups peanut or corn oil
Cranberry-Ginger Dipping Sauce (recipe follows)

1. In a small bowl, combine soy sauce, sesame oil, cilantro, scallion, orange zest, and sugar until well mixed. Toss with duck.

2. Place 1 won ton wrapper in palm of your hand with 1 corner pointing toward you. Using a chopstick or finger dipped in water, lightly moisten edges of wrapper. Place about 1 teaspoon filling in center and fold corner nearest you over filling, tucking in point to enclose completely, rolling wrapper to within 1 inch of top corner. Just inside wrapper, on either side of filling, moisten with water and press to seal. Moisten 2 side corners with water, overlap the points slightly, and pinch them together to seal. As each won ton is completed, arrange in a single layer on a large baking sheet or platter and cover with plastic wrap. Repeat with remaining wrappers and filling. Cover and refrigerate 1 hour or as long as 2 days.

3. In a wok or large heavy saucepan, heat oil to 350°F on a deep-frying thermometer over medium-high heat. Cook won tons in batches without crowding, turning occasionally, until crisp and golden, about 2 minutes. Drain on paper towels as you fry the rest. (If made in advance, keep warm in a 250° oven up to 1 hour. Fried won tons can also be kept covered in the refrigerator up to 2 days. Recrisp in a 450° oven until wrappers are once again crisp and sizzling hot, about 5 minutes.) Serve hot or warm.

* *Available in Asian markets and many supermarkets.*

334 CRANBERRY-GINGER DIPPING SAUCE

Prep: 5 minutes Cook: 10 minutes Makes: about 2 cups

1 cup sugar
1 (12-ounce) bag fresh cranberries, rinsed and drained
¼ cup chopped crystallized ginger
1 tablespoon dry vermouth
1 teaspoon soy sauce
Dash of cayenne

1. In a medium saucepan, combine sugar with 1 cup water. Bring to a boil over medium heat and cook 5 minutes.

2. Add cranberries, return to a boil, and cook, stirring once or twice, just until their skins pop, about 5 minutes. Stir in ginger, vermouth, soy sauce, and cayenne. Remove from heat and let cool. (If made in advance, cover and refrigerate up to 1 week.) Serve at room temperature.

SAVORY CURRANT AND ALMOND TARTLETS

Prep: 20 minutes Cook: 30 minutes Makes: 36

2 shallots, minced
1½ teaspoons butter
1 (17¼-ounce) package frozen puff pastry sheets, thawed as package directs
2 (3-ounce) packages cream cheese, softened
1 egg
¼ cup grated Parmesan cheese
½ teaspoon salt
¼ teaspoon freshly ground pepper
⅛ teaspoon grated nutmeg
1 cup heavy cream
½ teaspoon bourbon or brandy
2 tablespoons currants or raisins
2 tablespoons slivered almonds, toasted

1. In a small frying pan, cook shallots in butter over medium heat until softened but not browned, 2 to 3 minutes. Remove from heat and let cool.

2. On a lightly floured work surface, roll out pastry sheets to a scant ⅛ inch thick. Using a 2½-inch cookie cutter, cut pastry into rounds and press into greased gem-size (1½-inch) muffin tins. Refrigerate or freeze while you make the filling. Preheat oven to 350°F and position rack in lower third of oven.

3. In a food processor or blender, combine cream cheese, egg, Parmesan cheese, salt, pepper, and nutmeg. Puree until well blended. Pour in cream and bourbon and process until smooth. Add currants, almonds, and cooked shallots and process, using an on/off motion, until almonds are just chopped. Using a small ladle, fill chilled pastry shells three-quarters full.

4. Bake tartlets 30 minutes, or until pastry is puffed and golden and filling is set. Serve warm or at room temperature.

336 CRISP BACON AND GINGER TRIANGLES

Prep: 15 minutes Cook: 7 to 10 minutes Makes: 24

These exotic flavors stand well on their own, but pepper jelly makes a delightful dipping sauce.

- **½ pound thinly sliced bacon (about 10 slices)**
- **4 ounces cream cheese, at room temperature**
- **1 tablespoon minced candied ginger**
- **1 scallion, minced**
- **½ teaspoon curry powder**
- **24 won ton wrappers**
- **2 to 4 cups peanut or corn oil**
- **½ cup red or green hot pepper jelly**

1. In a large skillet, cook bacon over medium heat until crisp, 5 to 7 minutes. Drain on paper towels and crumble or chop into small bits.

2. In a small bowl, combine cream cheese, ginger, crumbled bacon, scallion, and curry. Mix well.

3. Lay won ton wrappers flat and brush edges lightly with water. Place 1 teaspoon of cream cheese mixture in one corner of each wrapper, leaving a ½-inch border. Fold diagonally to form a triangle, pressing moistened edges together to seal.

4. Fill a wok or heavy saucepan with 2 inches of oil and heat over medium-high heat until oil registers 350°F on a deep-frying thermometer. Deep-fry won ton triangles in batches, turning once, until crisp and lightly golden, 2 to 3 minutes. Drain well and allow to cool for 5 minutes before serving. Heat pepper jelly until melted and serve in a small bowl for dipping.

337 SHRIMP-FILLED WON TONS

Prep: 1 hour Chill: 1 hour Cook: 15 to 20 minutes
Makes: about 70

Enjoy these plain or with prepared Chinese hot mustard, sweet and sour, or plum sauce.

¾ pound medium shrimp, shelled and deveined
1 (8-ounce) can water chestnuts, drained
¼ cup chopped fresh cilantro
3 scallions, chopped
2 tablespoons soy sauce
1 garlic clove, minced
¼ teaspoon Asian sesame oil*
3 drops of Chinese hot chili oil*
Dash of salt
1 (1-pound) package won ton wrappers*
2 to 4 cups peanut or corn oil

1. In a food processor, combine shrimp, water chestnuts, cilantro, scallions, soy sauce, garlic, sesame oil, hot chili oil, and salt. Process until mixed but still slightly chunky.

2. Place 1 won ton wrapper in palm of your hand with 1 corner pointing toward you. Using a chopstick or finger dipped in water, lightly moisten edges of wrapper. Place about 1 teaspoon filling in center and fold corner nearest you over filling, tucking in point to enclose completely, rolling wrapper to within 1 inch of top corner. Just inside wrapper, on either side of filling, moisten with water and press to seal. Moisten 2 side corners with water, overlap points slightly, and pinch them together to seal. As each won ton is completed, arrange in a single layer on a large baking sheet or platter and cover with plastic wrap. Repeat with remaining wrappers and filling. Cover and refrigerate 1 hour or as long as 2 days.

3. In a wok or large heavy saucepan, heat oil to 350°F on a deep-frying thermometer over medium-high heat. Cook won tons a few at a time, turning occasionally, until crisp and golden, about 2 minutes. Drain on paper towels as you fry the rest. (If made in advance, keep warm in a 250° oven up to 1 hour. Fried won tons can also be kept covered in the refrigerator up to 2 days. Recrisp in a 450° oven until wrappers are once again crisp and sizzling hot, about 5 minutes.) Serve warm.

* *Available in Asian markets and many supermarkets.*

338 CALIFORNIA WON TONS

Prep: 50 minutes Chill: 1 hour
Cook: 15 to 29 minutes total Makes: about 70

California cuisine meets ancient China in this blend of flavors.

1½ cups herbed cream cheese, purchased or homemade (page 11), or ¾ pound goat cheese
2 tablespoons chopped oil-packed sun-dried tomatoes or roasted red bell pepper
1 (1-pound) package won ton wrappers*
2 to 4 cups peanut or corn oil

1. In a food processor, combine herbed cream cheese and sun-dried tomatoes. Process until mixed but still slightly chunky.

2. Place 1 won ton wrapper in palm of your hand with 1 corner pointing toward you. Using a chopstick or finger dipped in water, lightly moisten edges of wrapper. Place about 1 teaspoon filling in center and fold corner nearest you over filling, tucking in point to enclose completely, rolling wrapper to within 1 inch of top corner. Just inside wrapper, on either side of filling, moisten with water and press to seal. Moisten 2 side corners with water, overlap points slightly, and pinch them together to seal. As each won ton is completed, arrange in a single layer on a large baking sheet or platter and cover with plastic wrap. Repeat with remaining wrappers and filling. Cover and refrigerate 1 hour or as long as 2 days.

3. In a wok or large heavy saucepan, heat oil over medium-high heat to 350°F on a deep-frying thermometer. Cook won tons in batches without crowding, turning occasionally, until crisp and golden, about 2 minutes. Drain on paper towels as you fry the rest. (If made in advance, keep warm in a 250° oven up to 1 hour. Fried won tons can also be kept covered in the refrigerator up to 2 days. Reheat in a 450° oven until wrappers are once again crisp and sizzling hot, about 5 minutes.) Serve hot or warm.

* *Available in Asian markets and many supermarkets.*

339 WON TONS WITH CRAB RANGOON FILLING

Prep: 1 hour Chill: 1 hour Cook: 15 to 20 minutes total
Makes: about 70

Enjoy these plain or with Cranberry-Ginger Dipping Sauce (page 197) or with bottled Asian plum sauce.

- **½ pound crab meat, picked over for bits of shell and cartilage**
- **1 (8-ounce) package cream cheese, softened**
- **2 scallions, chopped**
- **½ teaspoon prepared white horseradish**
- **½ teaspoon fresh lemon juice**
- **⅛ teaspoon hot pepper sauce**
- **Dash of salt**
- **1 (1-pound) package won ton wrappers***
- **2 to 4 cups peanut or corn oil**

1. In a food processor, combine crab meat, cream cheese, scallions, horseradish, lemon juice, hot sauce, and salt. Process with an on/off motion until mixed but still slightly chunky.

2. Place 1 won ton wrapper in palm of your hand with 1 corner pointing toward you. Using a chopstick or finger dipped in water, lightly moisten edges of wrapper. Place about 1 teaspoon filling in center and fold corner nearest you over filling, tucking in point to enclose completely, rolling wrapper to within 1 inch of top corner. Just inside wrapper, on either side of filling, moisten with water and press to seal. Moisten 2 side corners with water, overlap points slightly, and pinch them together to seal. As each won ton is completed, arrange in a single layer on a large baking sheet or platter and cover with plastic wrap. Repeat with remaining wrappers and filling. Cover and refrigerate 1 hour or as long as 2 days.

3. In a wok or large heavy saucepan, heat 2 inches of oil to 350°F on a deep-frying thermometer over medium-high heat. Cook won tons in batches without crowding, turning occasionally, until crisp and golden, about 2 minutes. Drain on paper towels as you fry the rest. (If made in advance, keep warm in a 250° oven up to 1 hour. Fried won tons can also be kept covered in the refrigerator up to 2 days. Recrisp in a 450° oven until wrappers are once again crisp and sizzling hot, about 5 minutes.) Serve hot or warm.

* *Available in Asian markets and many supermarkets.*

Chapter 14

Biscuits, Muffins, Breads, and Crackers

In the eyes of an appetizer lover, this chapter is worth a lot of dough. Actually, it covers a lot of territory and includes many flour-based recipes, from Beaten Biscuits and Tiny Puffs—perfect for stuffing with bits of ham or turkey or one of our savory spreads or mousses—to Zucchini Madeleines and Southern Cheddar Pecan Wafers, made for nibbling on their own.

Special snacks, such as Irish Bread Sticks, Bess Brownell's Blue Devils, and Poppadums, are surprisingly easy to prepare. When serving cheese on a buffet, see what kind of reactions you get with fragrant Rosemary Fougasse, a beautifully shaped French bread, or Double Olive Bread, in place of ordinary bread or crackers.

This chapter also contains three spectacular ways to present a wheel of Brie. One tucks it inside a puff pastry wrapper, another in a rich, homemade basket of brioche. Perhaps the most spectacular, though, is also the easiest—a golden brown wreath of braided bread, made with frozen dough from the supermarket.

340 BEATEN BISCUITS

Prep: 5 minutes Cook: 25 minutes Makes: 24

This is an old-time Southern favorite. Before food processors, the dough was beaten with a rolling pin. This is one time you don't have to worry about overprocessing the dough. Beaten Biscuits are often filled with thinly sliced country ham, chicken salad, or other creamy fillings to make tiny appetizer sandwiches.

2 cups flour
1 stick (4 ounces) unsalted butter
1 teaspoon salt
½ cup ice water

1. Preheat oven to 350°F. In a food processor, combine flour, butter, and salt. Process until mixture is consistency of cornmeal. With machine on, add ice water in a slow steady stream. Process until dough forms a ball, then process 2 minutes longer.

2. Roll dough into an 8x10-inch rectangle about ⅛ inch thick, then fold dough in half. Cut out biscuits with a round 1-inch cookie cutter. Arrange on an ungreased baking sheet.

3. Bake biscuits 25 to 30 minutes, until crisp and very lightly browned. While still warm, use tines of a fork to split biscuits in half; let cool. If made in advance, store airtight.

341 BESS BROWNELL'S BLUE DEVILS

Prep: 10 minutes Cook: 14 minutes Makes: 40

Bess hates to cook but loves to eat. Here's one of her tasty appetizers that's always a hit.

1 (10-ounce) package refrigerated flaky biscuits
1 stick (4 ounces) butter
1 cup crumbled blue cheese (4 ounces)

1. Preheat oven to 400°F. Separate dough into individual biscuits and cut into quarters. Arrange in a single layer in an ungreased 9x13-inch baking pan.

2. In a small saucepan, melt butter over medium heat. Add blue cheese and cook, stirring, until cheese is melted and mixture is well blended, about 3 minutes. Pour over biscuits and bake until dough has absorbed most of cheese mixture and tops are nicely browned, about 11 minutes. Let cool in pan 2 to 3 minutes before removing with a spatula. Serve warm.

342 OYSTER-STUFFED BISCUITS

Prep: 10 minutes Cook: 10 minutes Makes: 18

1 (8-ounce) package refrigerated biscuits
1 (3¾-ounce) can smoked oysters

1. Preheat oven to 425°F. Separate biscuits and cut each into quarters. On a clean work surface, roll each quarter until about ¼ inch thick.

2. Drain oysters and wrap each in dough to cover completely. Place seam-side down on ungreased baking sheet and bake 10 minutes, or until golden brown.

343 SWISS BISCUITS

Prep: 15 minutes Cook: 15 minutes Makes: about 24

To serve to adults, cut these with a standard 2½-inch round biscuit cutter. For children, let them choose their favorite cookie cutters and help cut the dough into the desired shapes.

2 cups shredded Swiss cheese (about 8 ounces)
2 sticks butter (½ pound), softened
¾ cup flour
½ teaspoon freshly ground pepper
¼ teaspoon cayenne
1 egg white, beaten
2 tablespoons grated Parmesan cheese

1. Preheat oven to 425°F. In a food processor, combine Swiss cheese, butter, flour, pepper, and cayenne. Process until well blended.

2. On a flat work surface, roll out dough ¼ inch thick and cut into desired shapes. Brush with beaten egg white and sprinkle with Parmesan cheese. Transfer to a baking sheet. Bake until biscuits are lightly browned, about 15 minutes.

344 ZUCCHINI MADELEINES

Prep: 15 minutes Stand: 30 minutes
Cook: 20 to 25 minutes Makes: 36

It's fun to find other uses for the shell-shaped pans used to make French dessert cakes. These savories taste like miniature frittatas.

- **1 pound zucchini, grated (about 4½ cups)**
- **1 tablespoon coarse (kosher) salt**
- **5 eggs**
- **½ cup olive oil**
- **¼ teaspoon cayenne**
- **1¼ cups grated Parmesan cheese (about 5 ounces)**
- **1 medium onion, minced**
- **2 tablespoons chopped mixed fresh herbs, such as parsley, chives, and thyme, or 2 teaspoons dried**
- **1 cup flour**
- **1 tablespoon baking powder**

1. In a colander, toss zucchini with salt. Let stand 30 minutes to draw out excess moisture.

2. Preheat oven to 350°F. In a large bowl, combine eggs, olive oil, and cayenne. Beat until well blended. Whisk in cheese, onion, and herbs. Squeeze zucchini dry with your hands and stir into egg mixture. Mix in flour and baking powder.

3. Fill greased madeleine pans with about 2 tablespoons zucchini mixture and bake until golden, 20 to 25 minutes. Serve warm or at room temperature. (If made in advance, cover and refrigerate up to 2 days.)

NOTE: *These can also be baked in gem-size (1¾-inch) muffin tins for 20 minutes. The small pans will take about 2 tablespoons batter per muffin and will make about 36.*

345 CORN MADELEINES

Prep: 10 minutes Cook: 10 to 15 minutes Makes: 12 to 14

These are a wonderful accompaniment to a platter of thinly sliced smoked salmon, fresh dill, and crème fraîche or sour cream.

- **1 cup flour**
- **1 cup yellow cornmeal**
- **2 tablespoons sugar**
- **2 teaspoons baking powder**
- **½ teaspoon salt**
- **2 eggs**
- **1 cup milk**
- **2 tablespoons melted butter**

1. Preheat oven to 400°F. In a medium bowl, combine flour, cornmeal, sugar, baking powder, and salt. Whisk gently until well blended. In a small bowl, beat eggs until well blended. Whisk in milk and melted butter.

2. As quickly and as lightly as possible, add egg mixture to dry ingredients and stir just enough to combine, about 16 strokes.

3. Fill greased madeleine pans with about 2 tablespoons corn batter and bake until risen and firm, 10 to 15 minutes. Let cool before serving.

346 GINGERBEAD MADELEINES WITH GINGER CREAM

Prep: 15 minutes Cook: 10 to 15 minutes Makes: 20 to 24

We enjoy this slightly sweet appetizer especially around the holidays.

2 eggs, separated
½ cup packed dark brown sugar
1 stick (4 ounces) butter, softened
1 teaspoon vanilla extract
1 cup flour
1 teaspoon baking powder
1½ teaspoons ground ginger
½ teaspoon cinnamon
¼ teaspoon ground cloves
¼ teaspoon ground allspice
Dash of grated nutmeg
2 tablespoons minced crystallized ginger (optional)
Dash of salt
Ginger Cream (recipe follows)

1. Preheat oven to 400°F. In a medium bowl, combine egg yolks and brown sugar. Mix until well blended. Beat in butter and vanilla. Sift together flour, baking powder, ginger, cinnamon, cloves, allspice, and nutmeg. Add egg yolk mixture and blend well. Stir in crystallized ginger, if desired.

2. In a medium bowl, beat egg whites with salt until soft peaks form. Gently fold into batter one-third at a time until just blended.

3. Fill greased madeleine pans with about 2 tablespoons batter and bake 10 to 15 minutes, until madeleines are risen and firm and spring back when touched lightly. Let cool. Serve at room temperature with ginger cream.

GINGER CREAM

Makes: 1¼ cups

1 (8-ounce) package cream cheese, softened
¼ cup minced crystallized ginger
2 teaspoons dark rum, or more to taste

In a small bowl, combine cream cheese, ginger, and rum. Blend until well mixed. If made in advance, cover and refrigerate up to 2 days. Serve at room temperature.

347 COCKTAIL SCONES

Prep: 10 minutes Cook: 15 minutes Makes: about 12 small scones

These tiny scones, split and filled with a dab of honey mustard and a sliver of smoky ham, make perfect cocktail fare. Scones are traditionally triangular, but an assortment of biscuit cutters will give you whimsical hearts and crescents.

2 cups flour
4 teaspoons baking powder
½ teaspoon salt
⅛ teaspoon cayenne
1 stick (4 ounces) cold butter
¾ cup plus 1 tablespoon buttermilk
Optional flavorings: ½ cup finely shredded Cheddar cheese; ¼ cup grated Parmesan or Romano cheese; ¼ cup currants; 1 or 2 jalapeño chiles, seeded and minced; 1 or more tablespoons chopped fresh herbs; 1 tablespoon poppy seeds

1. Preheat oven to 425°F. In a large bowl, sift together flour, baking powder, salt, and cayenne.

2. Cut butter into ½-inch cubes. Using a fork or pastry blender, cut butter into flour until mixture resembles coarse crumbs. Make a well in center and pour in ¾ cup buttermilk and any one of the optional flavorings. As quickly and as lightly as possible, stir until flour mixture is moistened.

3. Turn dough out onto a lightly floured work surface. Knead 2 or 3 times and roll or pat into a 1-inch-thick rectangle about 4 by 8½ inches. Cut dough into squares with a knife or other shapes with a biscuit cutter. Roll out scraps once and repeat. Arrange scones 1 inch apart on an ungreased baking sheet and brush with remaining 1 tablespoon buttermilk. (If made in advance, cover loosely with a tea towel and store at room temperature up to 4 hours.)

4. Bake scones until just golden, about 15 minutes.

348 DOUBLE-CORN MINI MUFFINS

Prep: 5 minutes Cook: 15 minutes Makes: 24

These moist corn muffins are a natural with baked ham. They make wonderful tiny sandwiches, too.

1 (8½-ounce) package corn muffin mix
1 egg
⅓ cup milk
1 (8½-ounce) can cream-style corn

1. Preheat oven to 400°F. Grease 2 gem-size (1¾-inch) muffin tins. Pour muffin mix into a medium bowl; create a well in center.

2. In a small bowl, beat egg with milk until well blended. Stir in creamed corn. Pour corn mixture into well in muffin mix. As quickly and as lightly as possible, blend ingredients just to moisten. (Do not try for a uniform batter; there will be some lumps.)

3. Spoon 2 tablespoons batter into prepared muffin tins and bake until cooked through, about 15 minutes.

349 MINI CORN MUFFINS WITH PROSCIUTTO

Prep: 15 minutes Cook: 15 minutes Makes: 24

½ cup yellow cornmeal
½ cup flour
2 tablespoons sugar
1¼ teaspoons baking powder
¼ teaspoon salt
3 ounces prosciutto or Black Forest Ham, minced
4 tablespoons melted butter
½ cup heavy cream
1 egg

1. Preheat oven to 400°F. In a medium bowl, combine cornmeal, flour, sugar, baking powder, and salt. Whisk gently until well mixed. Stir in minced prosciutto.

2. In a small bowl, combine melted butter, cream, and egg. Whisk until well blended. Make a well in center of dry ingredients and pour in egg mixture. As quickly and as lightly as possible, fold egg mixture into dry ingredients.

3. Drop 2 tablespoons batter into greased gem-sized (1¾-inch) muffin tins and bake until golden brown and cooked through, about 15 minutes.

350 SOUTHERN CHEDDAR PECAN WAFERS

Prep: 10 minutes Chill: 1 hour Cook: 10 to 12 minutes Makes: 48

1 stick (4 ounces) butter, softened
2 cups shredded sharp Cheddar cheese (about 8 ounces)
1 cup flour
¼ teaspoon salt
⅛ teaspoon cayenne
48 pecan halves (about 8 ounces)

1. Preheat oven to 425°F. In a medium bowl or in a food processor, blend butter and cheese until well mixed. Mix in flour, salt, and cayenne until well blended.

2. Divide dough into 3 equal portions; form each piece into a cylinder 1 inch in diameter. Wrap tightly in plastic wrap, twisting ends to seal. Refrigerate or freeze until firm, about 1 hour.

3. Remove plastic wrap and with a large sharp knife, cut the dough into slices ⅛ inch thick. Arrange in a single layer on an ungreased baking sheet and top each with a pecan half, pressing down gently. Bake until wafers are firm and just lightly browned at the edges, 10 to 12 minutes.

351 CHEDDAR SESAME WAFERS

Prep: 10 minutes Cook: 10 to 12 minutes Makes: 30

4 tablespoons butter, softened
1 cup grated sharp Cheddar cheese (about 4 ounces)
⅛ teaspoon cayenne
⅛ teaspoon salt
2 tablespoons heavy cream
½ teaspoon baking powder
½ cup flour
¼ cup yellow cornmeal
3 tablespoons sesame seeds

1. Preheat oven to 375°F. In a food processor, combine butter, cheese, cayenne, salt, and cream. Process until well blended. Add baking powder, flour, and cornmeal and process to a stiff dough, about 30 seconds.

2. Pinch off 2 teaspoons dough at a time and form into ¾-inch balls, then flatten into disks about 1½ inches in diameter and ¼ inch thick. Press one side of each disk in sesame seeds and place seed-side up on a baking sheet.

3. Bake until tops just begin to brown, 10 to 12 minutes. Transfer to a rack and let cool.

352 THUMBPRINT COCKTAIL COOKIES

Prep: 30 minutes Cook: 15 to 20 minutes Makes: 72

These pretty treats, with their shimmering centers of red and green, are ideal for holiday buffets. These also freeze very well.

- **4 cups shredded sharp Cheddar cheese (1 pound)**
- **2 sticks (8 ounces) butter, softened**
- **2 eggs, separated**
- **Dash of salt**
- **Dash of cayenne**
- **2 cups flour**
- **1½ cups chopped pistachios or walnuts (6 ounces)**
- **About ½ cup red and/or green hot pepper jelly**

1. Preheat oven to 350°F. In a food processor, combine Cheddar cheese and butter and process until well blended. Add egg yolks, salt, and cayenne and blend until mixed. Add flour and process until well blended.

2. In a small bowl, whisk egg whites until foamy. Place nuts in another bowl. Shape rounded tablespoons of dough into balls and roll first in egg white and then in chopped nuts. Arrange balls 1 inch apart on a baking sheet. Using a thumb or a floured thimble, make an indentation in the center of each ball.

3. Bake until cooked through and edges are lightly browned, 10 to 15 minutes. Let cool on a rack. When cool, fill centers with a dab of hot pepper jelly.

353 CHEESY PINE NUT PUFFS

Prep: 10 minutes Cook: 30 minutes Makes: 24

- **1 cup milk**
- **1 stick (4 ounces) butter, cut into bits**
- **1 cup flour**
- **3 eggs**
- **¼ cup finely chopped Gruyère or Swiss cheese**
- **¼ cup minced ham**
- **⅓ cup pine nuts (pignoli)**

1. Preheat oven to 425°F. In a medium saucepan, combine milk and butter. Place over medium heat until butter melts. Stir in flour. Cook, stirring constantly, until batter leaves sides of pan and forms a ball. Remove from heat. Beat in eggs, one at a time, making sure each egg is fully incorporated before adding the next. Fold in cheese, ham, and pine nuts.

2. Scoop with 2 spoons into 1-inch balls and arrange 2 inches apart on a greased baking sheet. (If mixture is too soft to handle, chill briefly.) Bake 15 minutes, then lower heat to 325° and bake until golden brown, 10 to 15 minutes longer. Serve warm or at room temperature.

354 CURRIED CHICKEN AND APRICOT PUFFS

Prep: 20 minutes Cook: 10 minutes Makes: 36

This versatile filling is equally good in filo cups or puff pastry shells and can be served hot or cold.

- **¼ cup coarsely chopped dried apricots**
- **2 scallions, cut into 1-inch pieces**
- **2 cups coarsely shredded cooked chicken (about 1 whole breast)**
- **1½ tablespoons mayonnaise**
- **1½ tablespoons sour cream**
- **1 teaspoon curry powder**
- **1 teaspoon fresh lemon juice**
- **¼ teaspoon salt**
- **Dash of cayenne**
- **¼ cup toasted slivered almonds (optional)**
- **35 Tiny Puffs or Tiny Cheese Puffs (recipes follow)**

1. In a food processor, finely chop apricots and scallions. Add chicken, mayonnaise, sour cream, curry powder, lemon juice, salt, cayenne, and almonds. Using an on/off motion, process until well mixed and finely chopped.

2. Using kitchen shears or a small serrated knife, cut tops of puffs about three-quarters through. Fill each puff with about 1 tablespoon chicken mixture, repositioning lid. (It's fine if a bit of filling peeks through.) Serve at room temperature, or bake 10 minutes in a 400°F oven.

355 TINY PUFFS

Prep: 30 minutes Cook: 19 to 20 minutes Makes: 60

Keeping a batch of these savory cream puffs in the freezer ensures frozen assets which can be pulled out any time you decide to entertain. If you do not have a food processor, beat in the eggs one at a time with a wooden spoon, making sure that each is fully incorporated before adding the next.

- **1 stick (4 ounces) butter, cut into tablespoons**
- **½ teaspoon sugar**
- **½ teaspoon salt**
- **1 cup flour**
- **4 eggs**
- **1 egg, beaten (optional, for glaze)**

1. Preheat oven to 400°F. In a medium saucepan, combine butter, sugar, and salt with 1 cup water. Bring to a boil over medium heat, adjusting heat as necessary so butter is fully melted when mixture boils. Reduce heat to low and add flour all at once, beating vigorously with a wooden spoon until dough is well blended and forms a ball, leaving a film on bottom and sides of pan, 1 to 2 minutes. Remove from heat and let cool 5 minutes.

2. Transfer dough to a food processor and process until broken into bits, 10 to 15 seconds. Add all 4 eggs and process until smooth and shiny, 30 to 45 seconds.

3. Using 2 spoons or a pastry bag fitted with a wide plain or fluted tip, drop small mounds (about 2 teaspoons each) on a parchment- or foil-lined baking sheet. To glaze puffs, brush tops with beaten egg and set aside 5 minutes. Brush again with egg.

4. Bake for 9 minutes. Reduce oven temperature to 350° and continue baking until puffed and golden brown, about 9 minutes longer. Let cool on a rack. (If made in advance, store airtight up to 1 day at room temperature. Freeze for longer storage. Before serving, bake frozen puffs for 5 to 10 minutes in a 400° oven until crisp.)

TINY CHEESE PUFFS

Prep: 35 minutes Cook: 19 to 20 minutes Makes: 60

Serve these by themselves or fill them with chicken, ham, or seafood. Making them in the food processor is a breeze, so it pays to make a full batch. What you don't use can be kept in the freezer.

2 ounces Gruyère or Swiss cheese, cut into ½-inch cubes (about ½ cup)
4 tablespoons butter
1 teaspoon sugar
½ teaspoon salt
1 cup flour
4 eggs
1 egg, beaten (optional, for glaze)

1. In a food processor, chop cheese into very small bits. Remove and reserve. (There is no need to wash work bowl.) Preheat oven to 400°F.

2. In a medium saucepan, combine butter, sugar, and salt with ⅔ cup water. Bring to a boil over medium heat, adjusting heat as necessary so butter is fully melted when mixture boils. Reduce heat to low and add flour all at once, beating vigorously with a wooden spoon until dough is well blended and forms a ball leaving a film on bottom and sides of pan, 1 to 2 minutes. Remove from heat and let cool 5 minutes.

3. Transfer dough to food processor and process until broken into bits, 10 to 15 seconds. Add all 4 eggs and process until smooth and shiny, 30 to 45 seconds. Add reserved cheese and process, using an on/off motion, until well mixed.

4. Using 2 spoons or a pastry bag fitted with a wide plain tip, drop small mounds (about 2 teaspoons each) 2 inches apart on a parchment- or foil-lined baking sheet. To glaze puffs, brush tops with beaten egg and set aside 5 minutes. Brush again with egg.

5. Bake 9 minutes. Reduce oven temperature to 350° and continue baking until puffed and golden brown, about 9 minutes longer. Let cool on a rack. (If made in advance, store airtight up to 1 day at room temperature. Freeze for longer storage. Before serving, bake in a 400° oven for 5 minutes, or until crisp.)

357 ALMOND STICKS

Prep: 10 minutes Cook: 20 minutes Makes: 60

1 stick (4 ounces) butter or margarine, softened
2 eggs
2 cups flour
½ pound blanched almonds, finely ground (1½ cups)
1 egg, slightly beaten
Salt (optional)

1. Preheat oven to 350°F. Beat butter until fluffy. Add eggs and ¼ cup water and mix well. Add flour and ground almonds. Stir thoroughly to blend.

2. On a lightly floured board, roll out dough about ⅜ inch thick. Cut into strips about ⅜ inch wide and 6 inches long. Arrange 1 inch apart on greased baking sheets. Brush tops with beaten egg. Sprinkle with salt, if desired.

3. Bake 15 to 20 minutes, until golden brown. Let cool on wire racks before serving. Store airtight up to 1 week.

358 SOUFFLÉED SALTINES

Prep: 20 minutes Cook: 20 to 25 minutes Makes: 24

These flaky crackers gained recognition several years ago when they began to appear at White House parties. Is it filo? Puff pastry? Pie crust? Only the cook will know for sure.

24 saltine crackers
Ice water
4 tablespoons butter, melted
Poppy seeds, sesame seeds, or coarse (kosher) salt, for topping

1. Preheat oven to 400°F. In one or more shallow pans of ice water, float a single layer of saltines until softened but not disintegrated, about 20 minutes. Remove with a slotted spatula, letting excess water drain off, and arrange in a single layer about 1½ inches apart on greased baking sheets.

2. Generously brush tops of crackers with melted butter, taking care not to press down. Top with a sprinkling of seeds or salt.

3. Bake until crackers are puffed and golden, 20 to 25 minutes. Serve warm, or let cool on a wire rack and store airtight. If made in advance, reheat 3 minutes in a 400° oven until crisp.

359 DOUBLE OLIVE BREAD

Prep: 10 minutes Rise: 45 minutes Cook: 30 minutes
Makes: 1 (7-inch) round loaf

This quickly assembled loaf is great with cheeses. You may also want to brush slices with extra-virgin olive oil and toast in the oven.

- **1/3 cup pitted and sliced kalamata olives**
- **1/3 cup sliced pimiento-stuffed olives**
- **1 (1-pound) loaf frozen white bread dough, thawed**
- **2 teaspoons extra-virgin olive oil**

1. On a lightly floured work surface, knead olives into bread dough. Form into a round loaf about 5 inches in diameter and brush with olive oil. Place on a lightly greased baking sheet, cover, and let rise in a warm draftfree place until almost doubled, about 1 hour.

2. Preheat oven to 375°F. Bake bread until loaf is golden brown on top and sounds hollow when tapped, about 30 minutes. Let cool on a wire rack. (If made in advance, store airtight up to 24 hours.) Serve slightly warm, at room temperature, or toasted.

360 SCALLION FOCACCIA

Prep: 10 minutes Rise: 45 minutes Cook: 20 minutes
Makes: a 11½ x 7½-inch loaf of flat bread

Cut this into small squares to eat as is, or split in half and fill for tiny appetizer sandwiches.

- **3 tablespoons olive oil**
- **2 teaspoons yellow cornmeal**
- **1 (1-pound) loaf frozen bread dough, thawed as package directs**
- **3/4 to 1 teaspoon coarse (kosher) salt**
- **3 scallions, chopped**

1. Brush an 11½ x 7½-inch baking pan with 1 tablespoon olive oil and sprinkle with cornmeal. Pat or roll out bread dough to fit pan; place in pan. Brush surface with 1 tablespoon olive oil and sprinkle with salt. Indent surface of dough by pressing all over with your fingertips. Cover with a kitchen towel and let rise in a warm, draftfree place 1 hour or until doubled in bulk. Press again all over with fingers. Preheat oven to 375°F.

2. Bake 15 minutes. In a small bowl, combine scallions with remaining 1 tablespoon olive oil. Sprinkle over surface of bread and continue baking until focaccia is golden brown and onions are lightly browned at the edges, about 5 minutes longer. Serve warm or at room temperature.

361 ROSEMARY FOUGASSE

Prep: 15 minutes Rise: 50 minutes Cook: 15 to 18 minutes
Makes: a 12 x 10½-inch loaf

The interesting shape and flavor of this bread from southern France make it a welcome addition to any gathering. As an added bonus, your kitchen will smell marvelous as it bakes! Serve this pull-apart bread with an assortment of cheeses—it is particularly delicious with goat cheese—and some good olives.

- **2 tablespoons chopped fresh rosemary or 2 teaspoons dried**
- **1 (1-pound) loaf frozen bread dough, thawed as package directs**
- **2 teaspoons yellow cornmeal**
- **1½ tablespoons extra-virgin olive oil**
- **1 garlic clove, minced**
- **¾ to 1 teaspoon coarse (kosher) salt**

1. On a lightly floured work surface, knead rosemary into bread dough. Let rest 5 minutes.

2. Roll out dough into a rough oval, about 11½ inches long and 10 inches wide. Using a sharp knife, make 1 vertical slash about 4 inches long in center of dough. Make 6 more slashes, radiating sunburst-fashion from the original cut. Lift and pull dough, stretching it and opening up slashes to about 1½ inches wide. (The dough should resemble a sand dollar.)

3. Arrange dough on a greased baking sheet sprinkled with cornmeal. In a small bowl, combine olive oil and garlic; brush generously over dough. Cover and let rise in a warm, draftfree place until nicely puffed, about 1 hour.

4. Preheat oven to 375°F. Sprinkle salt over dough and bake until loaf is golden brown outside and sounds hollow when bottom is tapped, 15 to 18 minutes. Let cool on a wire rack. Serve warm or at room temperature.

362 IRISH BREAD STICKS

Prep: 30 minutes Cook: 15 to 20 minutes Makes: 30

1 medium white-skinned potato (about ⅓ pound), peeled
1 stick (4 ounces) butter, softened
1 cup flour
½ teaspoon salt
2 tablespoons chopped parsley
1 egg
1 tablespoon cream or milk
3 tablespoons grated Parmesan cheese
3 tablespoons sesame seeds
1 tablespoon caraway seeds
2 teaspoons coarse (kosher) salt
¼ teaspoon paprika

1. Preheat oven to 375°F. Cut potato into quarters. In a small saucepan of boiling salted water, cook potato over medium-high heat until fork-tender, about 10 minutes; drain. In a medium bowl, mash potato. Stir in butter, flour, salt, and parsley until well blended.

2. Roll generous tablespoons of dough into cylinders 2 inches long. Arrange on a foil- or parchment-lined baking sheet. In a small bowl, beat egg with cream until well blended. Brush over potato sticks.

3. In a small bowl, combine Parmesan cheese, sesame seeds, caraway seeds, coarse salt, and paprika. Stir until well mixed. Roll potato sticks in seed mixture to coat.

4. Bake until golden brown and cooked through, about 15 minutes. Serve warm or at room temperature. Store airtight up to 3 days or freeze.

363 POPPADUMS

Prep: 5 minutes Cook: 4 to 5 seconds each Makes: about 15

These crisp and delicate lentil wafers should not be overlooked, for they are wonderful either just on their own or dipped in curry- or yogurt-based sauces. Look for them in Indian food shops or other international markets.

2 to 4 cups peanut oil or other vegetable oil
1 (4-ounce) bag or box of poppadums, about 5 inches in diameter, plain or spiced

1. In a large wok or skillet, heat oil to 375°F on a deep-frying thermometer.

2. Using tongs, slide poppadums into hot oil one at a time. Deep-fry until puffed and golden, 4 to 5 seconds. Drain on paper towels. Serve warm or at room temperature.

364 BRIOCHE BASKET FOR BRIE

Prep: 30 minutes Rise: 2 hours Cook: 45 minutes
Chill: overnight Serves: 12

This gorgeous golden basket makes the perfect setting for a whole wheel of Brie. Or use the inside bread to make tea sandwiches filled with your choice of savory spreads and set them back into the loaf. The lid turns the presentation into an edible surprise package. Be sure and begin a day ahead as the dough must be refrigerated overnight.

¾ cup sugar
¾ teaspoon salt
3 (¼-ounce) envelopes active dry yeast
5½ cups flour
2 sticks (½ pound) butter
¾ cup milk
7 large eggs

1. In the bowl of a large heavy-duty mixer fitted with the paddle attachment,* combine sugar, salt, yeast, and 2 cups of flour. In a small saucepan, combine butter and milk. Place over medium heat until butter is melted and mixture is lukewarm, 110° to 115°F on an instant-reading thermometer. With mixer on low speed, add liquid to dry ingredients and beat until just combined. Increase speed to medium and beat for 2 minutes. Gradually mix in 6 eggs, one at a time, and 1½ cups flour, beating 2 minutes longer. Add another 1½ cups flour and beat on low 5 minutes.

2. Place dough in a large greased bowl. Cover with a towel and let rise in a warm, draft-free place until doubled in bulk, about 1 hour. Punch dough down, then cover with plastic wrap and refrigerate overnight.

3. The next day, punch dough down, then turn out onto a lightly floured work surface. Cover with an inverted bowl and let rest 15 minutes. Grease a 10-inch springform pan. Pat dough into pan, smoothing top. Cover with an inverted bowl and let rise until doubled in bulk, about 1 hour. Preheat oven to 325°F.

4. Beat remaining egg with 2 teaspoons water to make a glaze. Brush egg glaze over dough. Bake 45 minutes, or until loaf is golden brown and sounds hollow when tapped. Let cool on a wire rack.

5. When cool, use a serrated knife to slice off top and reserve for a lid. Hollow out bread with a fork, leaving a 1-inch border around edges.

* *If you do not own a heavy-duty mixer, use a wooden spoon to incorporate all the eggs into the dough. When all the flour has been added, turn out onto a lightly floured work surface. Knead by hand until shiny and elastic, about 10 minutes.*

365 WREATH OF BRIE

Prep: 10 minutes   Rise: 30 minutes   Cook: 25 minutes
Makes: 1 (13-inch) bread ring

To do justice to this elaborate presentation, look for a perfectly ripe wheel of Brie, creamy and mellow. The rind should be a golden ivory, with white overlay. If the cheese is pure white, it is unripe.

1 pound frozen white or wheat bread dough, thawed
1 egg
1 tablespoon cream or milk
¼ cup sesame or poppy seeds
1 (2-pound) wheel of Brie cheese

1. Grease outside of a 9-inch round cake pan and invert onto a greased baking sheet.

2. Roll out bread dough into a rope about 29 inches long. Using a sharp knife or kitchen shears, cut dough in half lengthwise and braid the two halves together. Wrap braided dough around cake pan on prepared baking sheet; pinch edges together to seal. Cover lightly with a kitchen towel and let rise in a warm place until almost doubled in size, about 30 minutes. Preheat oven to 425°F.

3. In a small bowl, mix egg with cream until well blended. Brush over dough and sprinkle with seeds. Bake 5 minutes. Reduce oven temperature to 350° and bake 20 minutes longer, or until bread is nicely browned and sounds hollow when tapped with a knife. Unmold from pan and let cool.

4. To serve, place a whole wheel of Brie in center of a serving platter or cutting board at least 15 inches in diameter. Surround with bread wreath.

Index

About the Authors

Lonnie Gandara and Peggy Fallon are culinary professionals who live and work in the San Francisco Bay area. The team has been teaching a sold-out holiday cooking class in appetizers and hors d'oeuvres for the past ten years. Gandara is also the author of the best-selling *365 Great Barbecue & Grilling Recipes* published by HarperCollins.